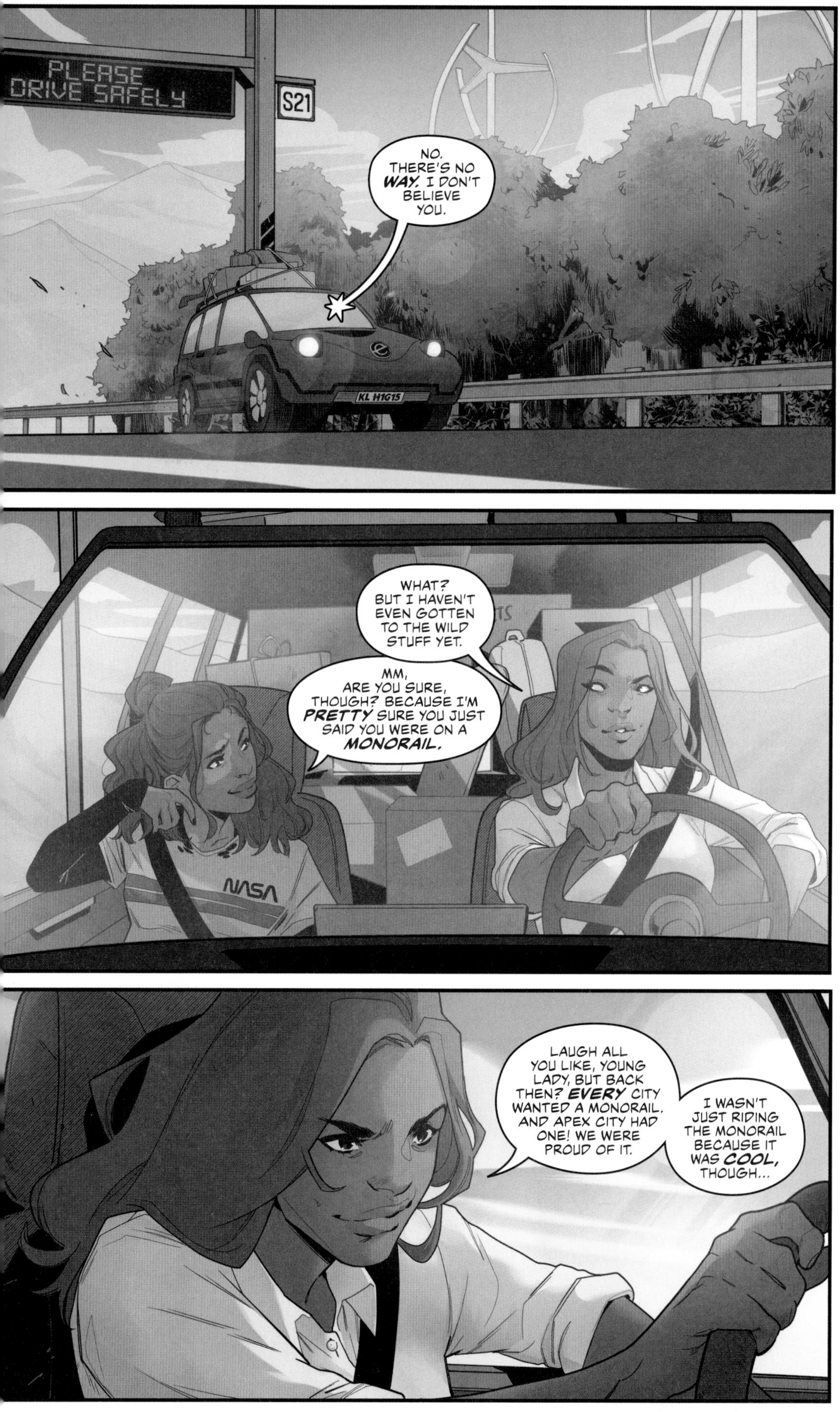
PLEASE DRIVE SAFELY
S21
NO. THERE'S NO WAY. I DON'T BELIEVE YOU.
KL H1G15
WHAT? BUT I HAVEN'T EVEN GOTTEN TO THE WILD STUFF YET.
MM, ARE YOU SURE, THOUGH? BECAUSE I'M PRETTY SURE YOU JUST SAID YOU WERE ON A MONORAIL.
NASA
LAUGH ALL YOU LIKE, YOUNG LADY, BUT BACK THEN? EVERY CITY WANTED A MONORAIL. AND APEX CITY HAD ONE! WE WERE PROUD OF IT.
I WASN'T JUST RIDING THE MONORAIL BECAUSE IT WAS COOL, THOUGH...

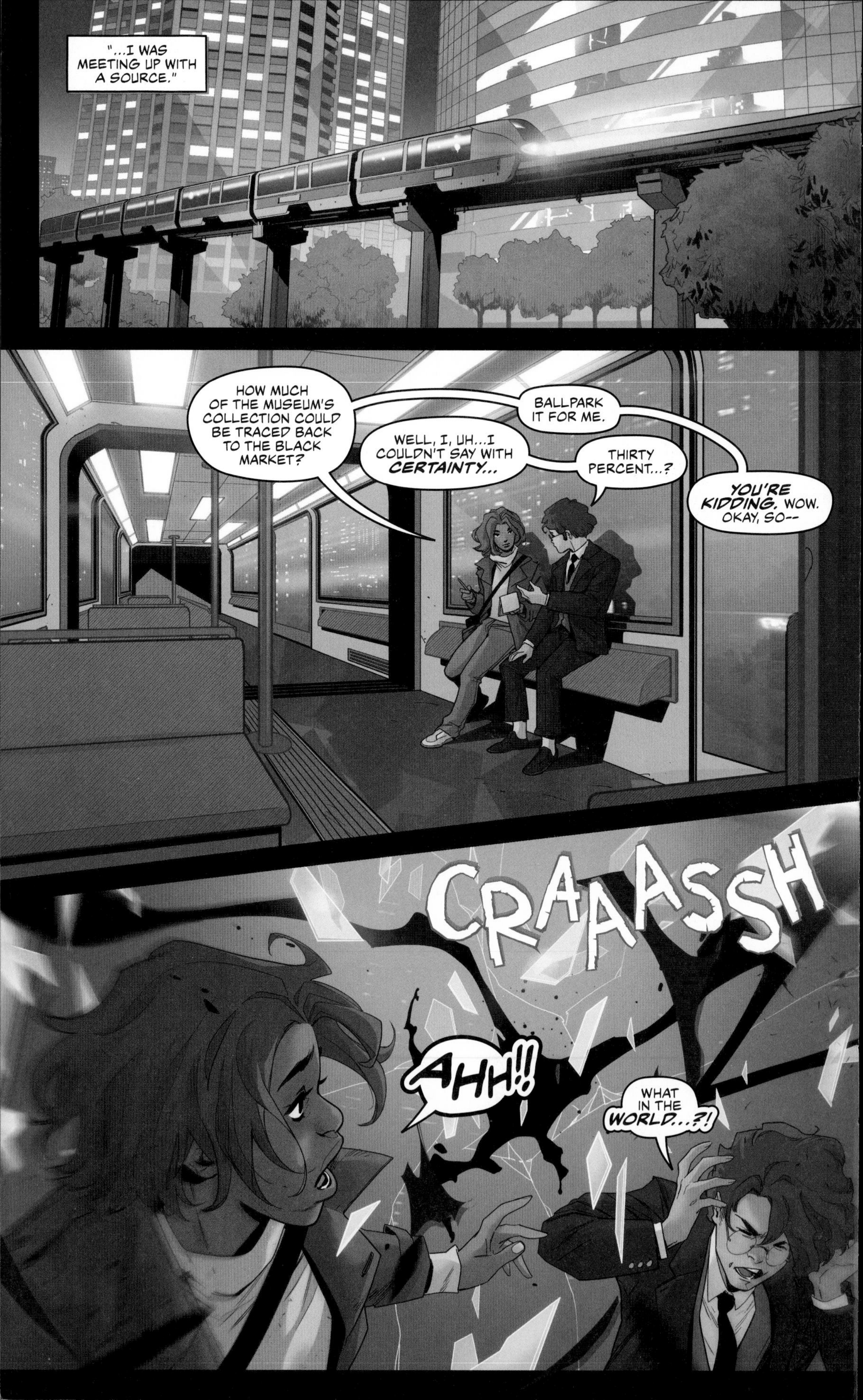
"...I WAS MEETING UP WITH A SOURCE."
HOW MUCH OF THE MUSEUM'S COLLECTION COULD BE TRACED BACK TO THE BLACK MARKET?
BALLPARK IT FOR ME.
WELL, I, UH...I COULDN'T SAY WITH CERTAINTY...
THIRTY PERCENT...?
YOU'RE KIDDING. WOW. OKAY, SO--
CRAAASSH
AHH!!
WHAT IN THE WORLD...?!

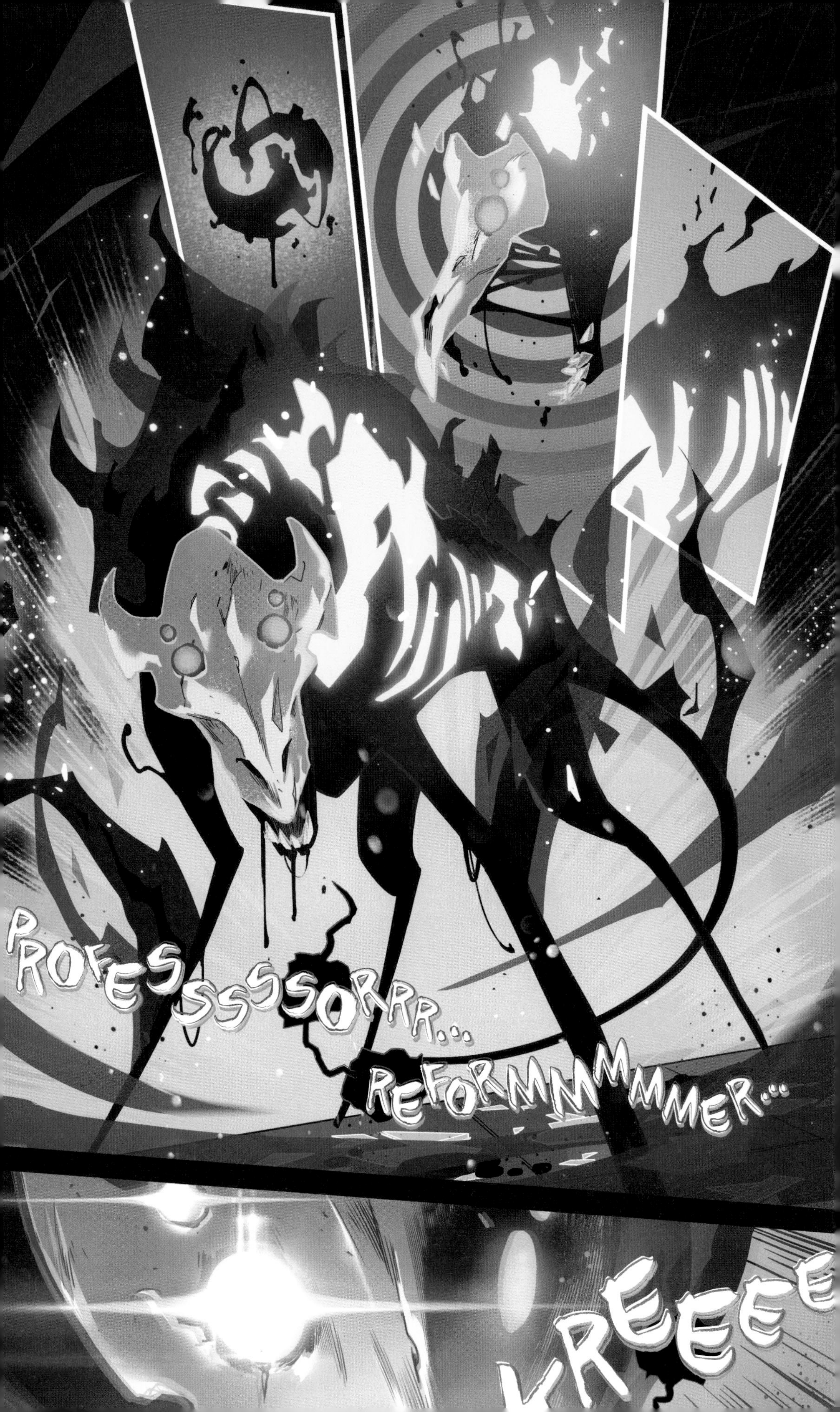
PROFESSSSSORRRR...
REFORMMMMMMER...
KREEEE

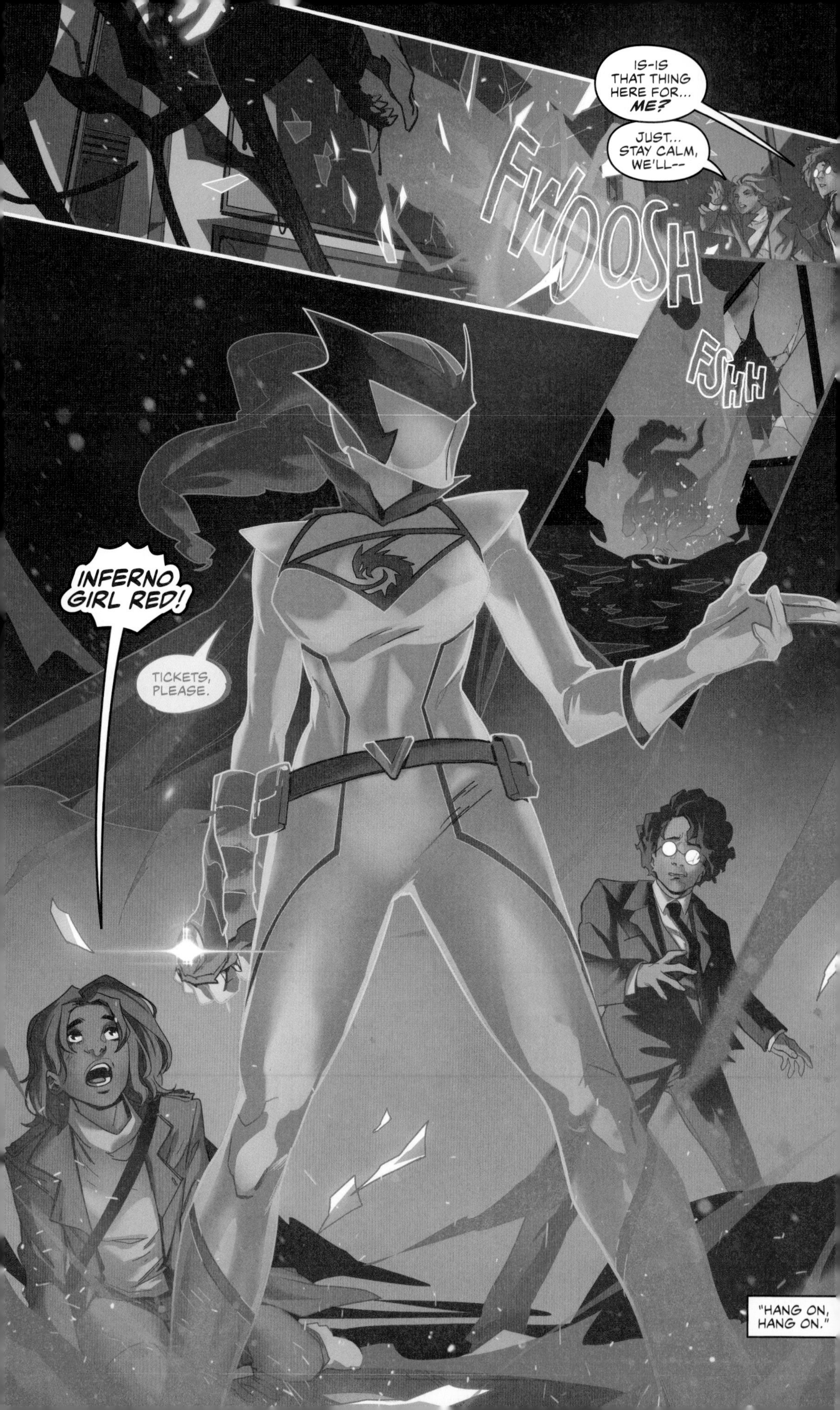
IS-IS THAT THING HERE FOR... ME?
JUST... STAY CALM, WE'LL--
FWOOSH
FSHH
INFERNO GIRL RED!
TICKETS, PLEASE.
"HANG ON, HANG ON."

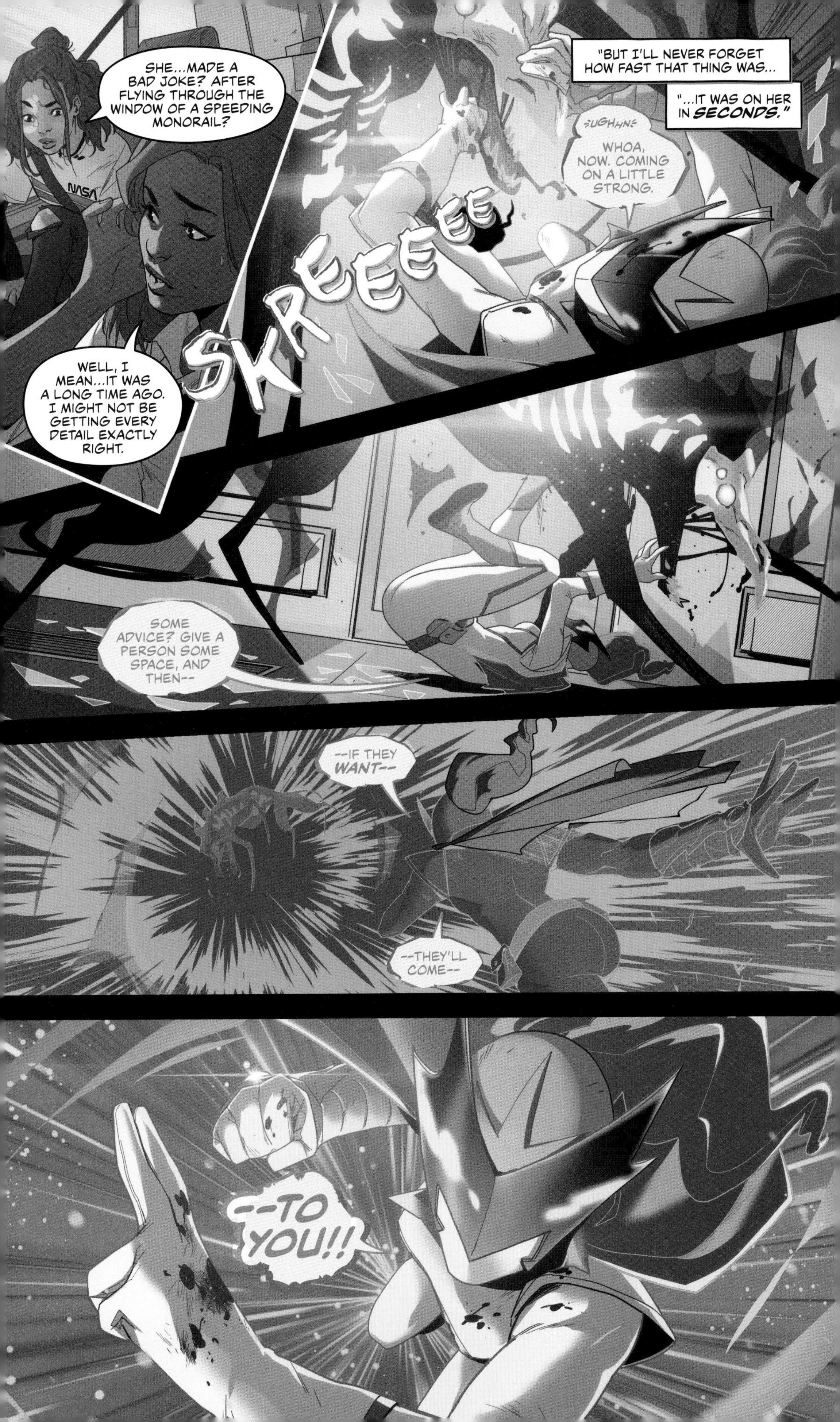
SHE...MADE A BAD JOKE? AFTER FLYING THROUGH THE WINDOW OF A SPEEDING MONORAIL?
WELL, I MEAN...IT WAS A LONG TIME AGO. I MIGHT NOT BE GETTING EVERY DETAIL EXACTLY RIGHT.
"BUT I'LL NEVER FORGET HOW FAST THAT THING WAS...
"...IT WAS ON HER IN SECONDS."
UGHHN
WHOA, NOW. COMING ON A LITTLE STRONG.
SKREEEEE
SOME ADVICE? GIVE A PERSON SOME SPACE, AND THEN--
--IF THEY WANT--
--THEY'LL COME--
--TO YOU!!

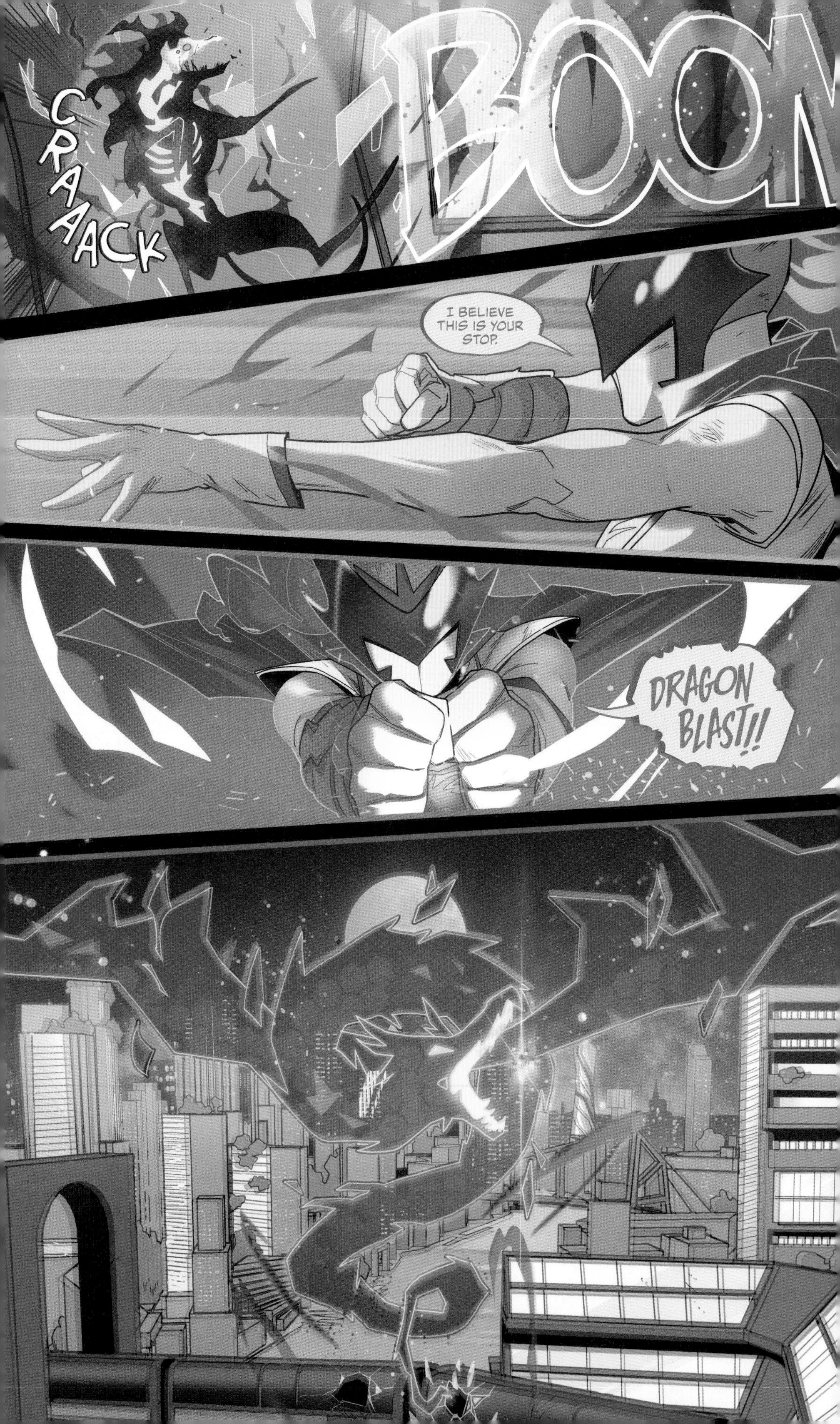
CRAAACK
BOOM
I BELIEVE THIS IS YOUR STOP.
DRAGON BLAST!!

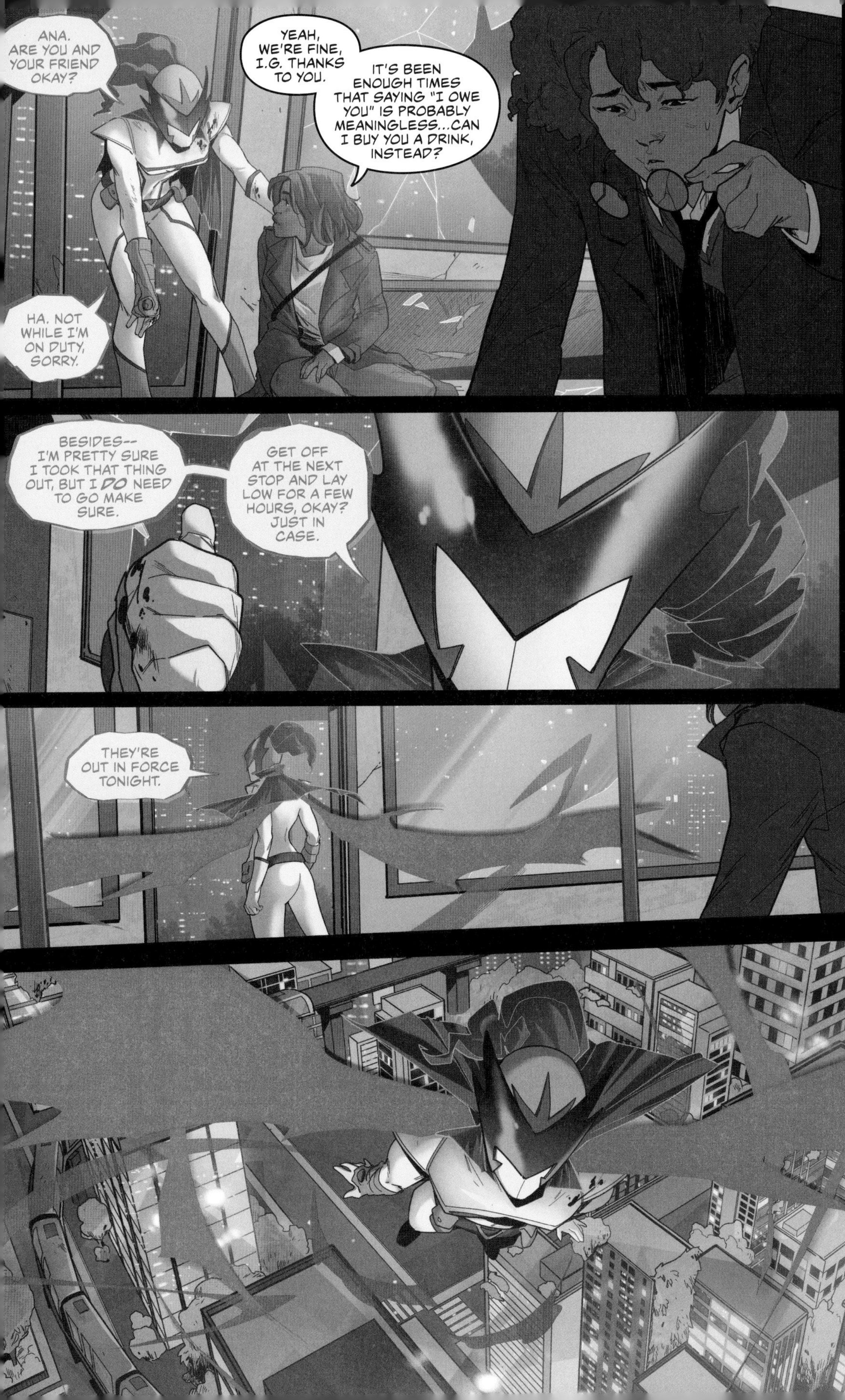
ANA. ARE YOU AND YOUR FRIEND OKAY?
YEAH, WE'RE FINE, I.G. THANKS TO YOU.
IT'S BEEN ENOUGH TIMES THAT SAYING "I OWE YOU" IS PROBABLY MEANINGLESS...CAN I BUY YOU A DRINK, INSTEAD?
HA. NOT WHILE I'M ON DUTY, SORRY.
BESIDES-- I'M PRETTY SURE I TOOK THAT THING OUT, BUT I *DO* NEED TO GO MAKE SURE.
GET OFF AT THE NEXT STOP AND LAY LOW FOR A FEW HOURS, OKAY? JUST IN CASE.
THEY'RE OUT IN FORCE TONIGHT.

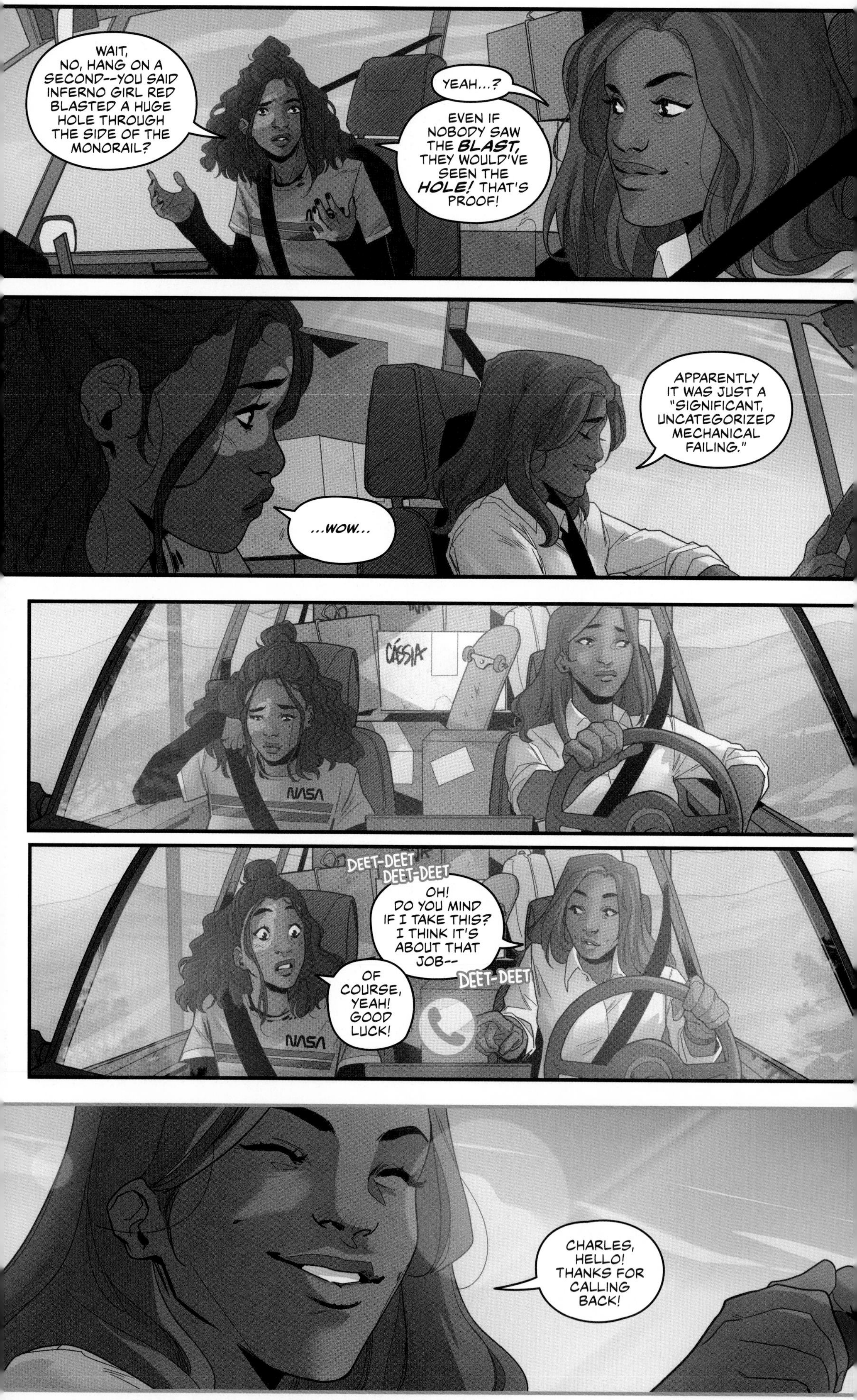
WAIT, NO, HANG ON A SECOND--YOU SAID INFERNO GIRL RED BLASTED A HUGE HOLE THROUGH THE SIDE OF THE MONORAIL?
YEAH...?
EVEN IF NOBODY SAW THE *BLAST,* THEY WOULD'VE SEEN THE *HOLE!* THAT'S PROOF!
APPARENTLY IT WAS JUST A "SIGNIFICANT, UNCATEGORIZED MECHANICAL FAILING."
...WOW...
CÁSSIA
NASA
DEET-DEET
DEET-DEET
OH! DO YOU MIND IF I TAKE THIS? I THINK IT'S ABOUT THAT JOB--
DEET-DEET
OF COURSE, YEAH! GOOD LUCK!
NASA
CHARLES, HELLO! THANKS FOR CALLING BACK!

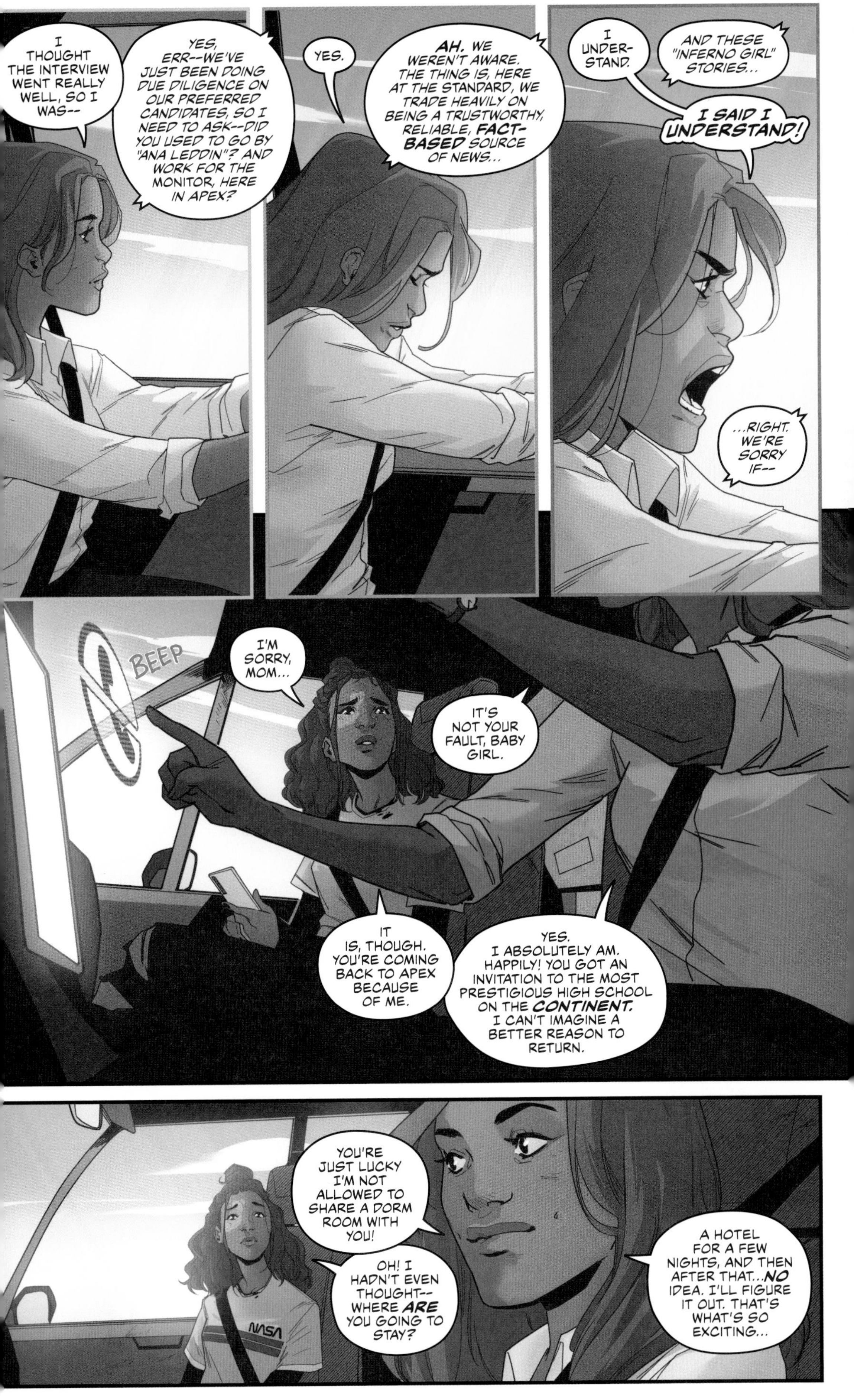
I THOUGHT THE INTERVIEW WENT REALLY WELL, SO I WAS--
YES, ERR--WE'VE JUST BEEN DOING DUE DILIGENCE ON OUR PREFERRED CANDIDATES, SO I NEED TO ASK--DID YOU USED TO GO BY "ANA LEDDIN"? AND WORK FOR THE MONITOR, HERE IN APEX?
YES.
AH. WE WEREN'T AWARE. THE THING IS, HERE AT THE STANDARD, WE TRADE HEAVILY ON BEING A TRUSTWORTHY, RELIABLE, FACT-BASED SOURCE OF NEWS...
I UNDER-STAND.
AND THESE "INFERNO GIRL" STORIES...
I SAID I UNDERSTAND!
...RIGHT. WE'RE SORRY IF--
BEEP
I'M SORRY, MOM...
IT'S NOT YOUR FAULT, BABY GIRL.
IT IS, THOUGH. YOU'RE COMING BACK TO APEX BECAUSE OF ME.
YES. I ABSOLUTELY AM. HAPPILY! YOU GOT AN INVITATION TO THE MOST PRESTIGIOUS HIGH SCHOOL ON THE CONTINENT. I CAN'T IMAGINE A BETTER REASON TO RETURN.
YOU'RE JUST LUCKY I'M NOT ALLOWED TO SHARE A DORM ROOM WITH YOU!
OH! I HADN'T EVEN THOUGHT--WHERE ARE YOU GOING TO STAY?
A HOTEL FOR A FEW NIGHTS, AND THEN AFTER THAT...NO IDEA. I'LL FIGURE IT OUT. THAT'S WHAT'S SO EXCITING...

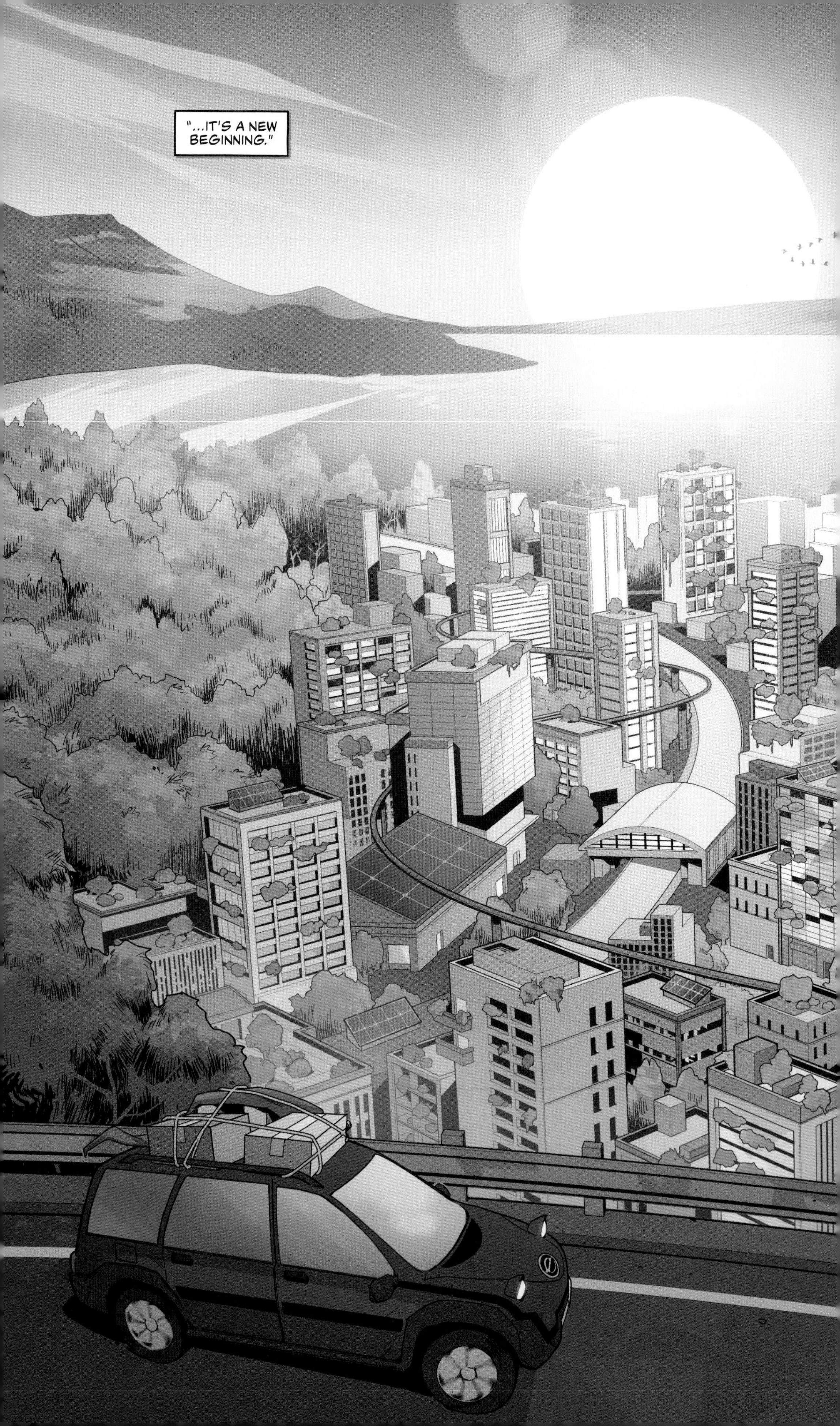
"...IT'S A NEW BEGINNING."

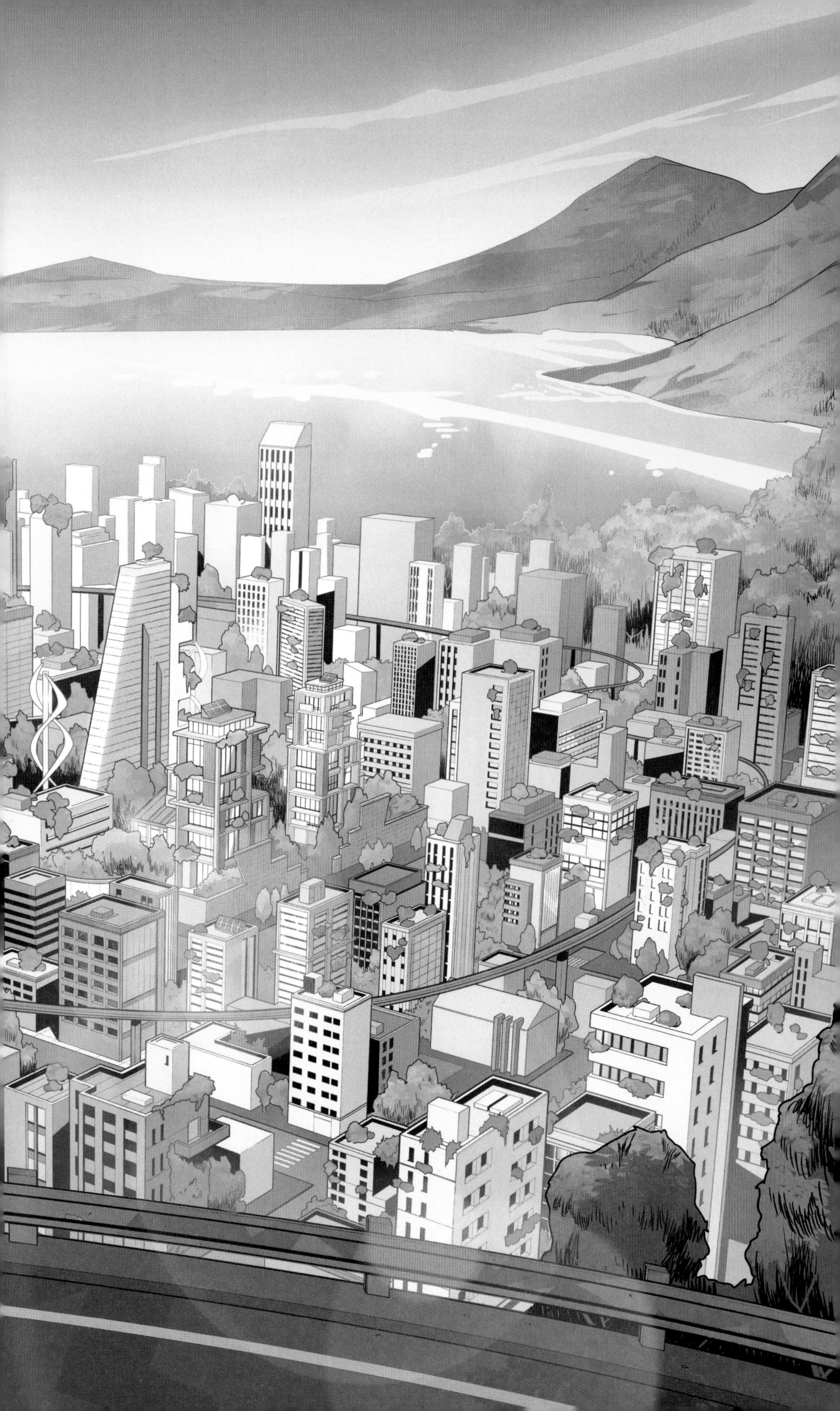

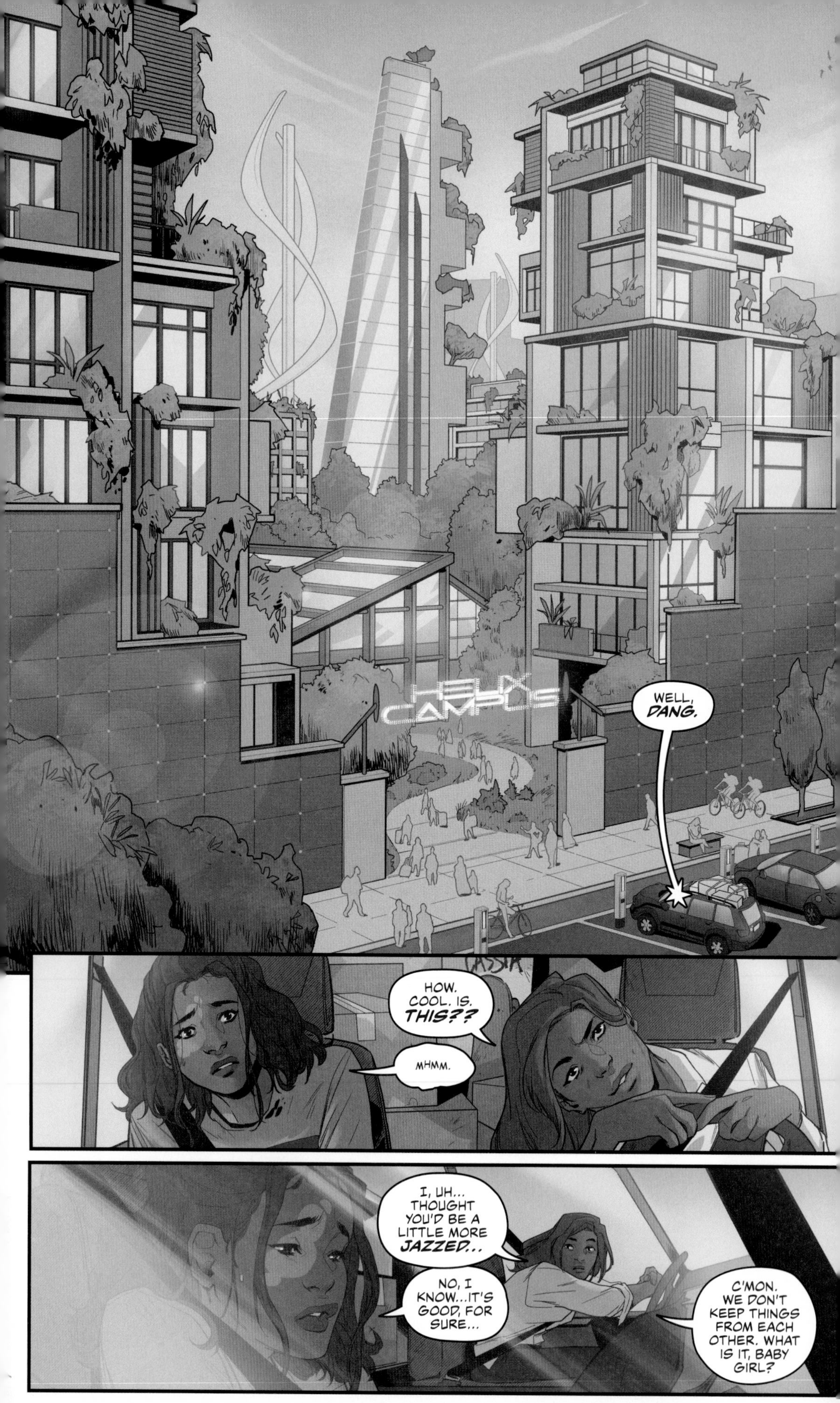
HELIX CAMPUS
WELL, DANG.
HOW. COOL. IS. THIS??
MHMM.
I, UH... THOUGHT YOU'D BE A LITTLE MORE JAZZED...
NO, I KNOW...IT'S GOOD, FOR SURE...
C'MON. WE DON'T KEEP THINGS FROM EACH OTHER. WHAT IS IT, BABY GIRL?

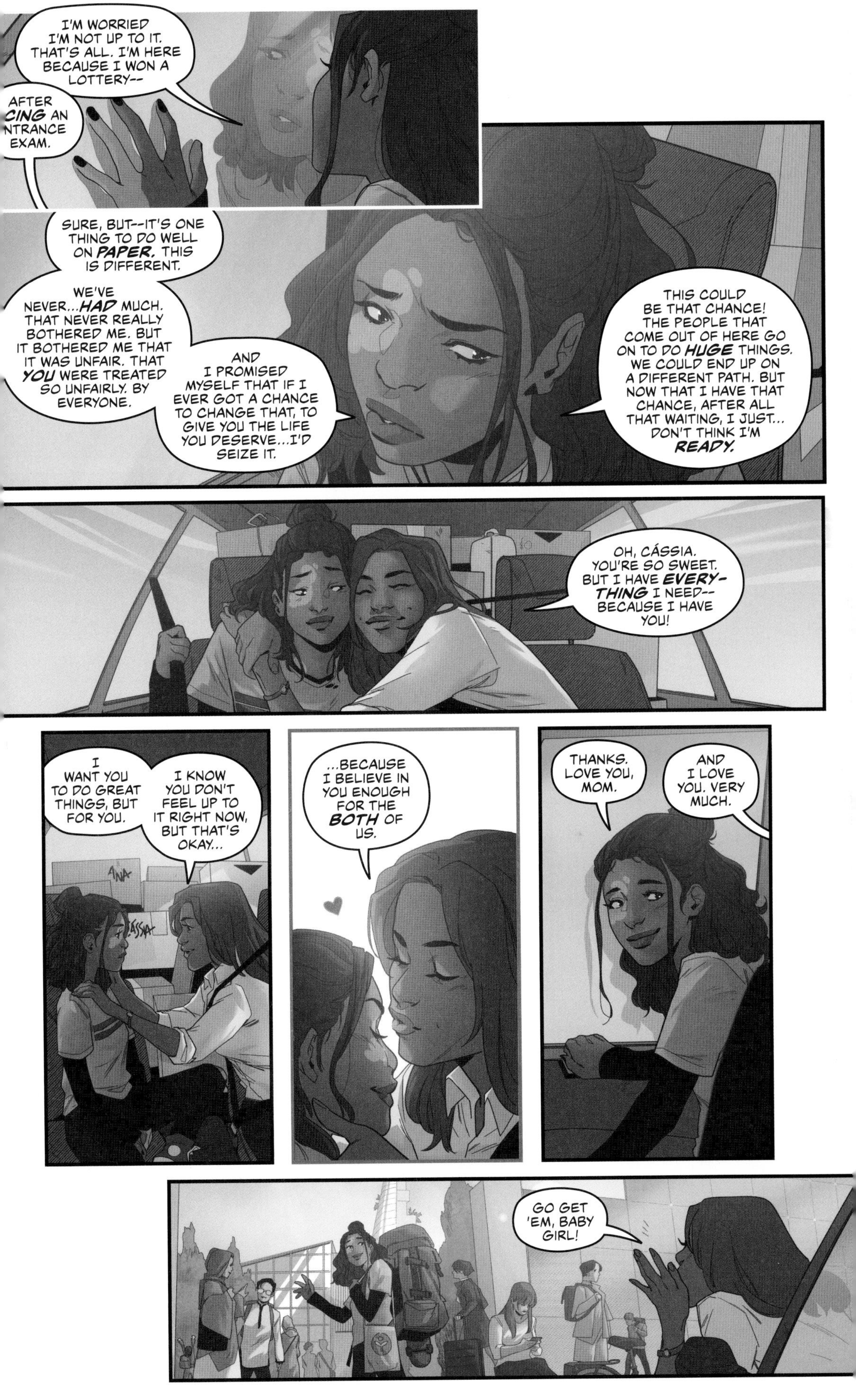
I'M WORRIED I'M NOT UP TO IT. THAT'S ALL. I'M HERE BECAUSE I WON A LOTTERY--
AFTER ACING AN ENTRANCE EXAM.
SURE, BUT--IT'S ONE THING TO DO WELL ON PAPER. THIS IS DIFFERENT.
WE'VE NEVER...HAD MUCH. THAT NEVER REALLY BOTHERED ME. BUT IT BOTHERED ME THAT IT WAS UNFAIR. THAT YOU WERE TREATED SO UNFAIRLY. BY EVERYONE.
AND I PROMISED MYSELF THAT IF I EVER GOT A CHANCE TO CHANGE THAT, TO GIVE YOU THE LIFE YOU DESERVE...I'D SEIZE IT.
THIS COULD BE THAT CHANCE! THE PEOPLE THAT COME OUT OF HERE GO ON TO DO HUGE THINGS. WE COULD END UP ON A DIFFERENT PATH. BUT NOW THAT I HAVE THAT CHANCE, AFTER ALL THAT WAITING, I JUST... DON'T THINK I'M READY.
OH, CÁSSIA. YOU'RE SO SWEET. BUT I HAVE EVERY-THING I NEED-- BECAUSE I HAVE YOU!
I WANT YOU TO DO GREAT THINGS, BUT FOR YOU.
I KNOW YOU DON'T FEEL UP TO IT RIGHT NOW, BUT THAT'S OKAY...
...BECAUSE I BELIEVE IN YOU ENOUGH FOR THE BOTH OF US.
THANKS. LOVE YOU, MOM.
AND I LOVE YOU. VERY MUCH.
GO GET 'EM, BABY GIRL!

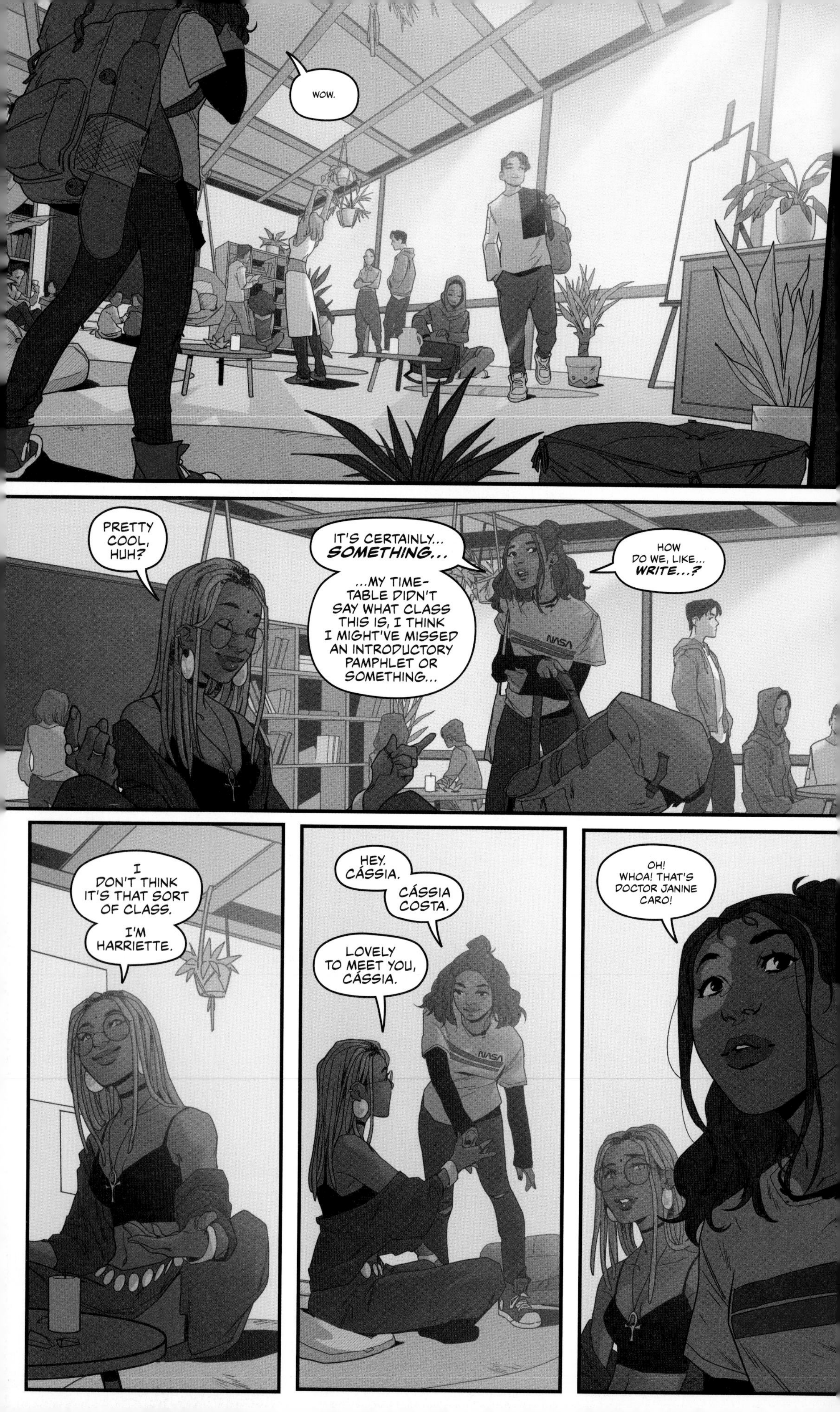
WOW.
PRETTY COOL, HUH?
IT'S CERTAINLY... SOMETHING...
...MY TIME-TABLE DIDN'T SAY WHAT CLASS THIS IS, I THINK I MIGHT'VE MISSED AN INTRODUCTORY PAMPHLET OR SOMETHING...
HOW DO WE, LIKE... WRITE...?
I DON'T THINK IT'S THAT SORT OF CLASS.
I'M HARRIETTE.
HEY. CÁSSIA.
CÁSSIA COSTA.
LOVELY TO MEET YOU, CÁSSIA.
OH! WHOA! THAT'S DOCTOR JANINE CARO!

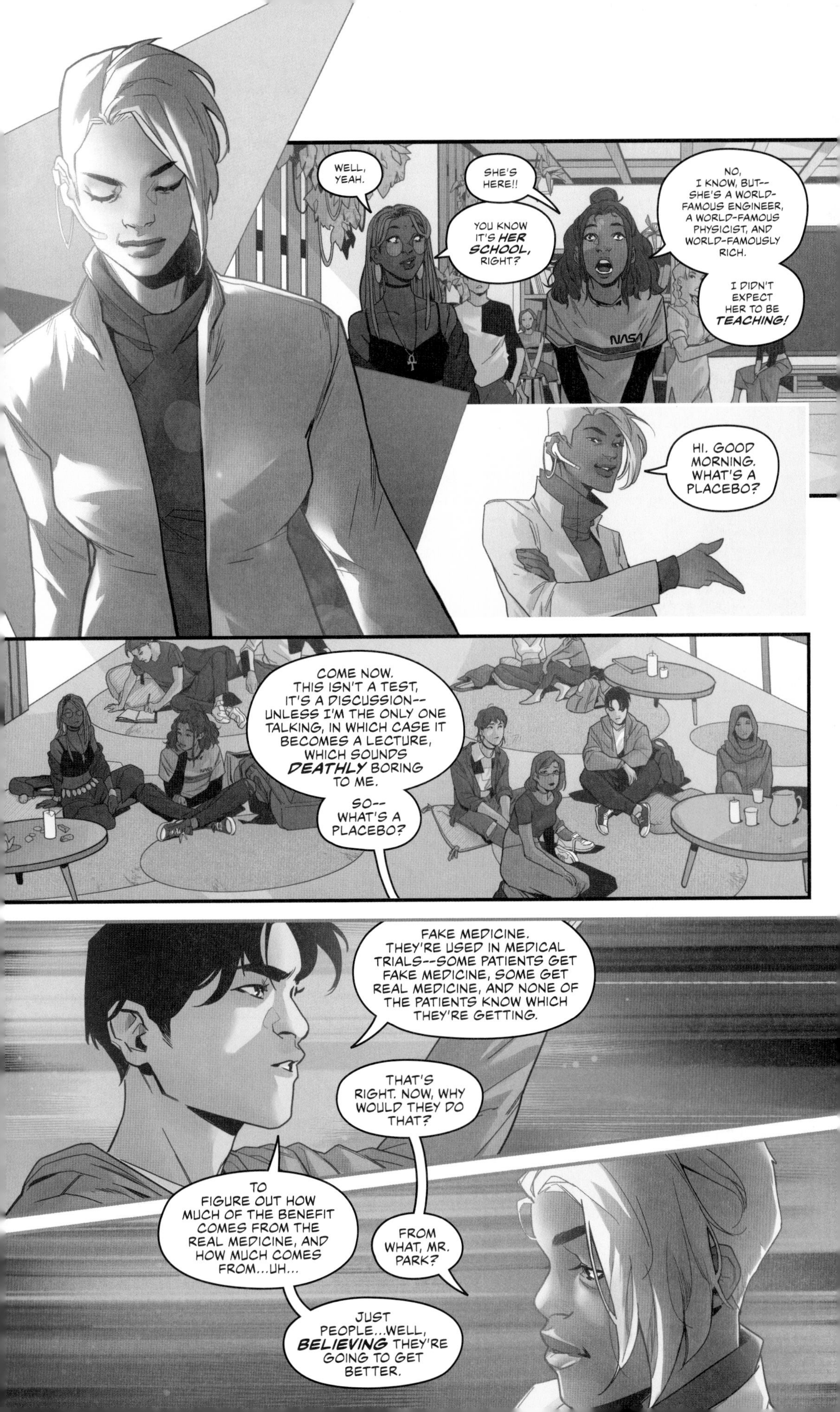
WELL, YEAH.
SHE'S HERE!!
YOU KNOW IT'S *HER SCHOOL,* RIGHT?
NO, I KNOW, BUT-- SHE'S A WORLD-FAMOUS ENGINEER, A WORLD-FAMOUS PHYSICIST, AND WORLD-FAMOUSLY RICH.
I DIDN'T EXPECT HER TO BE *TEACHING!*
HI. GOOD MORNING. WHAT'S A PLACEBO?
COME NOW. THIS ISN'T A TEST, IT'S A DISCUSSION-- UNLESS I'M THE ONLY ONE TALKING, IN WHICH CASE IT BECOMES A LECTURE, WHICH SOUNDS *DEATHLY* BORING TO ME.
SO-- WHAT'S A PLACEBO?
FAKE MEDICINE. THEY'RE USED IN MEDICAL TRIALS--SOME PATIENTS GET FAKE MEDICINE, SOME GET REAL MEDICINE, AND NONE OF THE PATIENTS KNOW WHICH THEY'RE GETTING.
THAT'S RIGHT. NOW, WHY WOULD THEY DO THAT?
TO FIGURE OUT HOW MUCH OF THE BENEFIT COMES FROM THE REAL MEDICINE, AND HOW MUCH COMES FROM...UH...
FROM WHAT, MR. PARK?
JUST PEOPLE...WELL, *BELIEVING* THEY'RE GOING TO GET BETTER.

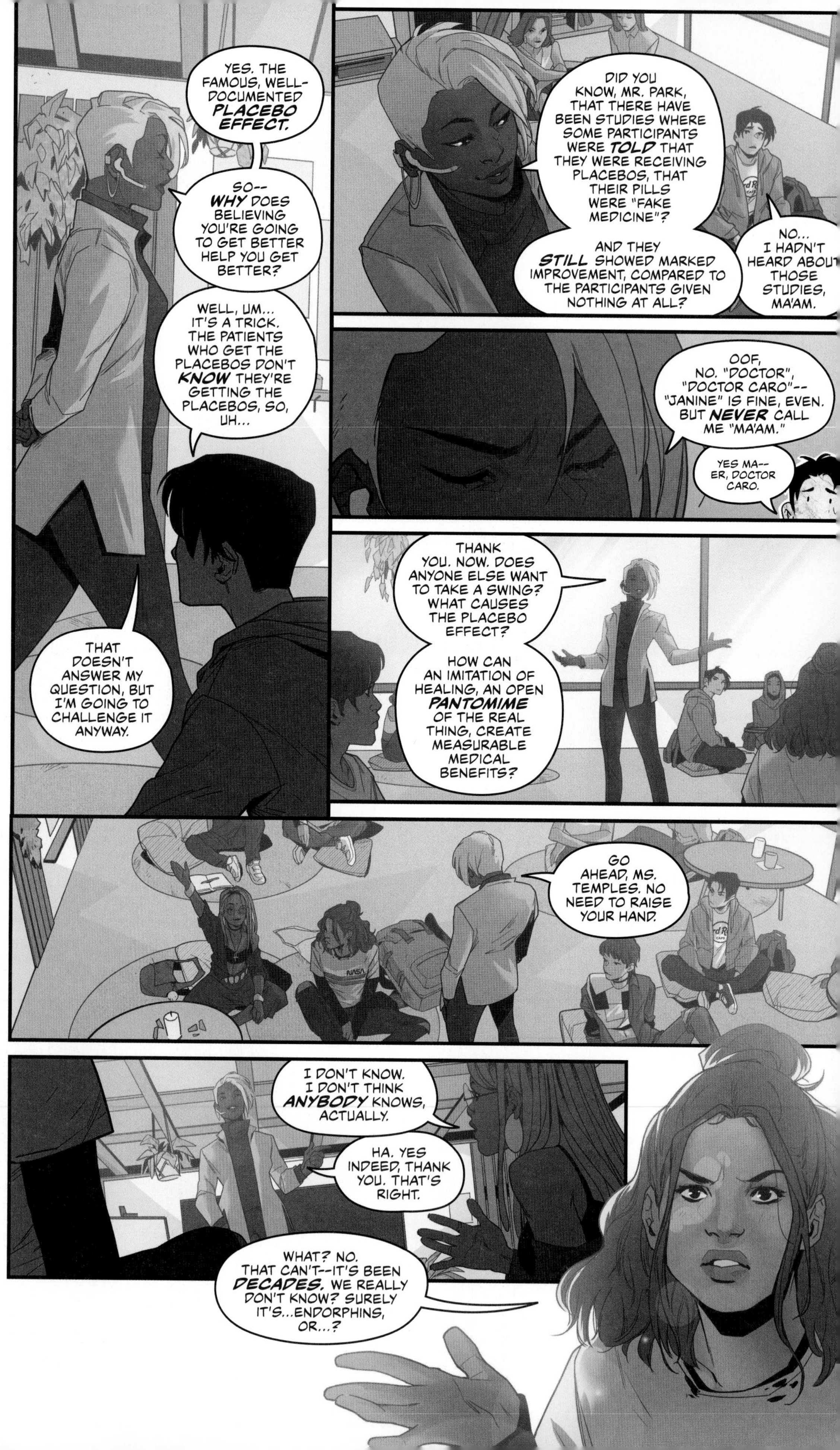
YES. THE FAMOUS, WELL-DOCUMENTED PLACEBO EFFECT.
SO-- WHY DOES BELIEVING YOU'RE GOING TO GET BETTER HELP YOU GET BETTER?
WELL, UM... IT'S A TRICK. THE PATIENTS WHO GET THE PLACEBOS DON'T KNOW THEY'RE GETTING THE PLACEBOS, SO, UH...
THAT DOESN'T ANSWER MY QUESTION, BUT I'M GOING TO CHALLENGE IT ANYWAY.
DID YOU KNOW, MR. PARK, THAT THERE HAVE BEEN STUDIES WHERE SOME PARTICIPANTS WERE TOLD THAT THEY WERE RECEIVING PLACEBOS, THAT THEIR PILLS WERE "FAKE MEDICINE"?
AND THEY STILL SHOWED MARKED IMPROVEMENT, COMPARED TO THE PARTICIPANTS GIVEN NOTHING AT ALL?
NO... I HADN'T HEARD ABOUT THOSE STUDIES, MA'AM.
OOF, NO. "DOCTOR", "DOCTOR CARO"-- "JANINE" IS FINE, EVEN. BUT NEVER CALL ME "MA'AM."
YES MA-- ER, DOCTOR CARO.
THANK YOU. NOW. DOES ANYONE ELSE WANT TO TAKE A SWING? WHAT CAUSES THE PLACEBO EFFECT?
HOW CAN AN IMITATION OF HEALING, AN OPEN PANTOMIME OF THE REAL THING, CREATE MEASURABLE MEDICAL BENEFITS?
GO AHEAD, MS. TEMPLES. NO NEED TO RAISE YOUR HAND.
I DON'T KNOW. I DON'T THINK ANYBODY KNOWS, ACTUALLY.
HA. YES INDEED, THANK YOU. THAT'S RIGHT.
WHAT? NO. THAT CAN'T--IT'S BEEN DECADES. WE REALLY DON'T KNOW? SURELY IT'S...ENDORPHINS, OR...?

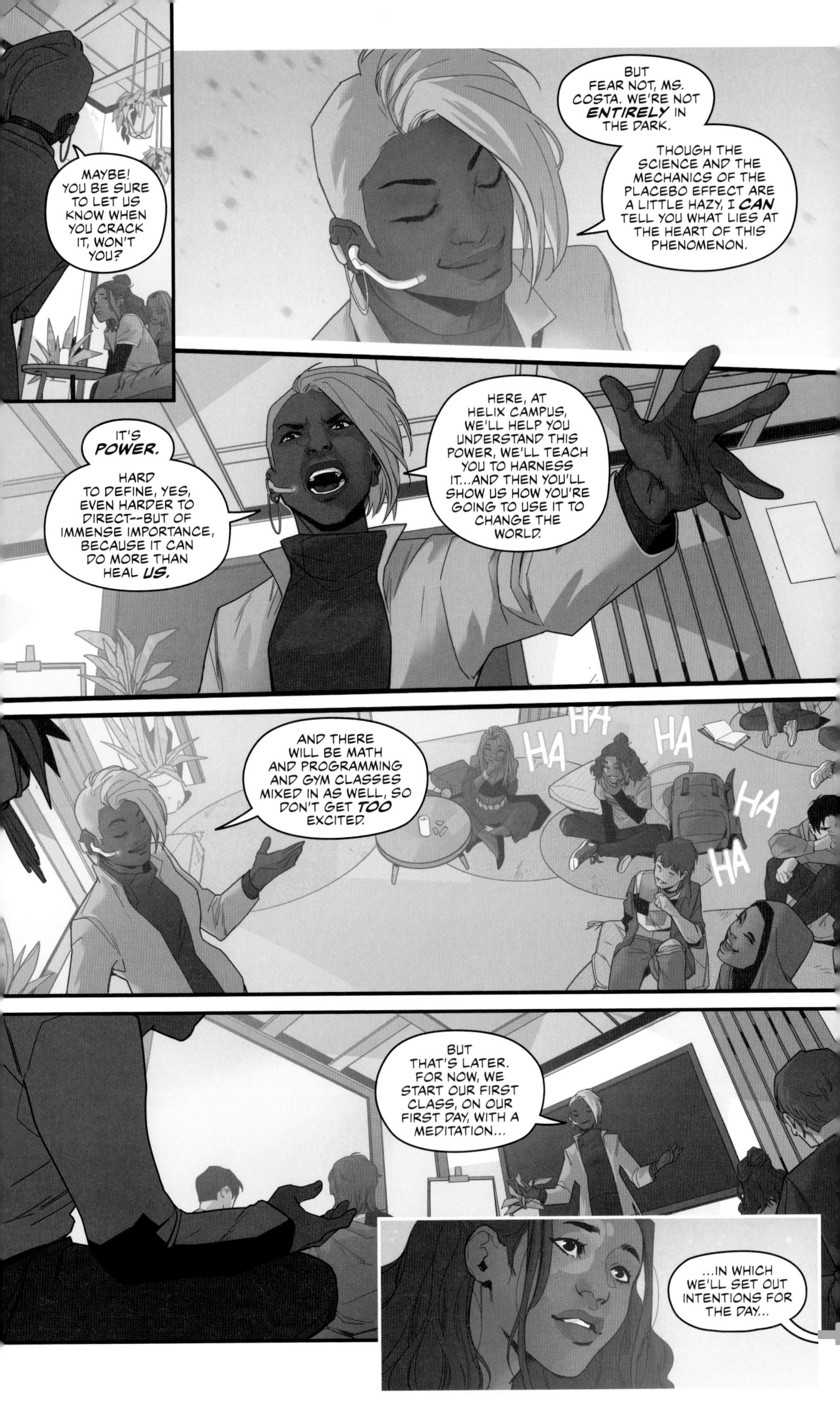

BUT FEAR NOT, MS. COSTA. WE'RE NOT ENTIRELY IN THE DARK.
THOUGH THE SCIENCE AND THE MECHANICS OF THE PLACEBO EFFECT ARE A LITTLE HAZY, I CAN TELL YOU WHAT LIES AT THE HEART OF THIS PHENOMENON.
MAYBE! YOU BE SURE TO LET US KNOW WHEN YOU CRACK IT, WON'T YOU?
IT'S POWER.
HARD TO DEFINE, YES, EVEN HARDER TO DIRECT--BUT OF IMMENSE IMPORTANCE, BECAUSE IT CAN DO MORE THAN HEAL US.
HERE, AT HELIX CAMPUS, WE'LL HELP YOU UNDERSTAND THIS POWER, WE'LL TEACH YOU TO HARNESS IT...AND THEN YOU'LL SHOW US HOW YOU'RE GOING TO USE IT TO CHANGE THE WORLD.
AND THERE WILL BE MATH AND PROGRAMMING AND GYM CLASSES MIXED IN AS WELL, SO DON'T GET TOO EXCITED.
HA HA HA HA HA
BUT THAT'S LATER. FOR NOW, WE START OUR FIRST CLASS, ON OUR FIRST DAY, WITH A MEDITATION...
...IN WHICH WE'LL SET OUT INTENTIONS FOR THE DAY...

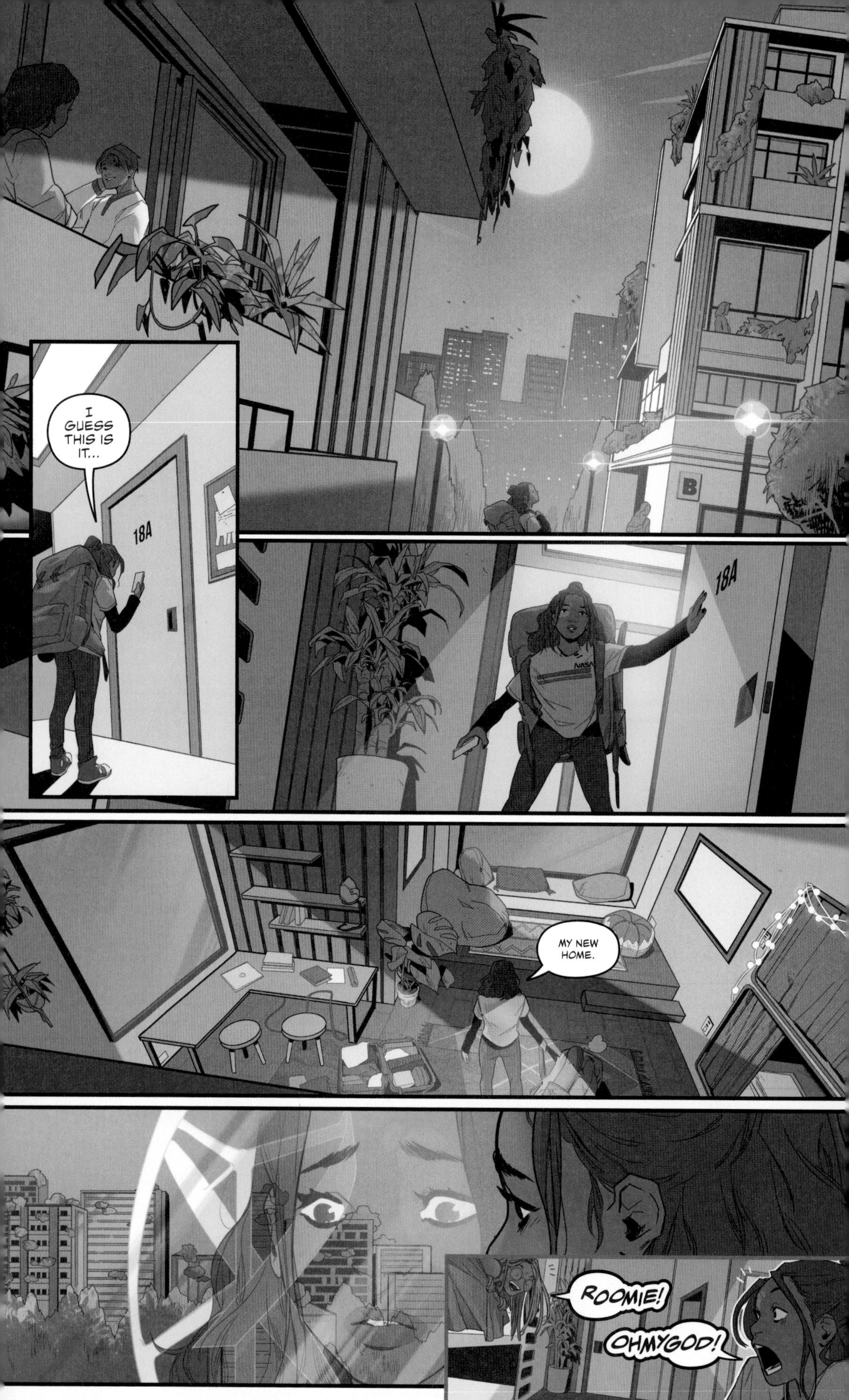

B
I GUESS THIS IS IT...
18A
18A
NASA
MY NEW HOME.
ROOMIE!
OHMYGOD!

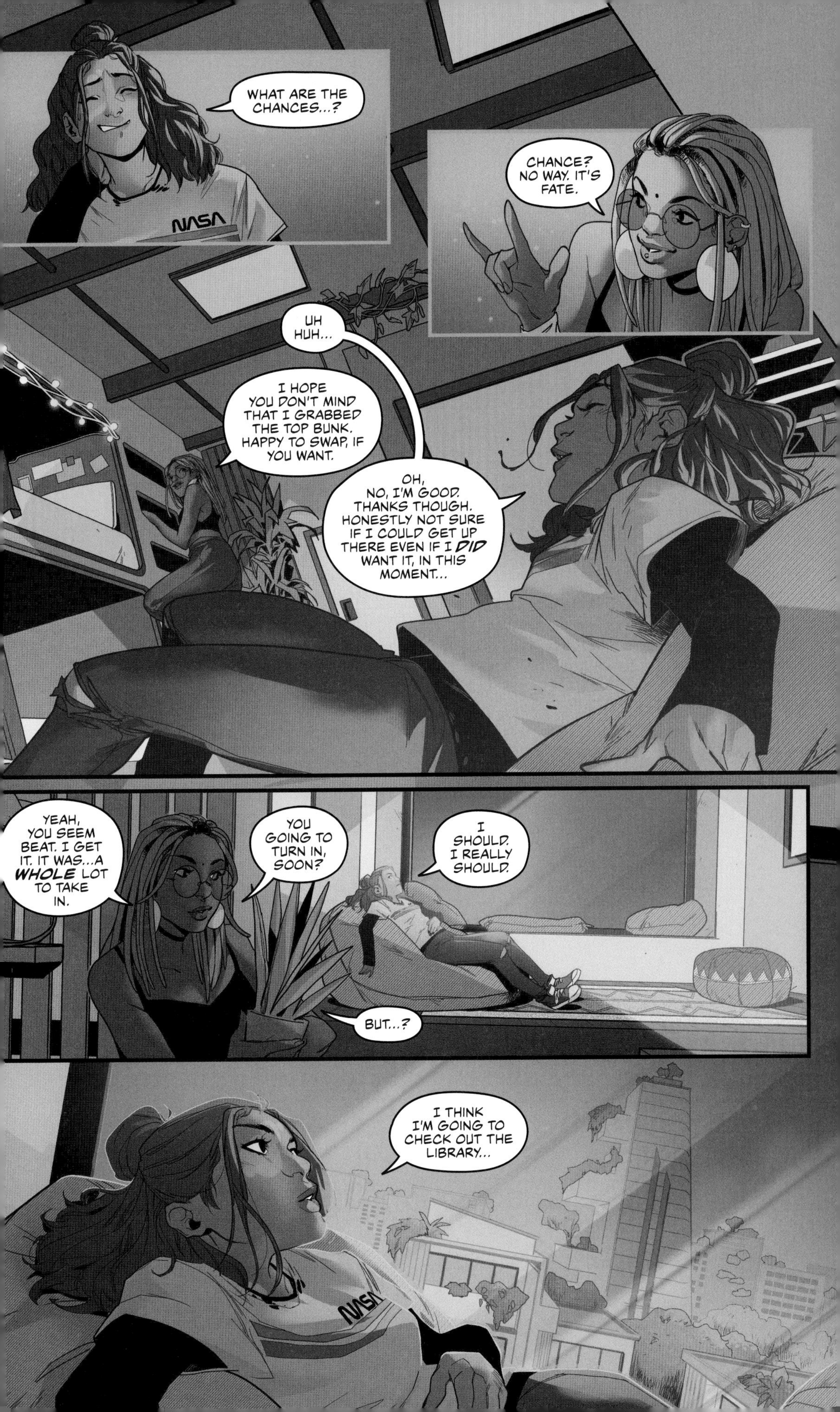
WHAT ARE THE CHANCES...?
CHANCE? NO WAY. IT'S FATE.
UH HUH...
I HOPE YOU DON'T MIND THAT I GRABBED THE TOP BUNK. HAPPY TO SWAP, IF YOU WANT.
OH, NO, I'M GOOD. THANKS THOUGH. HONESTLY NOT SURE IF I COULD GET UP THERE EVEN IF I DID WANT IT, IN THIS MOMENT...
YEAH, YOU SEEM BEAT. I GET IT. IT WAS...A WHOLE LOT TO TAKE IN.
YOU GOING TO TURN IN, SOON?
I SHOULD. I REALLY SHOULD.
BUT...?
I THINK I'M GOING TO CHECK OUT THE LIBRARY...

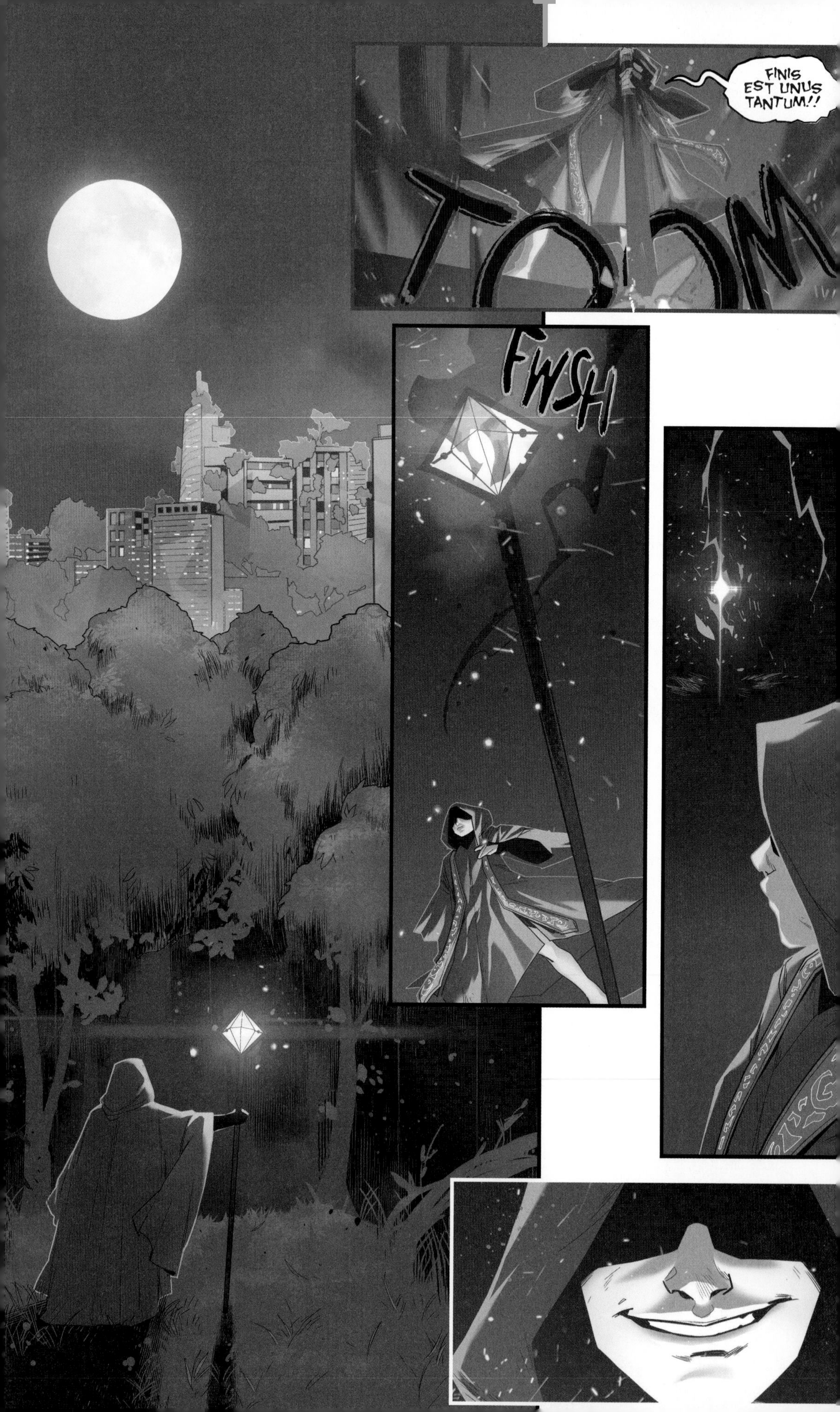
FINIS EST UNUS TANTUM!!
TOOOM
FWSH

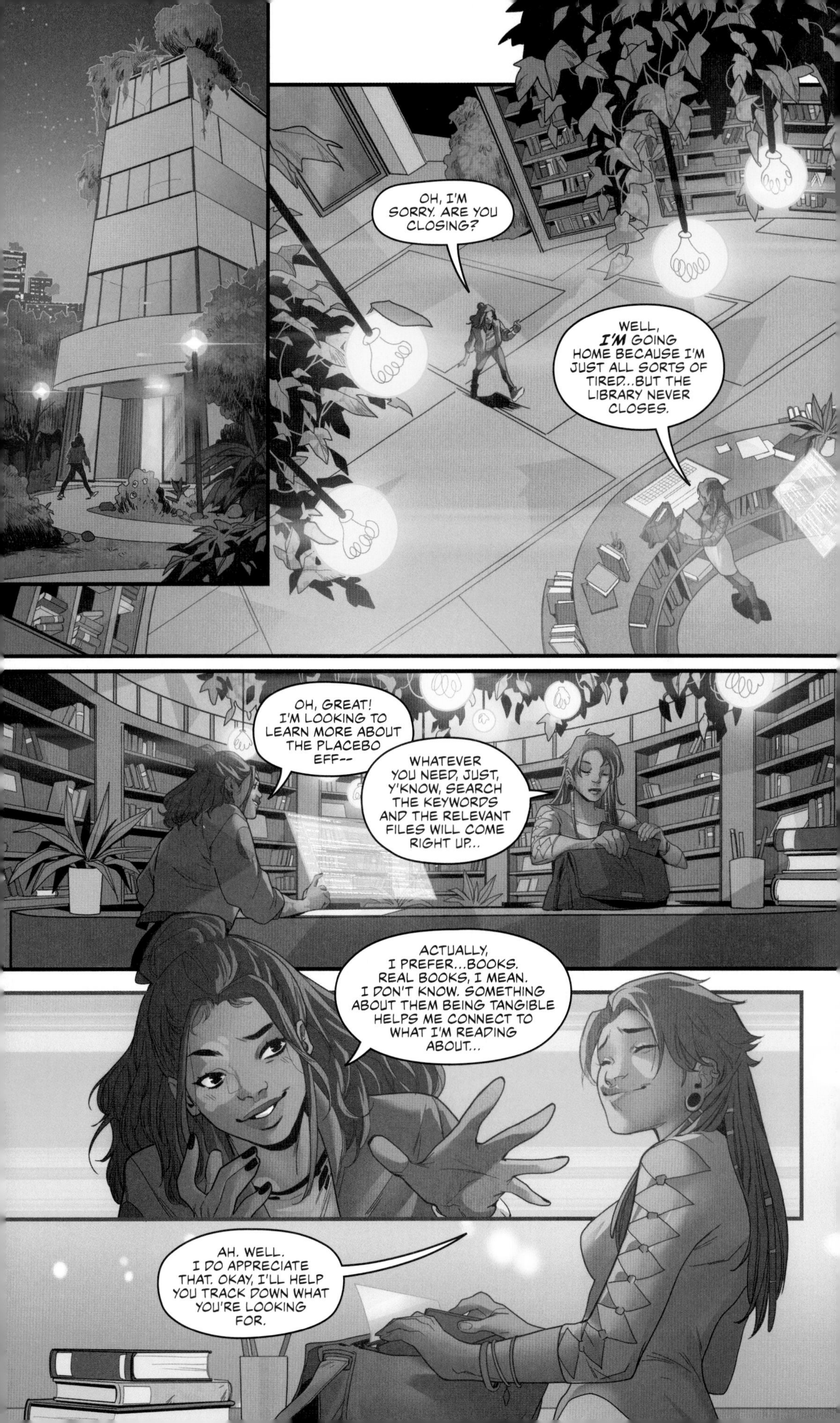

OH, I'M SORRY. ARE YOU CLOSING?
WELL, *I'M* GOING HOME BECAUSE I'M JUST ALL SORTS OF TIRED...BUT THE LIBRARY NEVER CLOSES.
OH, GREAT! I'M LOOKING TO LEARN MORE ABOUT THE PLACEBO EFF--
WHATEVER YOU NEED, JUST, Y'KNOW, SEARCH THE KEYWORDS AND THE RELEVANT FILES WILL COME RIGHT UP...
ACTUALLY, I PREFER...BOOKS. REAL BOOKS, I MEAN. I DON'T KNOW. SOMETHING ABOUT THEM BEING TANGIBLE HELPS ME CONNECT TO WHAT I'M READING ABOUT...
AH. WELL. I DO APPRECIATE THAT. OKAY, I'LL HELP YOU TRACK DOWN WHAT YOU'RE LOOKING FOR.

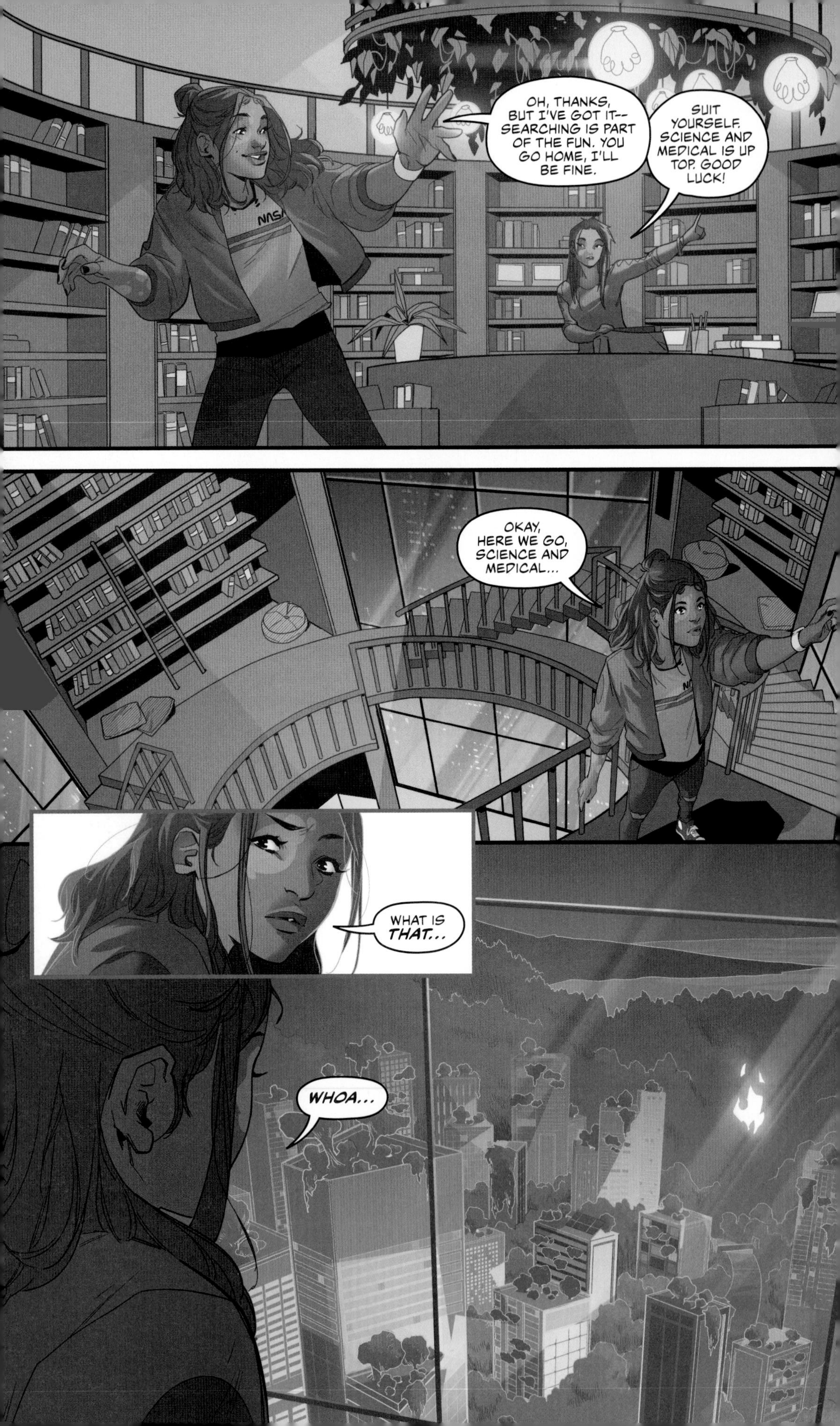
OH, THANKS, BUT I'VE GOT IT-- SEARCHING IS PART OF THE FUN. YOU GO HOME, I'LL BE FINE.
SUIT YOURSELF. SCIENCE AND MEDICAL IS UP TOP. GOOD LUCK!
OKAY, HERE WE GO, SCIENCE AND MEDICAL...
WHAT IS *THAT...*
WHOA...

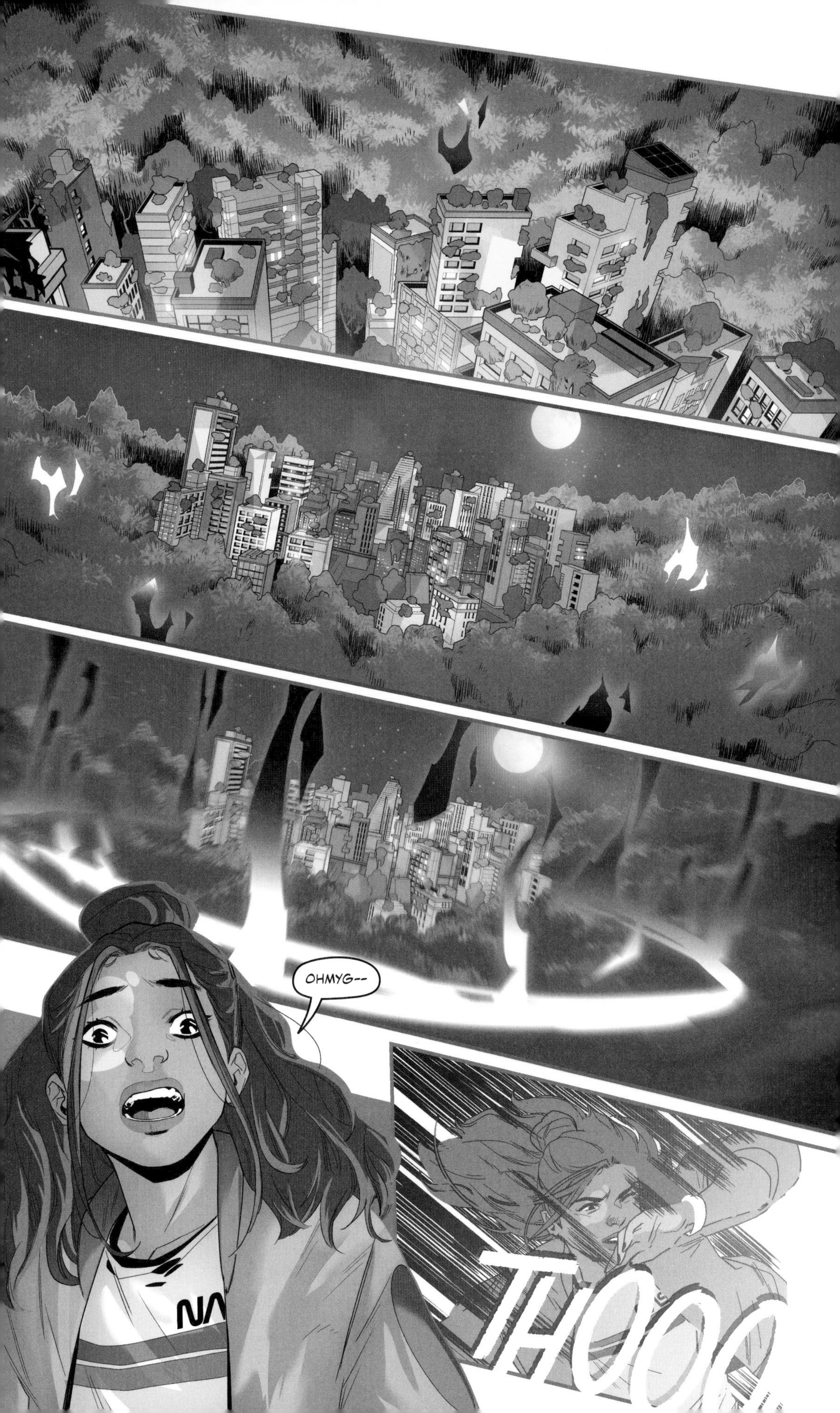
OHMYG--
THOO

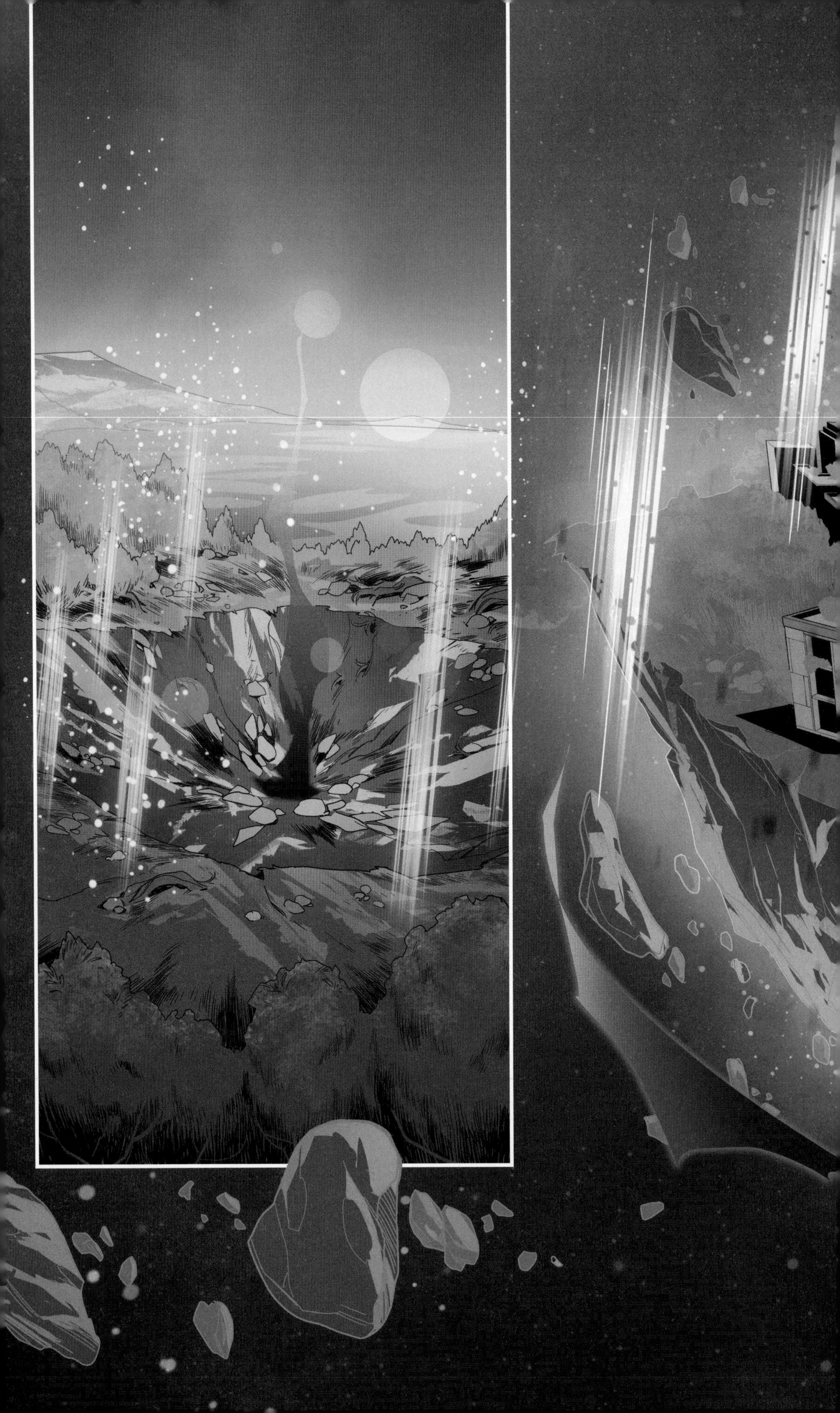

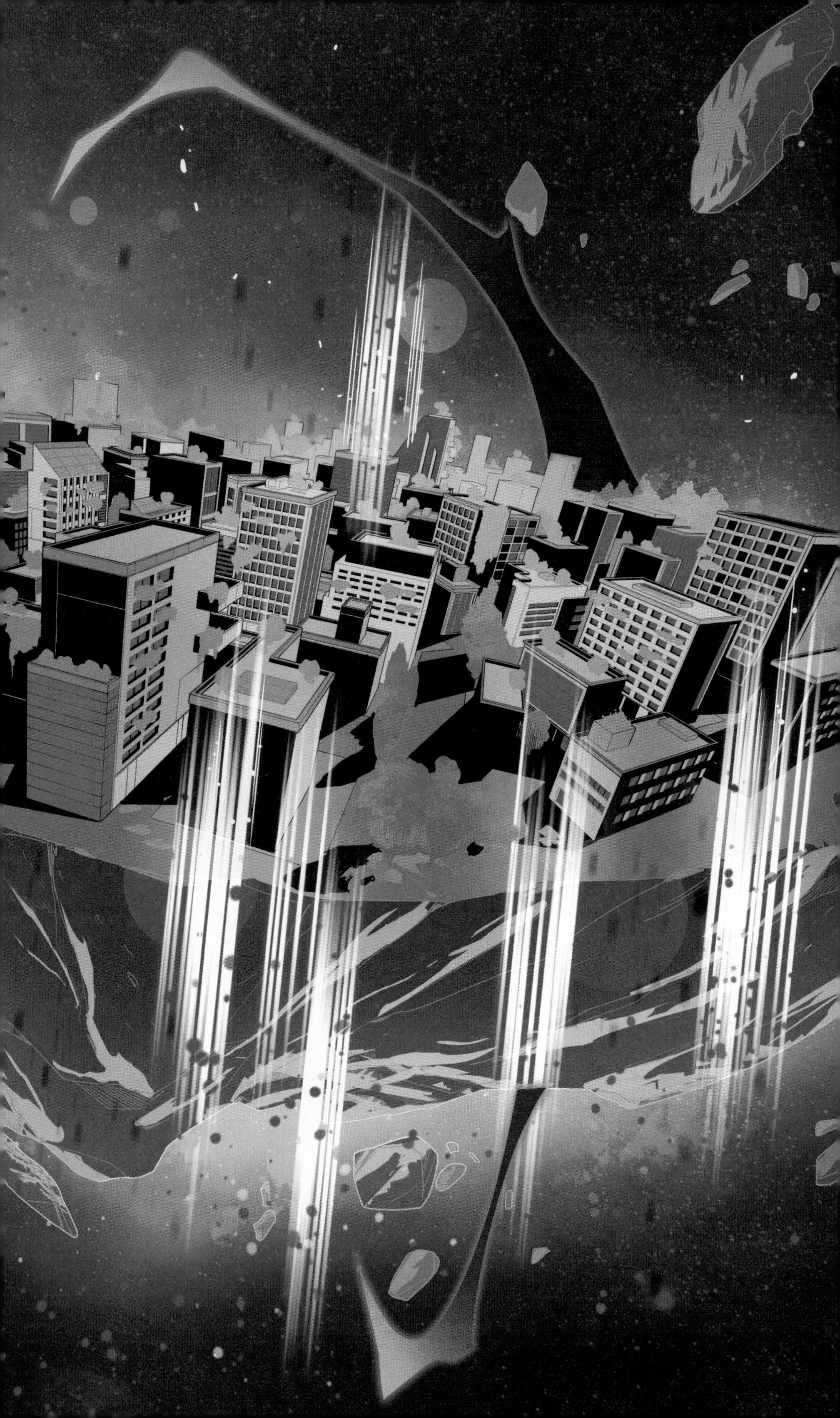

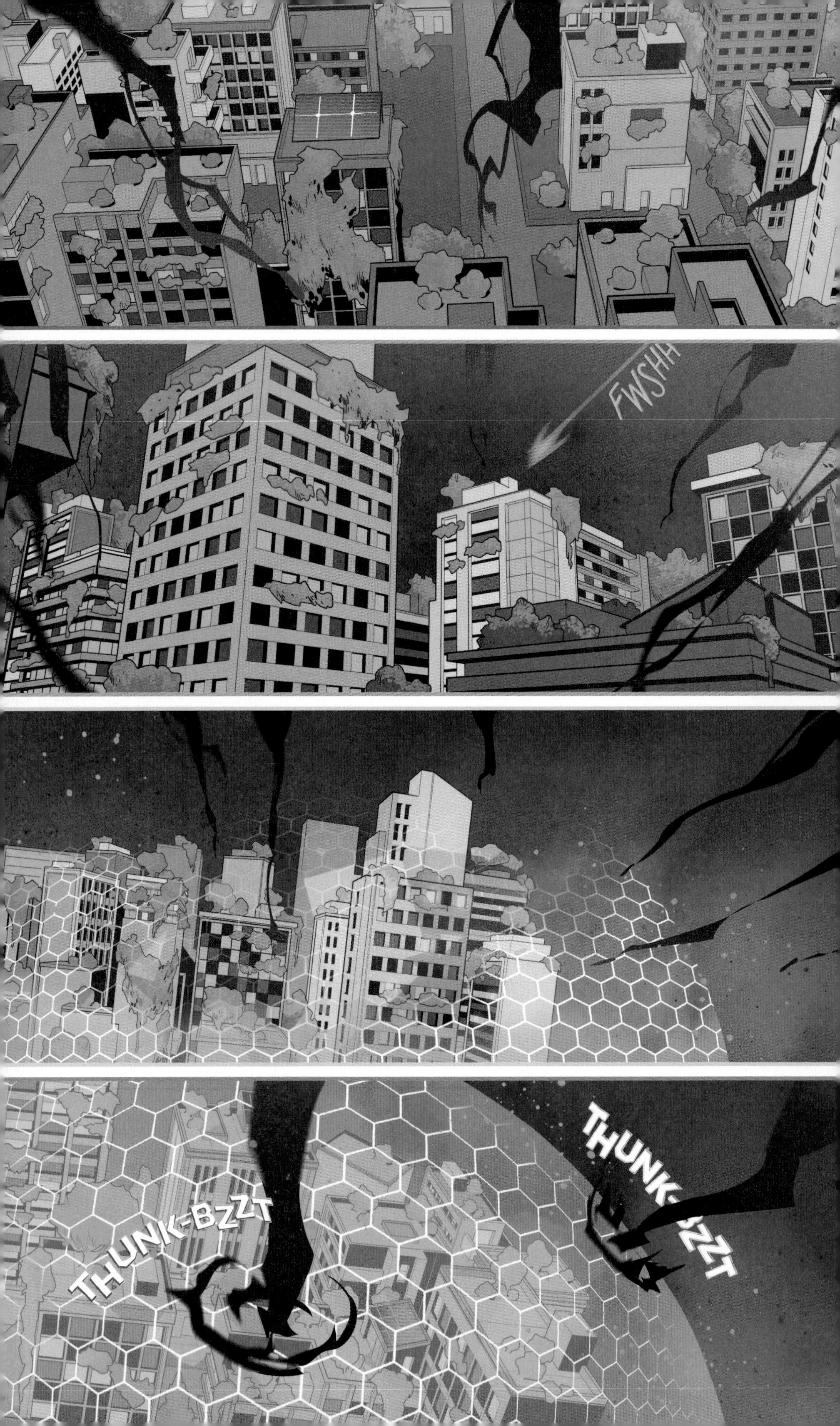
FWSHH
THUNK-BZZT
THUNK-BZZT

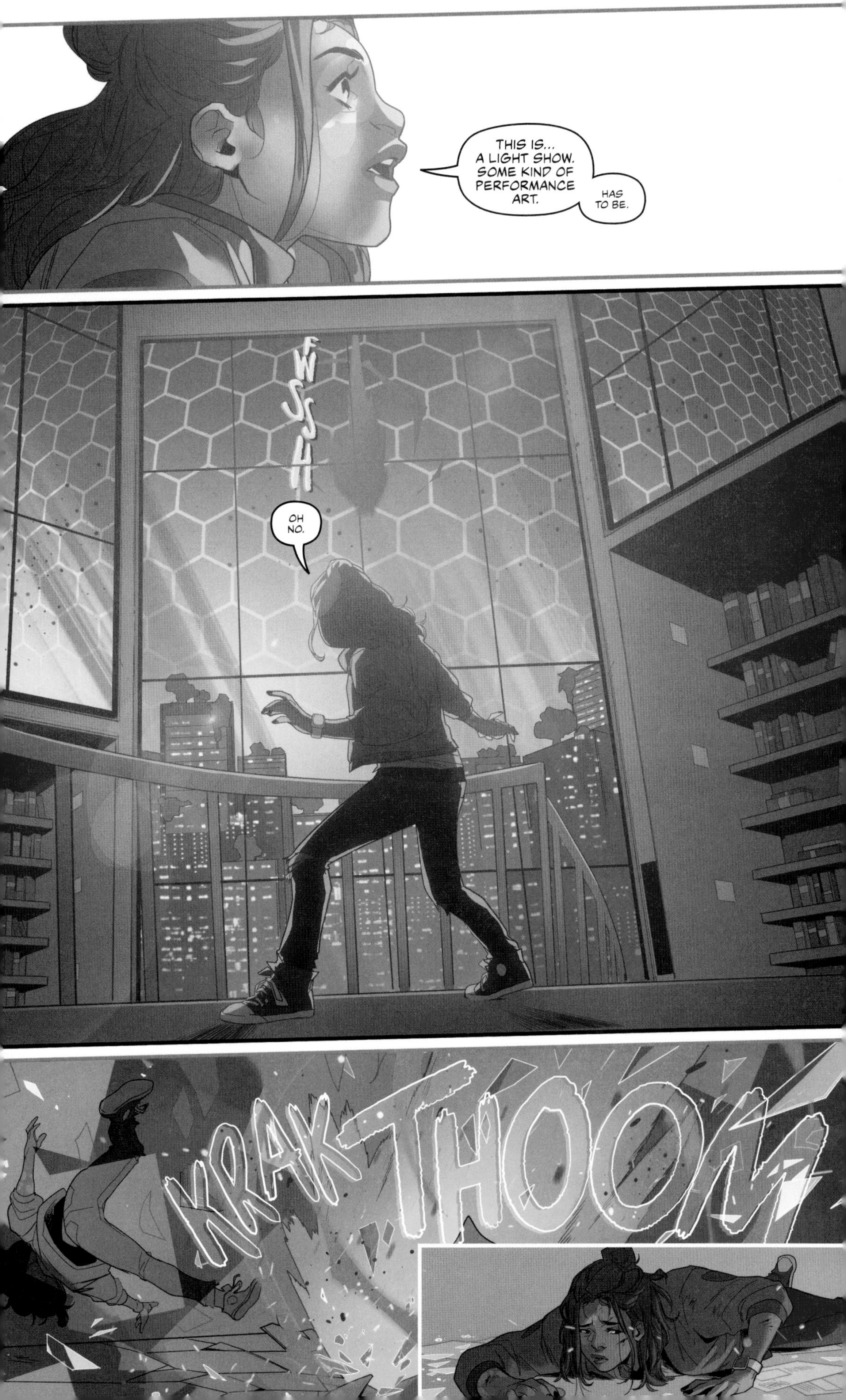
THIS IS... A LIGHT SHOW. SOME KIND OF PERFORMANCE ART.
HAS TO BE.
FWSSH
OH NO.
KRAKTHOOM

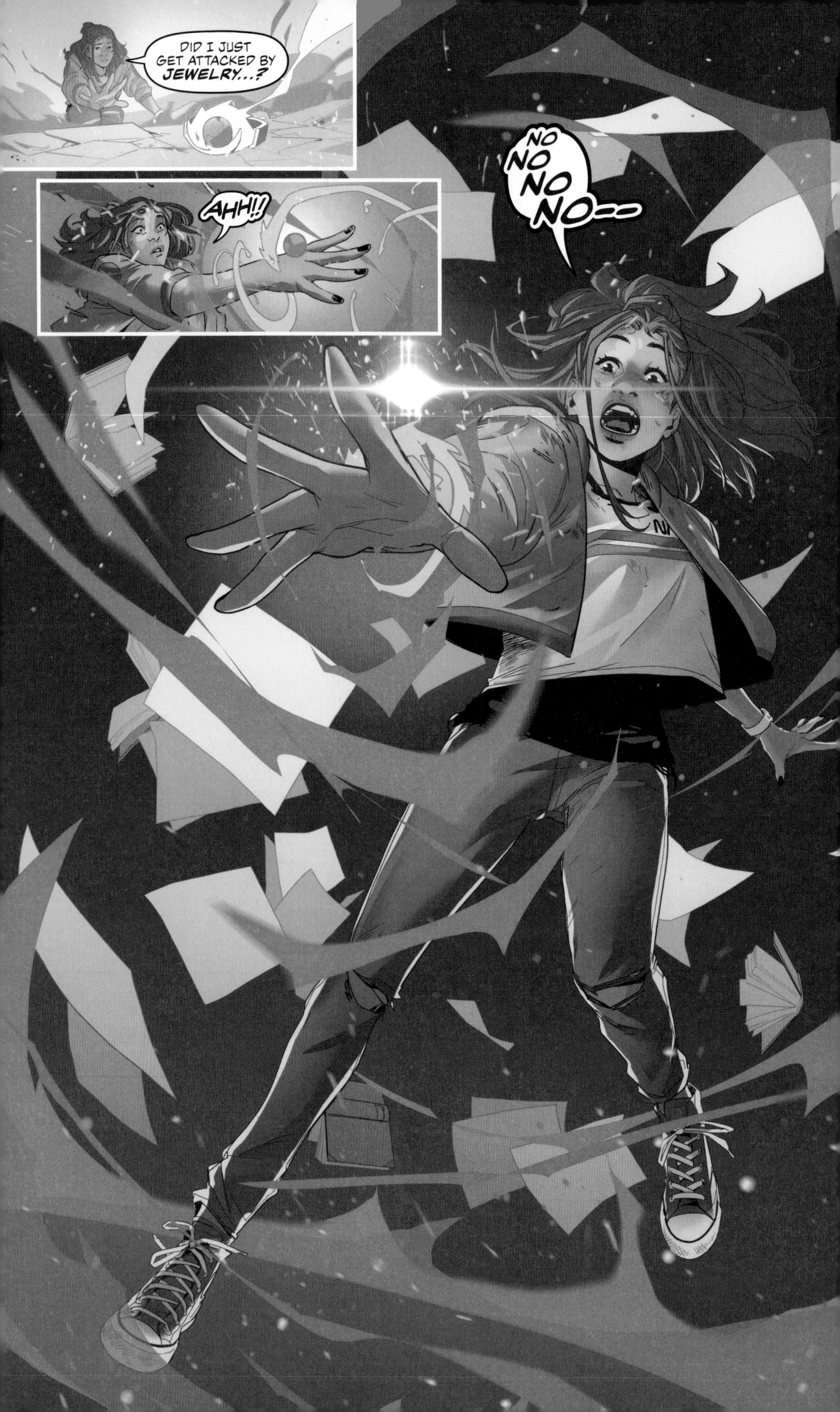
DID I JUST GET ATTACKED BY JEWELRY...?
AHH!!
NO NO NO NO--

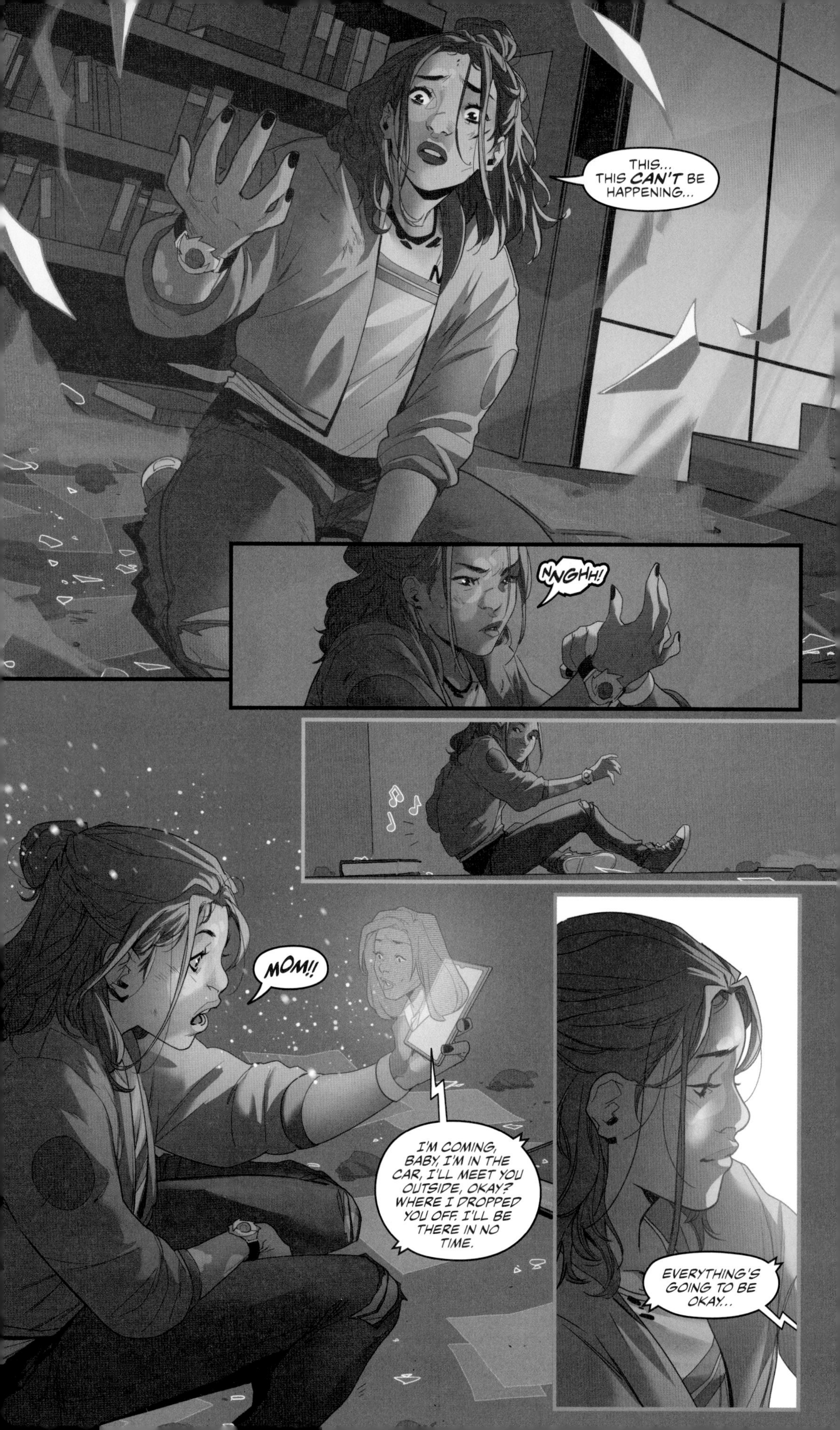
THIS... THIS CAN'T BE HAPPENING...
NNGHH!
MOM!!
I'M COMING, BABY, I'M IN THE CAR, I'LL MEET YOU OUTSIDE, OKAY? WHERE I DROPPED YOU OFF. I'LL BE THERE IN NO TIME.
EVERYTHING'S GOING TO BE OKAY...

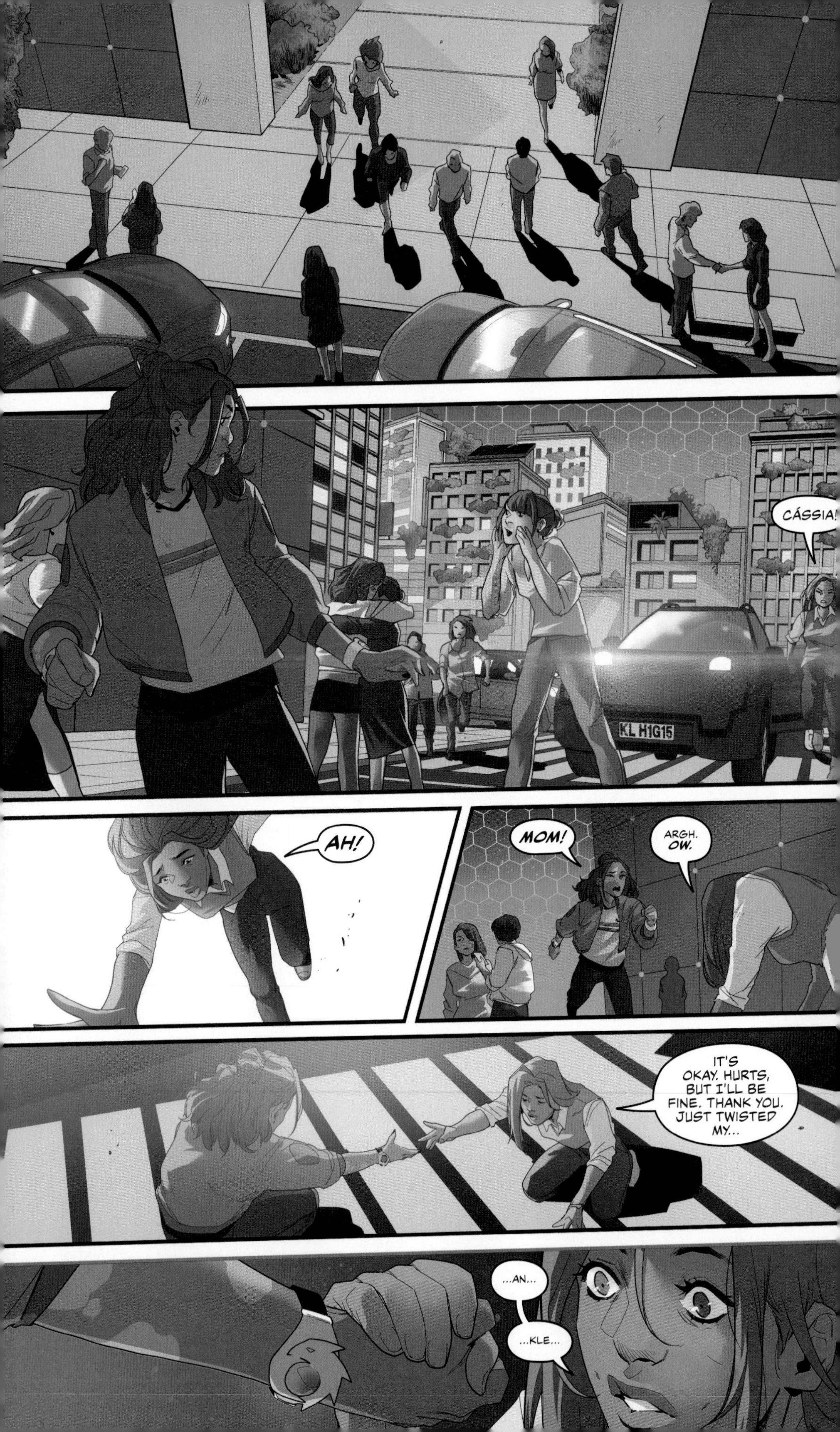
KL H1G15
CÁSSIA!
AH!
MOM!
ARGH. OW.
IT'S OKAY. HURTS, BUT I'LL BE FINE. THANK YOU. JUST TWISTED MY...
...AN...
...KLE...

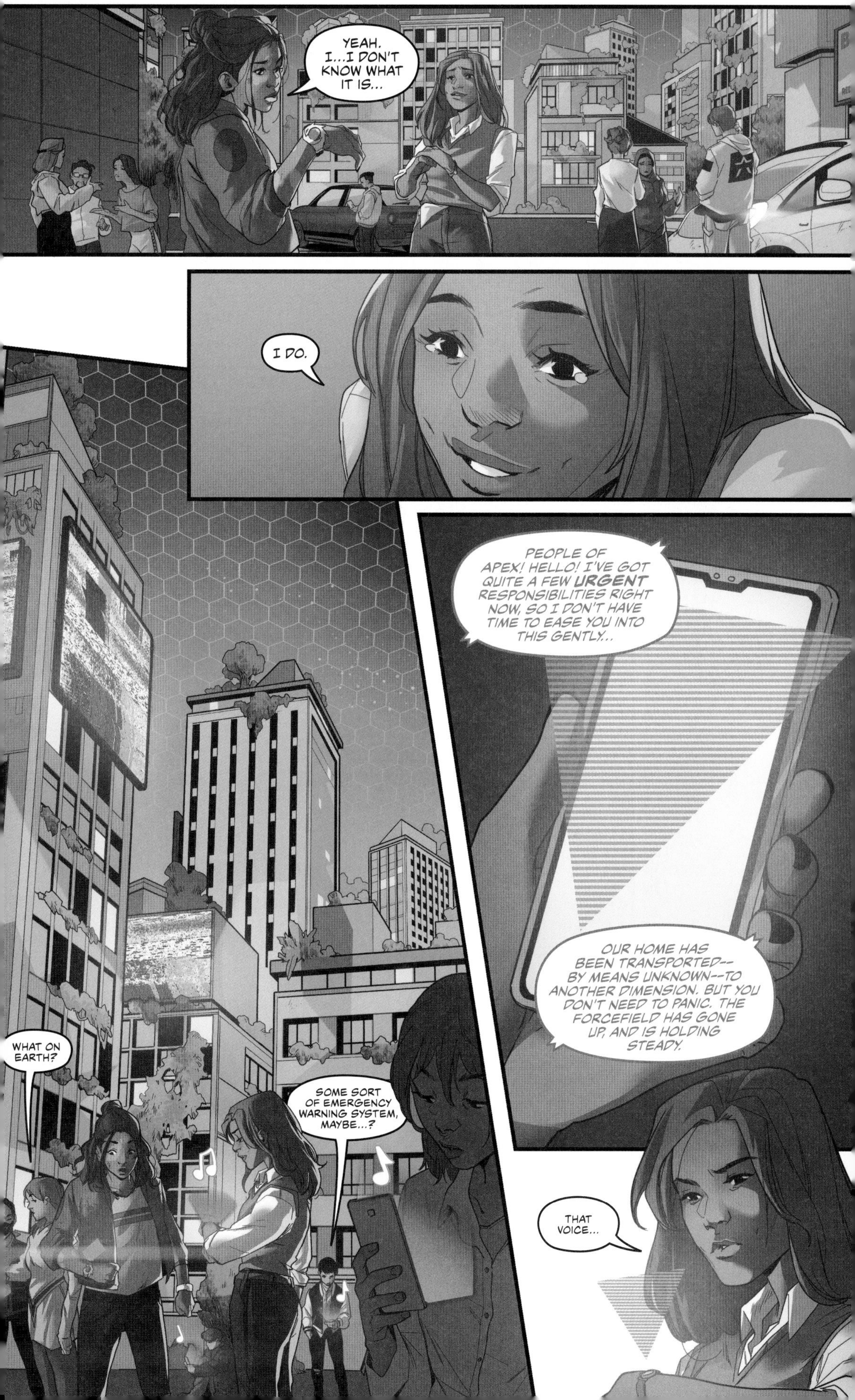
YEAH. I...I DON'T KNOW WHAT IT IS...
I DO.
WHAT ON EARTH?
SOME SORT OF EMERGENCY WARNING SYSTEM, MAYBE...?
PEOPLE OF APEX! HELLO! I'VE GOT QUITE A FEW URGENT RESPONSIBILITIES RIGHT NOW, SO I DON'T HAVE TIME TO EASE YOU INTO THIS GENTLY...
OUR HOME HAS BEEN TRANSPORTED--BY MEANS UNKNOWN--TO ANOTHER DIMENSION. BUT YOU DON'T NEED TO PANIC. THE FORCEFIELD HAS GONE UP, AND IS HOLDING STEADY.
THAT VOICE...

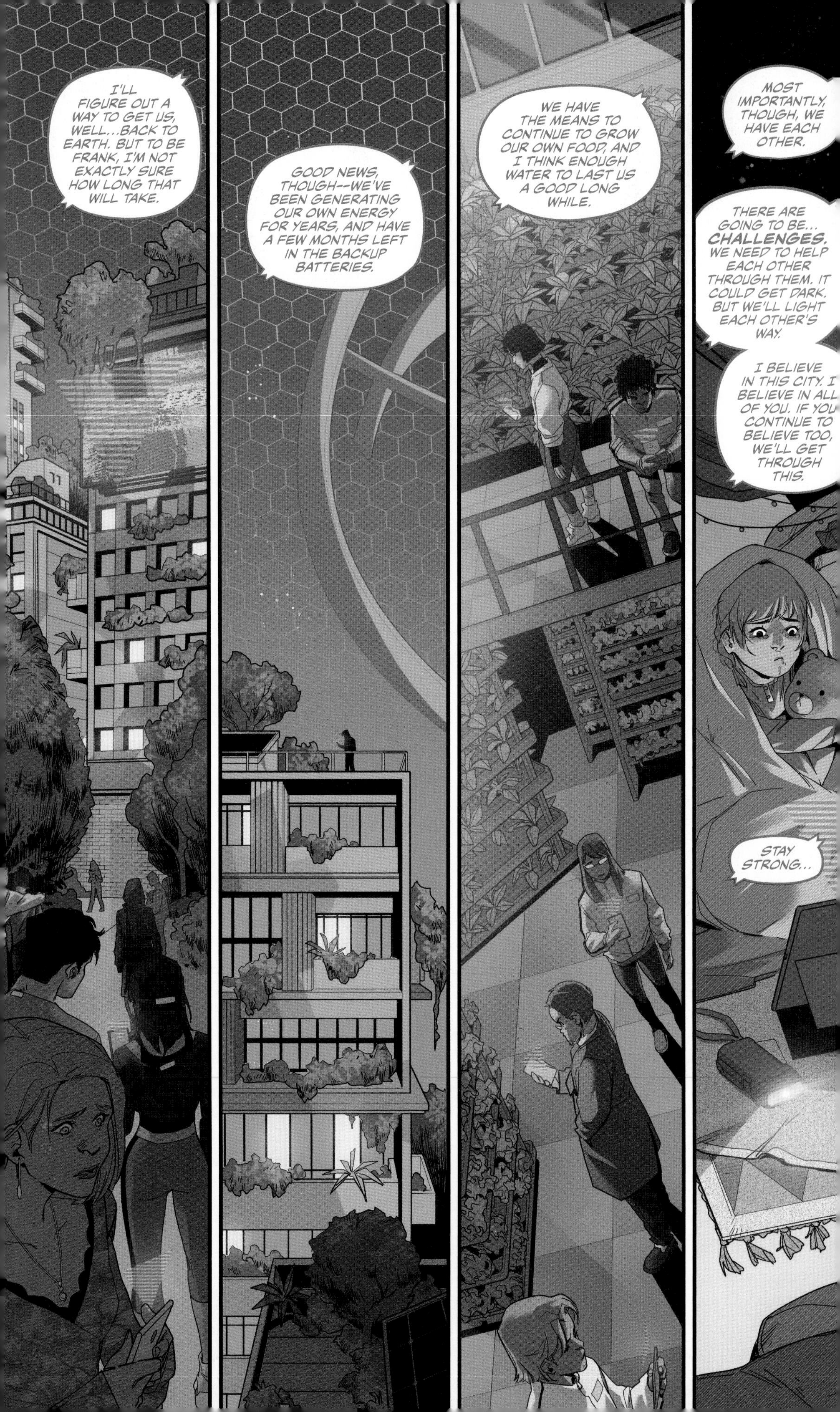
I'LL FIGURE OUT A WAY TO GET US, WELL...BACK TO EARTH. BUT TO BE FRANK, I'M NOT EXACTLY SURE HOW LONG THAT WILL TAKE.
GOOD NEWS, THOUGH--WE'VE BEEN GENERATING OUR OWN ENERGY FOR YEARS, AND HAVE A FEW MONTHS LEFT IN THE BACKUP BATTERIES.
WE HAVE THE MEANS TO CONTINUE TO GROW OUR OWN FOOD, AND I THINK ENOUGH WATER TO LAST US A GOOD LONG WHILE.
MOST IMPORTANTLY, THOUGH, WE HAVE EACH OTHER.
THERE ARE GOING TO BE... **CHALLENGES.** WE NEED TO HELP EACH OTHER THROUGH THEM. IT COULD GET DARK. BUT WE'LL LIGHT EACH OTHER'S WAY.
I BELIEVE IN THIS CITY. I BELIEVE IN ALL OF YOU. IF YOU CONTINUE TO BELIEVE TOO, WE'LL GET THROUGH THIS.
STAY STRONG...

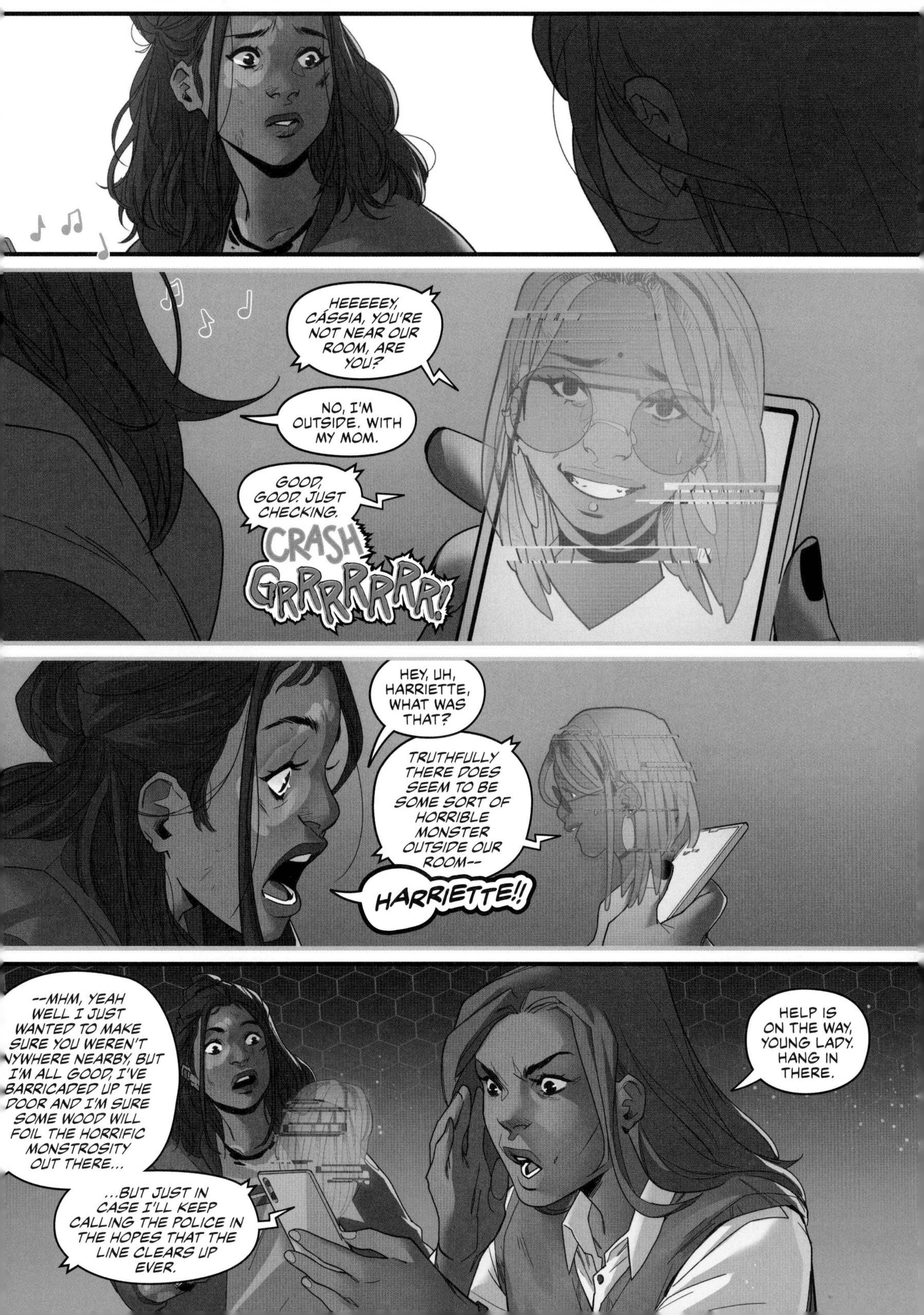
HEEEEEY, CÁSSIA, YOU'RE NOT NEAR OUR ROOM, ARE YOU?
NO, I'M OUTSIDE. WITH MY MOM.
GOOD, GOOD. JUST CHECKING.
CRASH
GRRRRRRR!
HEY, UH, HARRIETTE, WHAT WAS THAT?
TRUTHFULLY THERE DOES SEEM TO BE SOME SORT OF HORRIBLE MONSTER OUTSIDE OUR ROOM--
HARRIETTE!!
--MHM, YEAH WELL I JUST WANTED TO MAKE SURE YOU WEREN'T NYWHERE NEARBY, BUT I'M ALL GOOD, I'VE BARRICADED UP THE DOOR AND I'M SURE SOME WOOD WILL FOIL THE HORRIFIC MONSTROSITY OUT THERE...
...BUT JUST IN CASE I'LL KEEP CALLING THE POLICE IN THE HOPES THAT THE LINE CLEARS UP EVER.
HELP IS ON THE WAY, YOUNG LADY. HANG IN THERE.

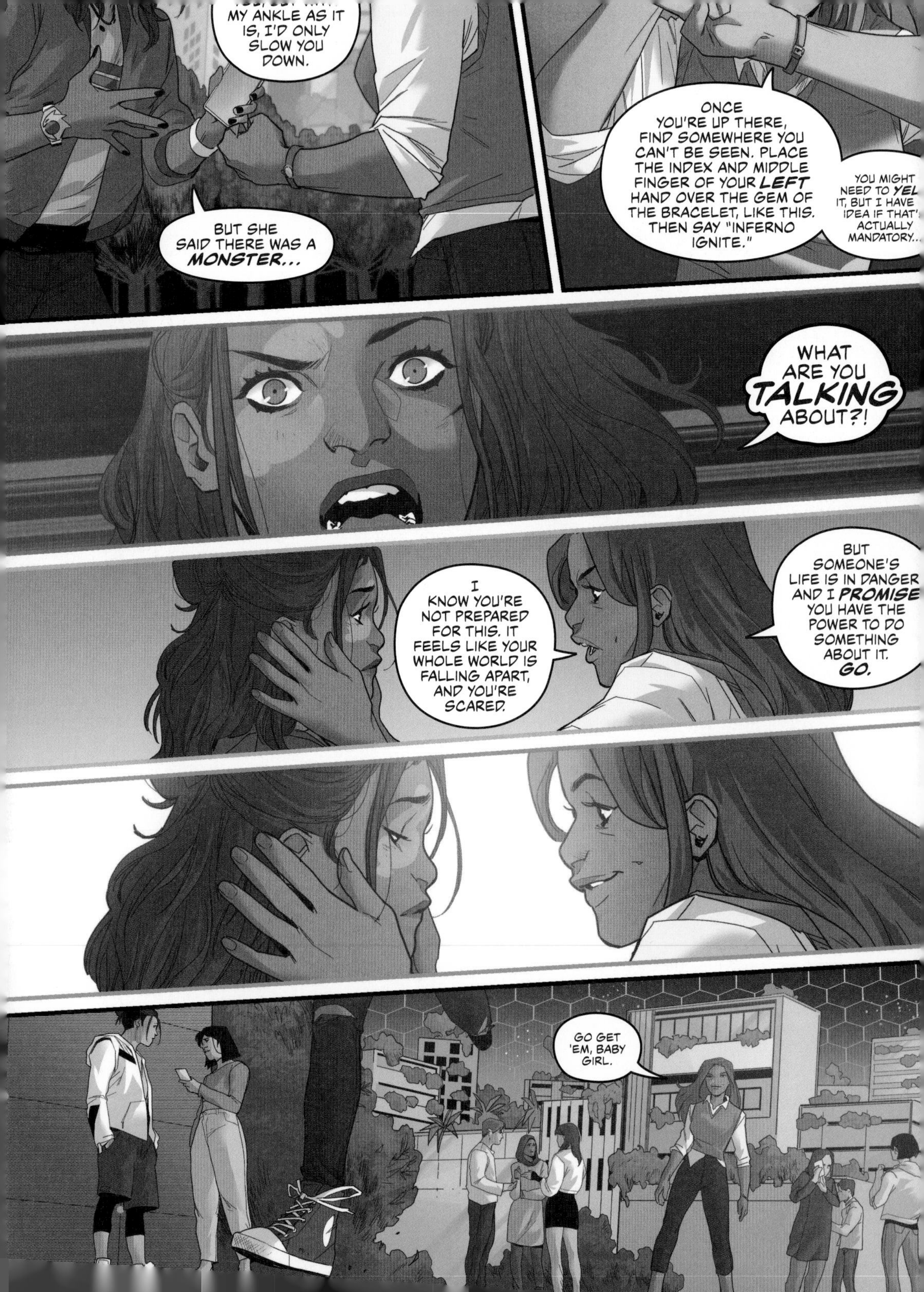
MY ANKLE AS IT IS, I'D ONLY SLOW YOU DOWN.
BUT SHE SAID THERE WAS A MONSTER...
ONCE YOU'RE UP THERE, FIND SOMEWHERE YOU CAN'T BE SEEN. PLACE THE INDEX AND MIDDLE FINGER OF YOUR LEFT HAND OVER THE GEM OF THE BRACELET, LIKE THIS. THEN SAY "INFERNO IGNITE."
YOU MIGHT NEED TO YEL IT, BUT I HAVE IDEA IF THAT' ACTUALLY MANDATORY...
WHAT ARE YOU TALKING ABOUT?!
I KNOW YOU'RE NOT PREPARED FOR THIS. IT FEELS LIKE YOUR WHOLE WORLD IS FALLING APART, AND YOU'RE SCARED.
BUT SOMEONE'S LIFE IS IN DANGER AND I PROMISE YOU HAVE THE POWER TO DO SOMETHING ABOUT IT. GO.
GO GET 'EM, BABY GIRL.

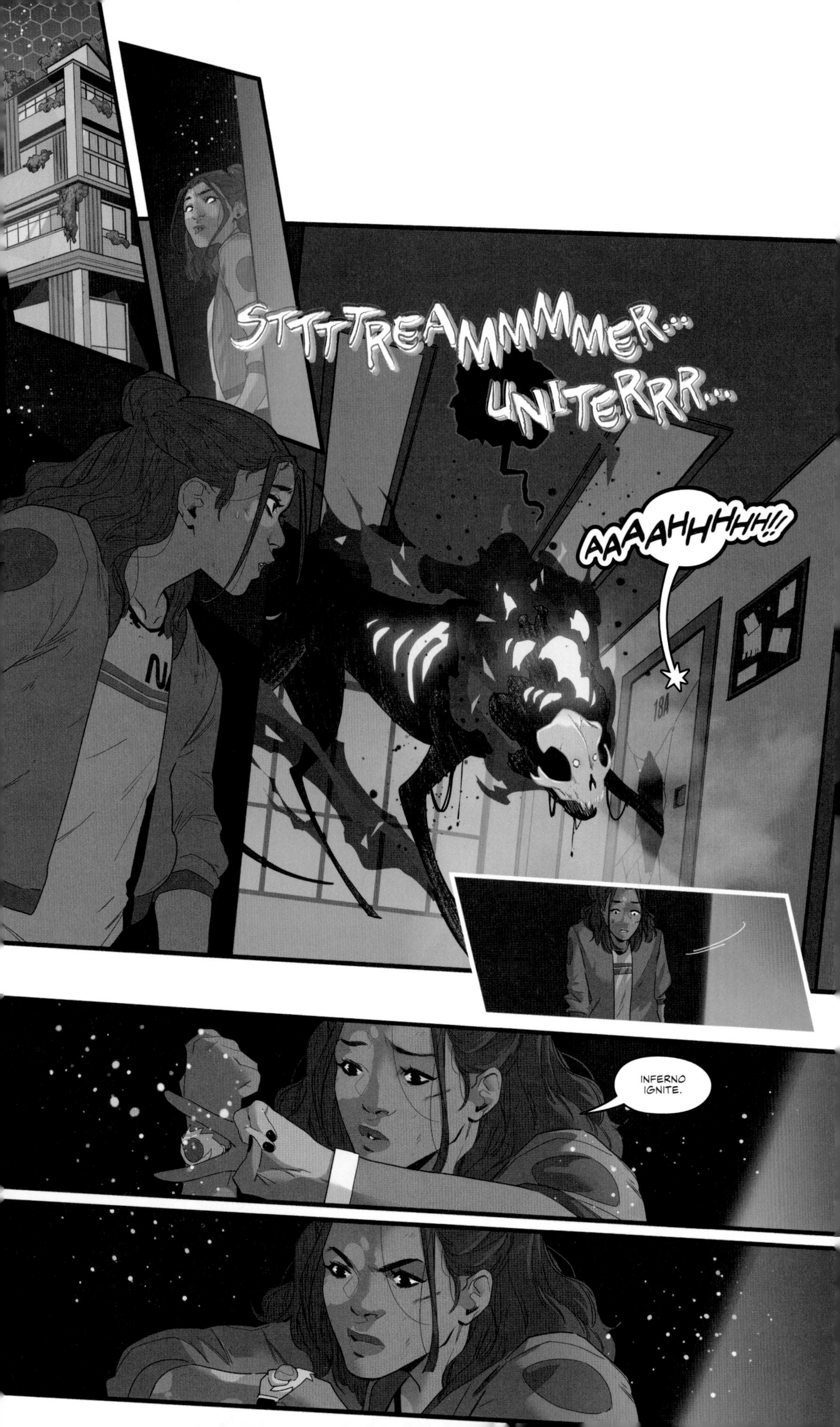
STTTTREAMMMMMER...
UNITERRR...
AAAAHHHHH!!
INFERNO IGNITE.

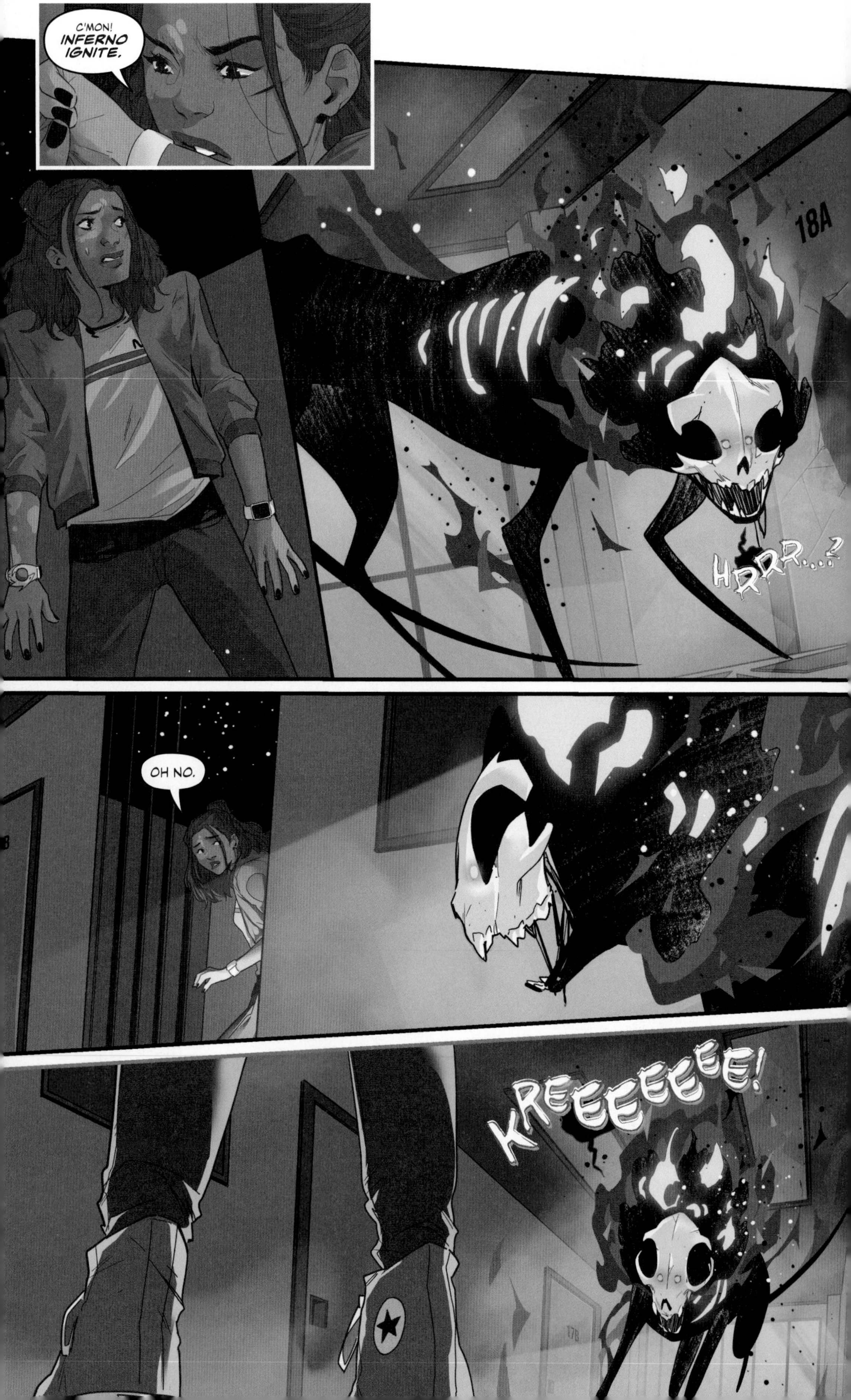
C'MON! INFERNO IGNITE.
18A
HRRR...?
OH NO.
KREEEEEEE!

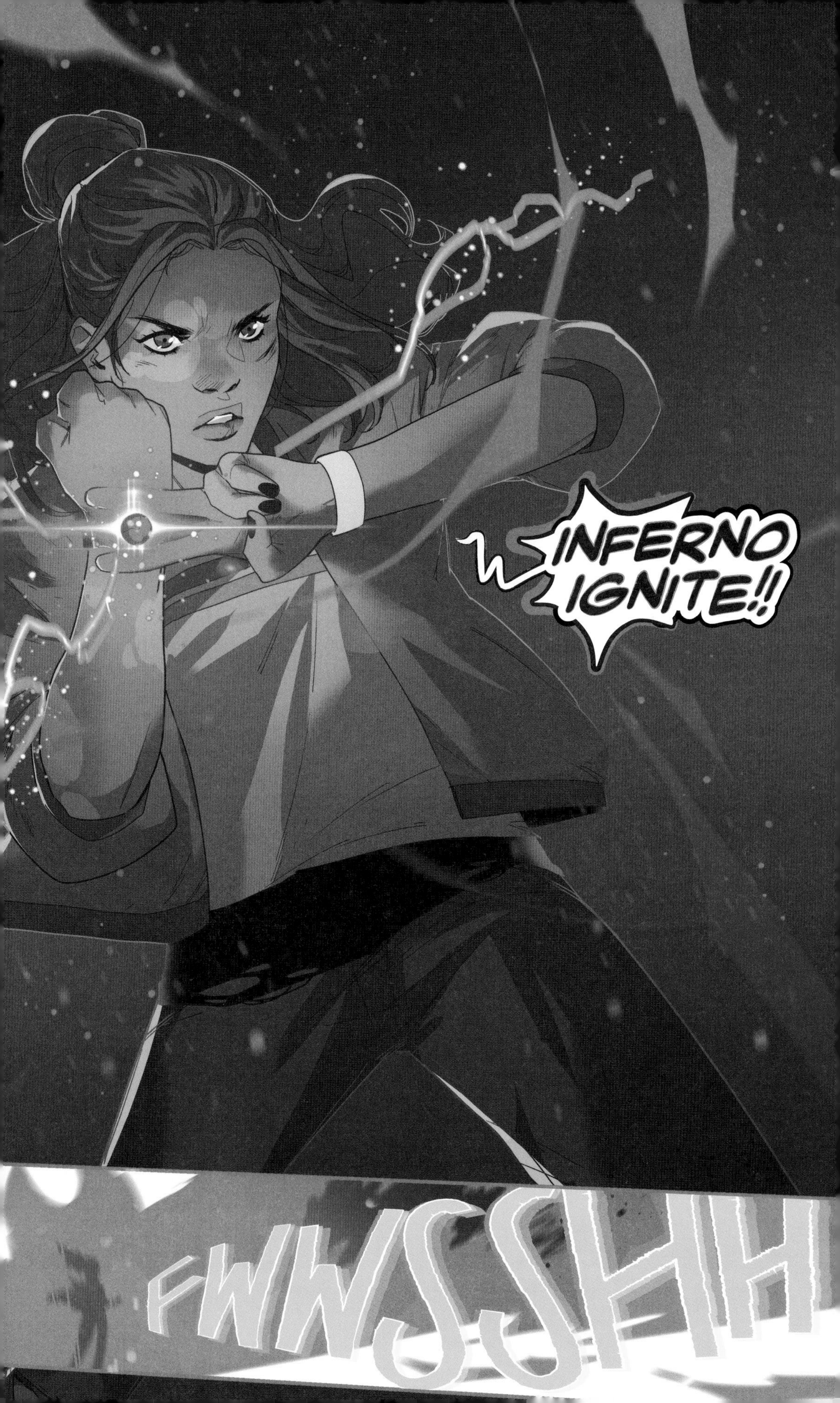
INFERNO IGNITE!!
FWWSSHH

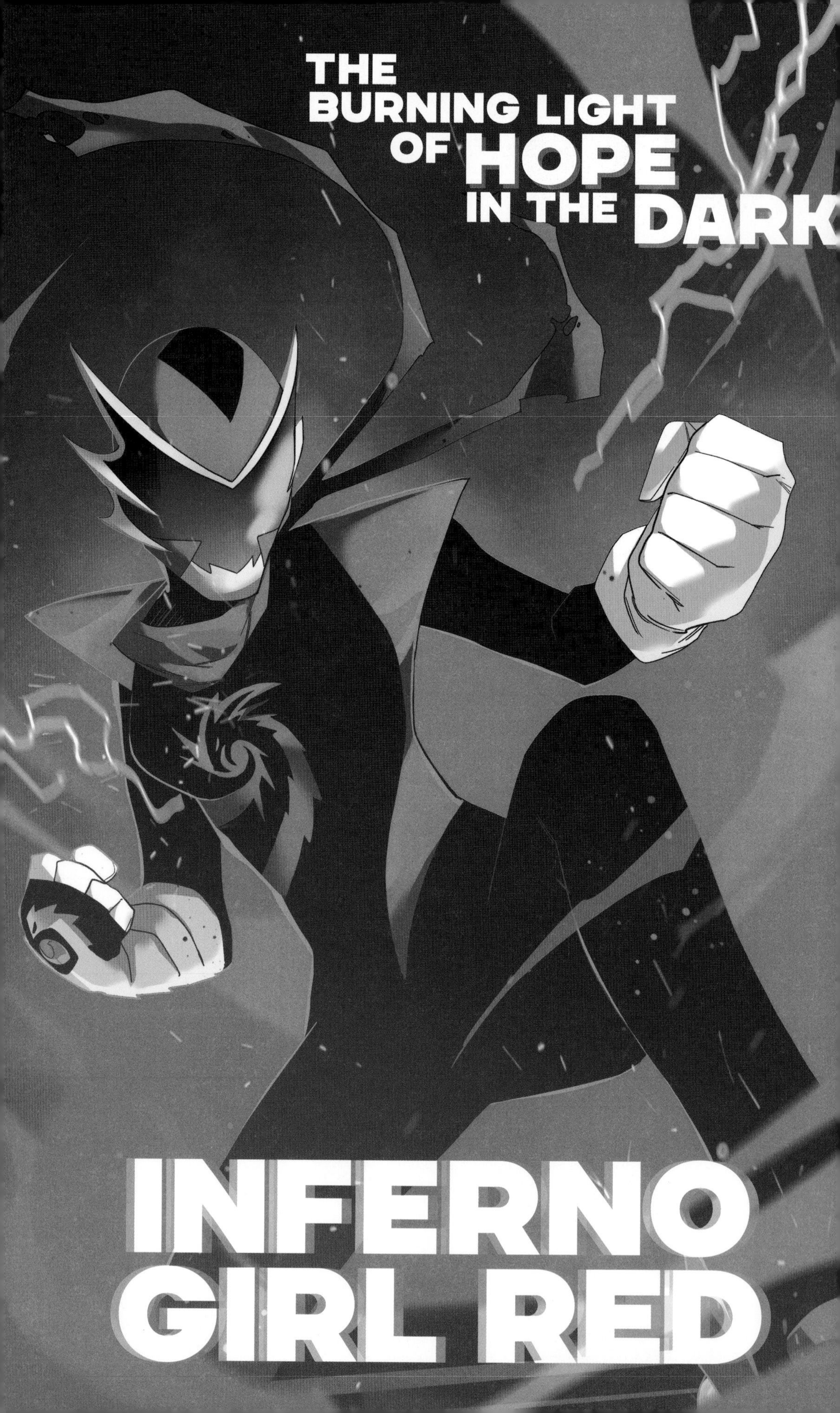
THE BURNING LIGHT OF HOPE IN THE DARK
INFERNO GIRL RED

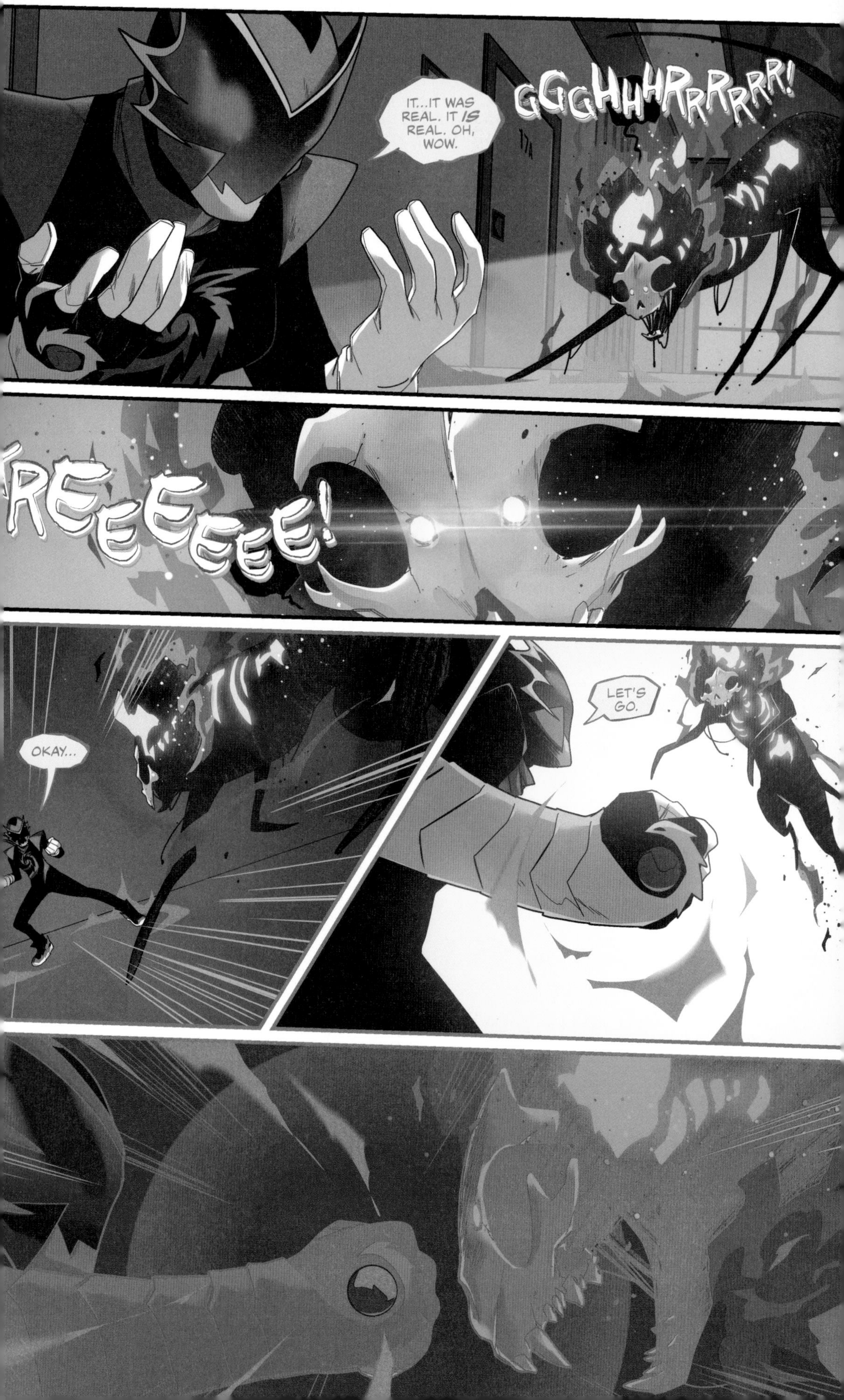

IT...IT WAS REAL. IT IS REAL. OH, WOW.
GGGHHHRRRRRR!
REEEEEEE!
OKAY...
LET'S GO.

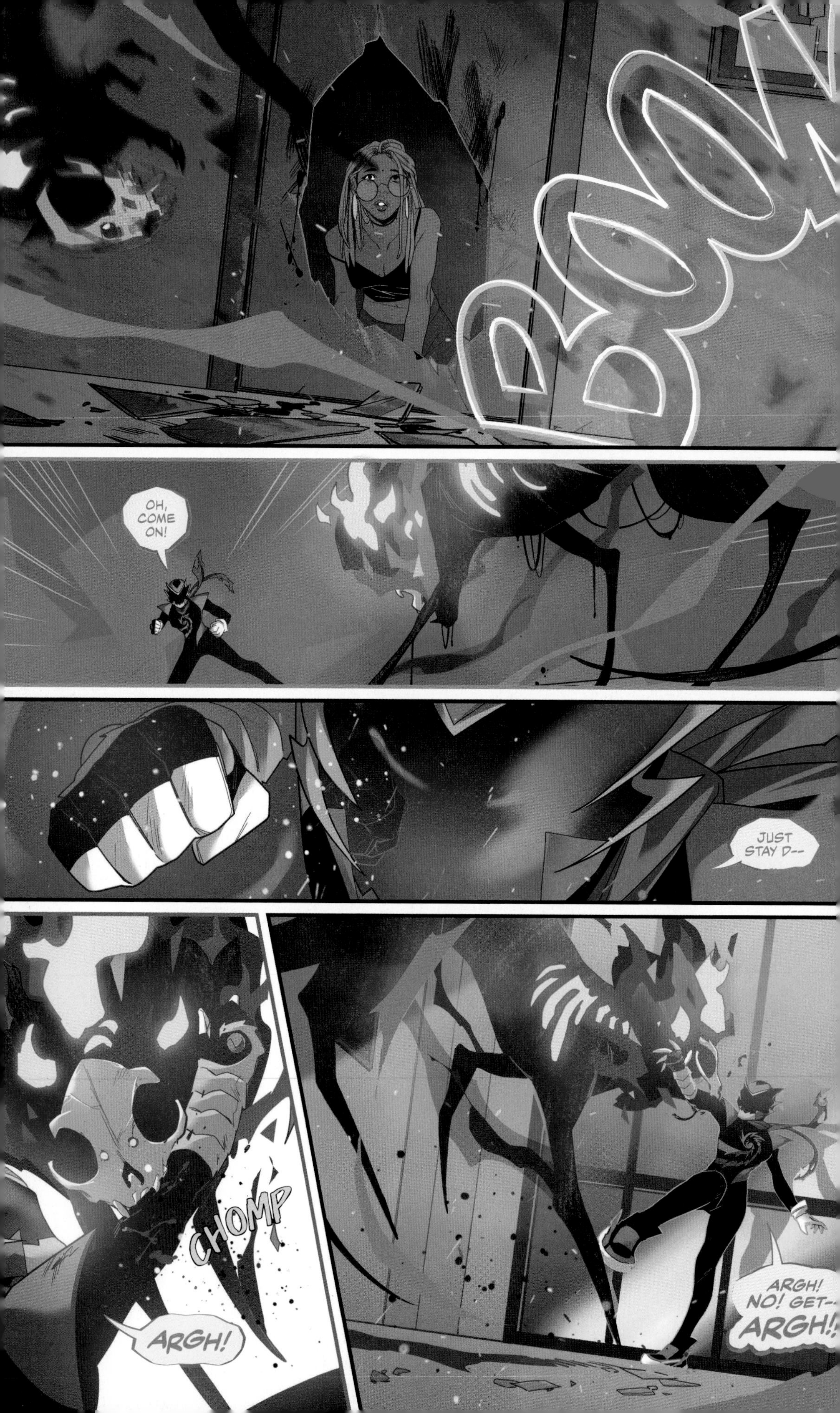
BOOM
OH, COME ON!
JUST STAY D--
CHOMP
ARGH!
ARGH! NO! GET-- ARGH!!

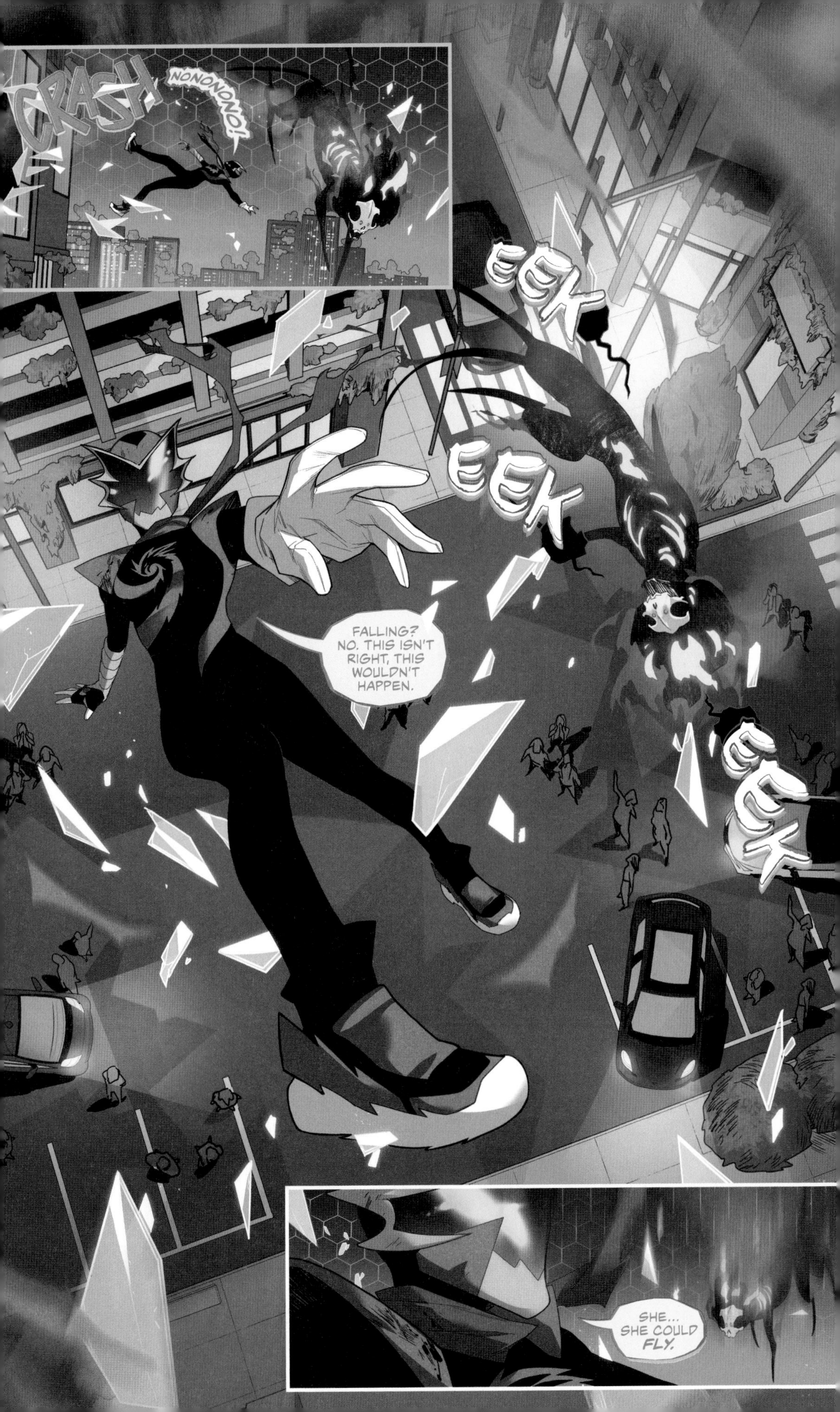
CRASH
NONONONO!
EEK
EEK
FALLING? NO. THIS ISN'T RIGHT, THIS WOULDN'T HAPPEN.
EEK
SHE... SHE COULD *FLY.*

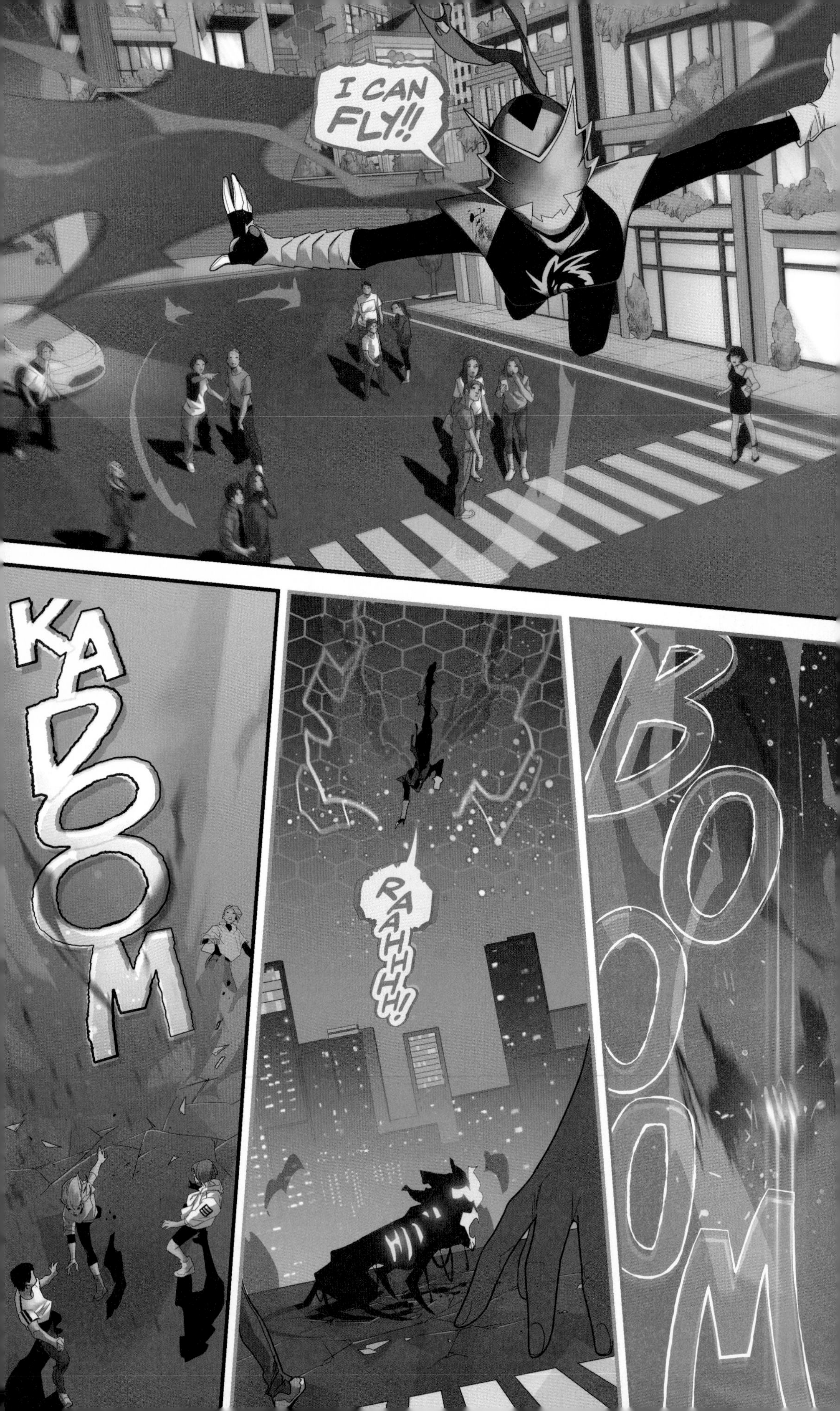
I CAN FLY!!
KADOOM
RAAHHHH!
BOOOOM

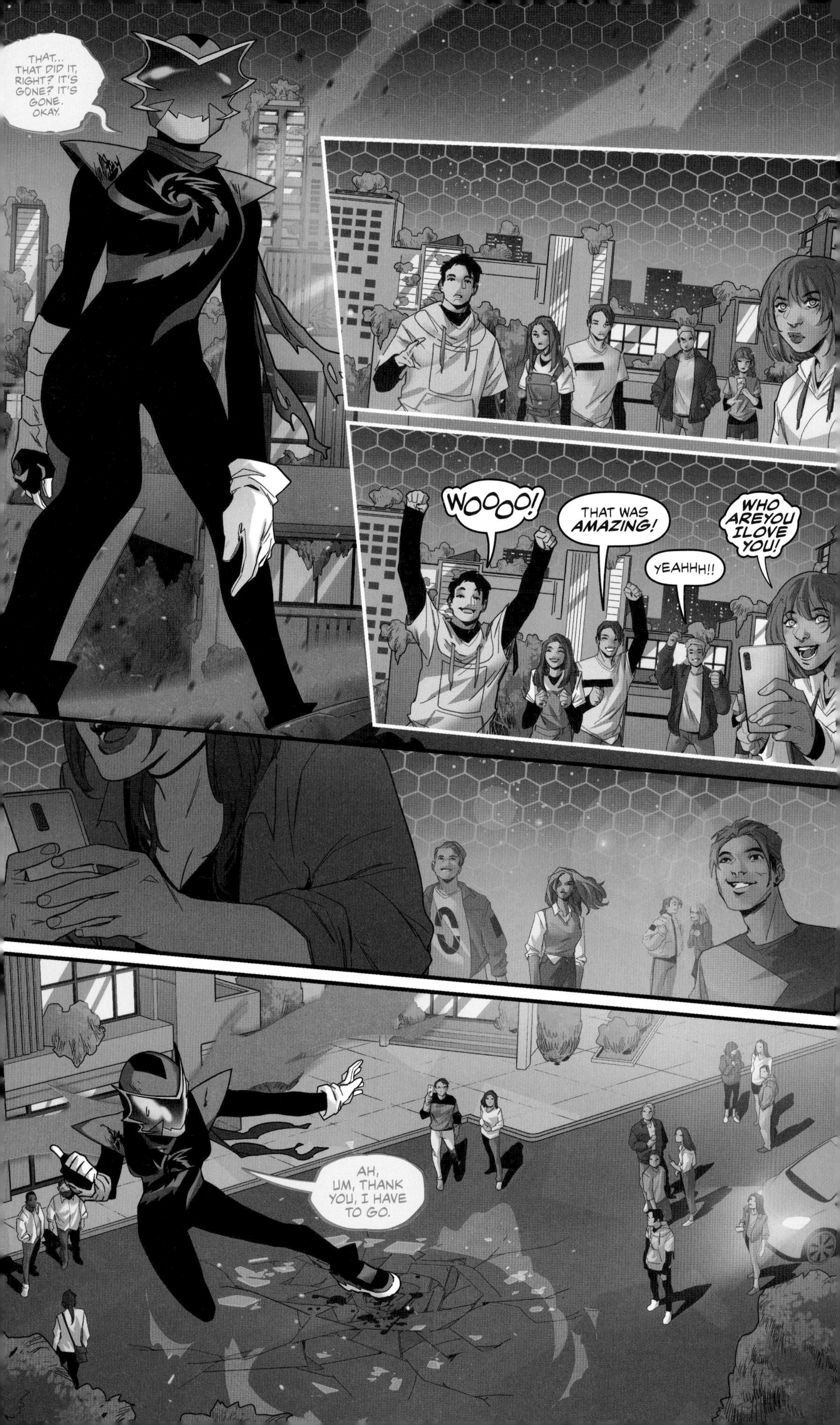
THAT... THAT DID IT, RIGHT? IT'S GONE? IT'S GONE. OKAY.
WOOOO!
THAT WAS AMAZING!
YEAHHH!!
WHO AREYOU ILOVE YOU!
AH, UM, THANK YOU, I HAVE TO GO.

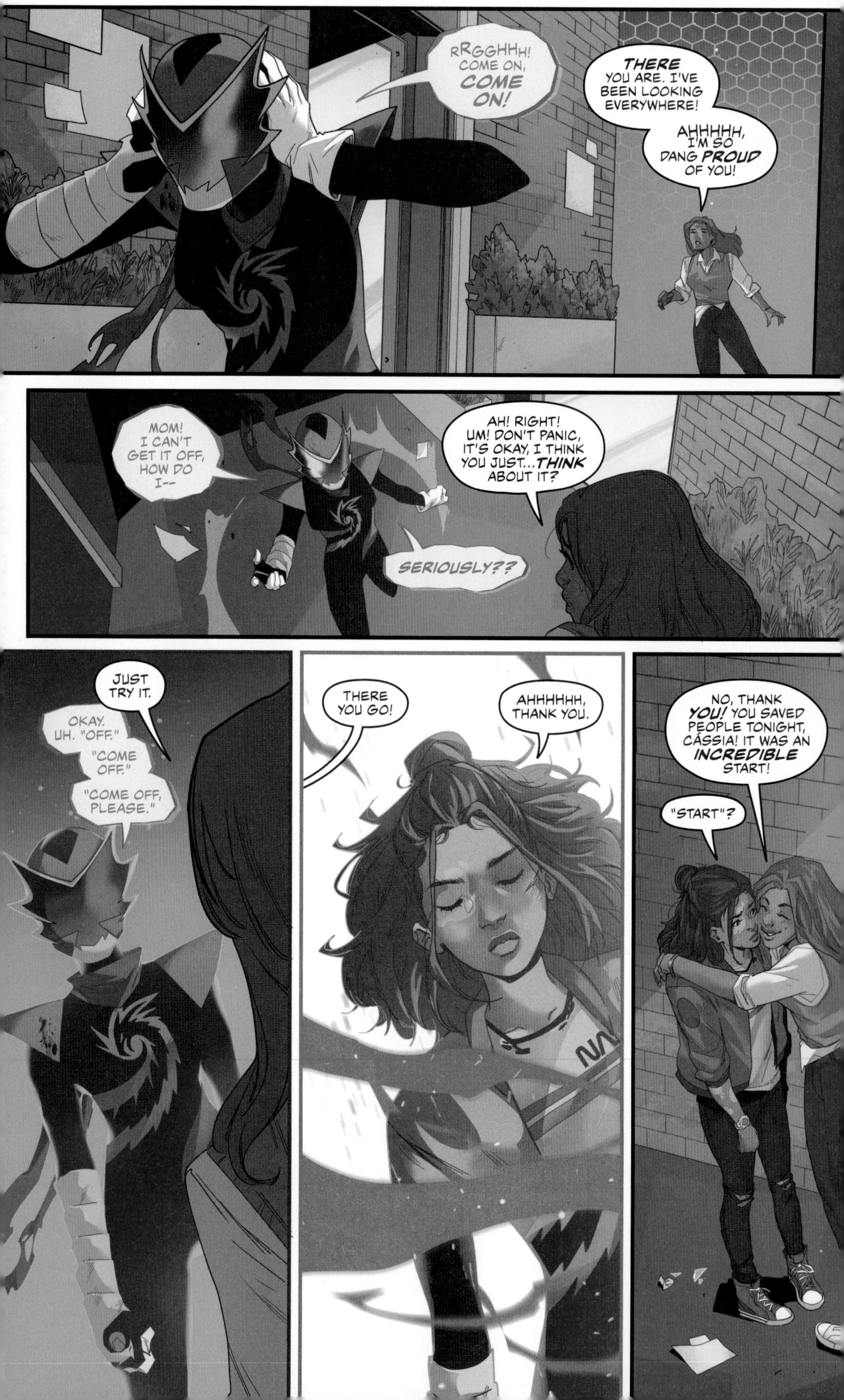
RRGGHHH! COME ON, COME ON!
THERE YOU ARE. I'VE BEEN LOOKING EVERYWHERE!
AHHHHH, I'M SO DANG PROUD OF YOU!
MOM! I CAN'T GET IT OFF, HOW DO I--
AH! RIGHT! UM! DON'T PANIC, IT'S OKAY, I THINK YOU JUST...THINK ABOUT IT?
SERIOUSLY??
JUST TRY IT.
OKAY. UH. "OFF."
"COME OFF."
"COME OFF, PLEASE."
THERE YOU GO!
AHHHHHH, THANK YOU.
NO, THANK YOU! YOU SAVED PEOPLE TONIGHT, CÁSSIA! IT WAS AN INCREDIBLE START!
"START"?

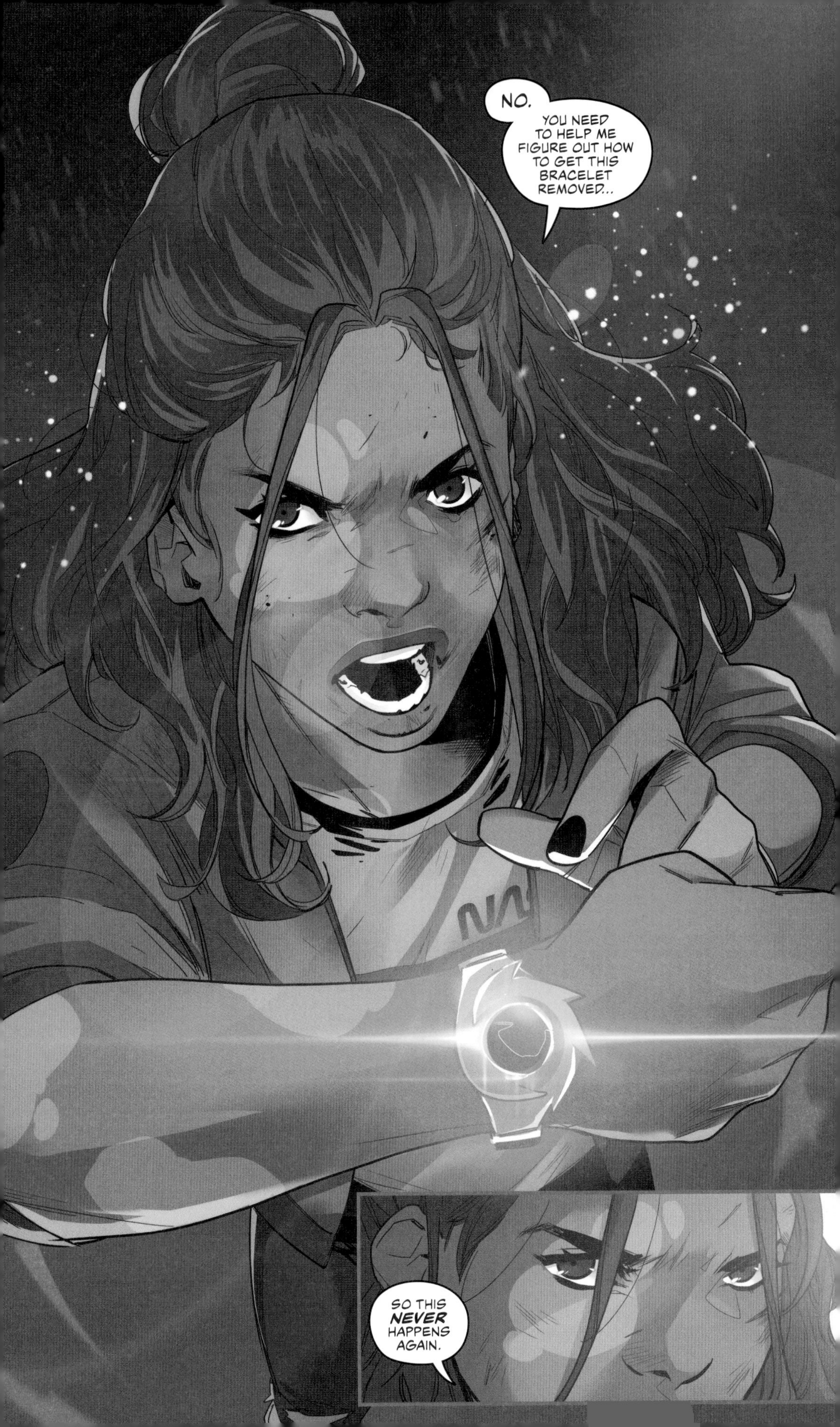
NO.
YOU NEED TO HELP ME FIGURE OUT HOW TO GET THIS BRACELET REMOVED...
SO THIS NEVER HAPPENS AGAIN.

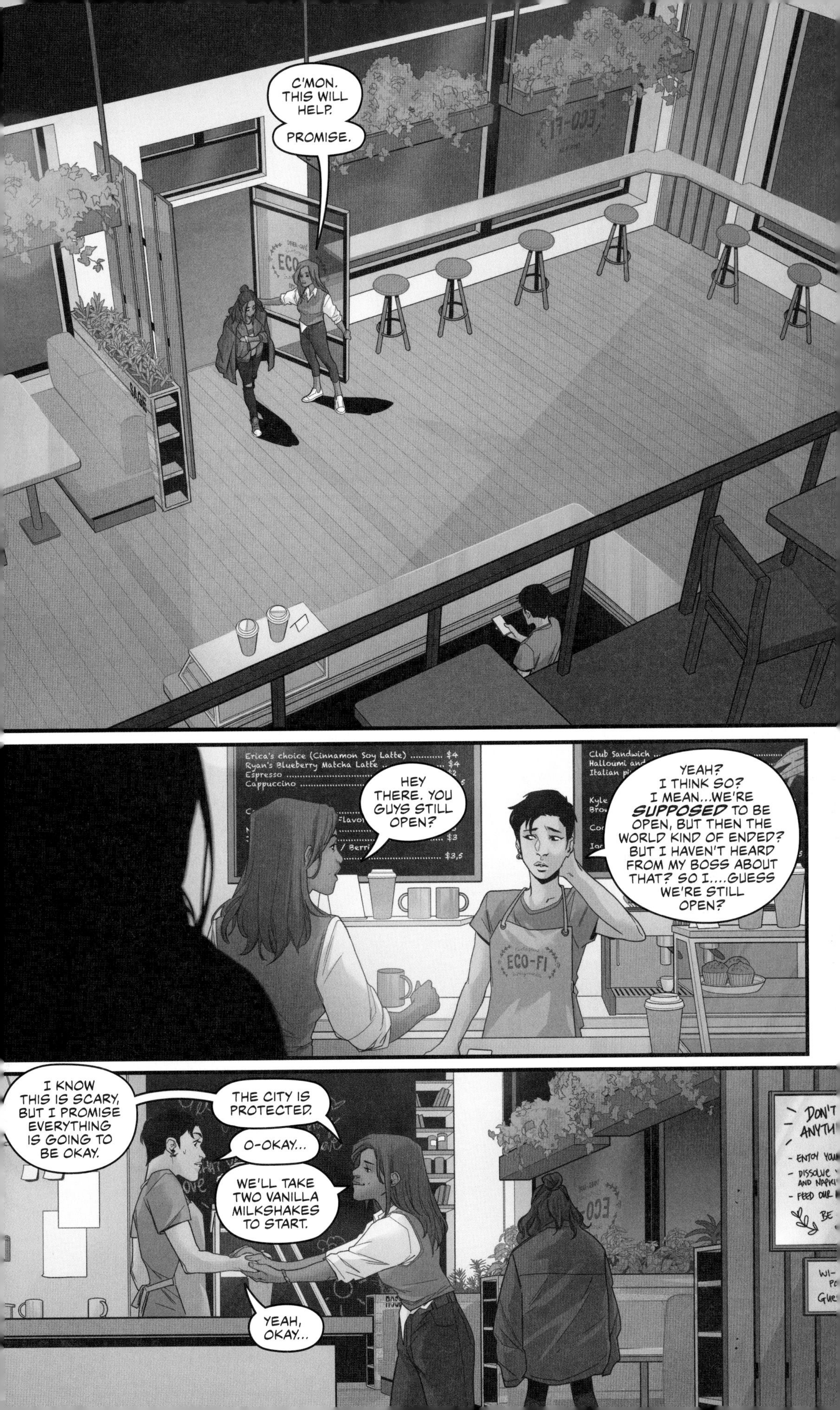

C'MON. THIS WILL HELP.
PROMISE.
Erica's choice (Cinnamon Soy Latte) $4
Ryan's Blueberry Matcha Latte
Espresso
Cappuccino
Club Sandwich
HEY THERE. YOU GUYS STILL OPEN?
YEAH? I THINK SO? I MEAN...WE'RE SUPPOSED TO BE OPEN, BUT THEN THE WORLD KIND OF ENDED? BUT I HAVEN'T HEARD FROM MY BOSS ABOUT THAT? SO I....GUESS WE'RE STILL OPEN?
ECO-FI
I KNOW THIS IS SCARY, BUT I PROMISE EVERYTHING IS GOING TO BE OKAY.
THE CITY IS PROTECTED.
O-OKAY...
WE'LL TAKE TWO VANILLA MILKSHAKES TO START.
YEAH, OKAY...

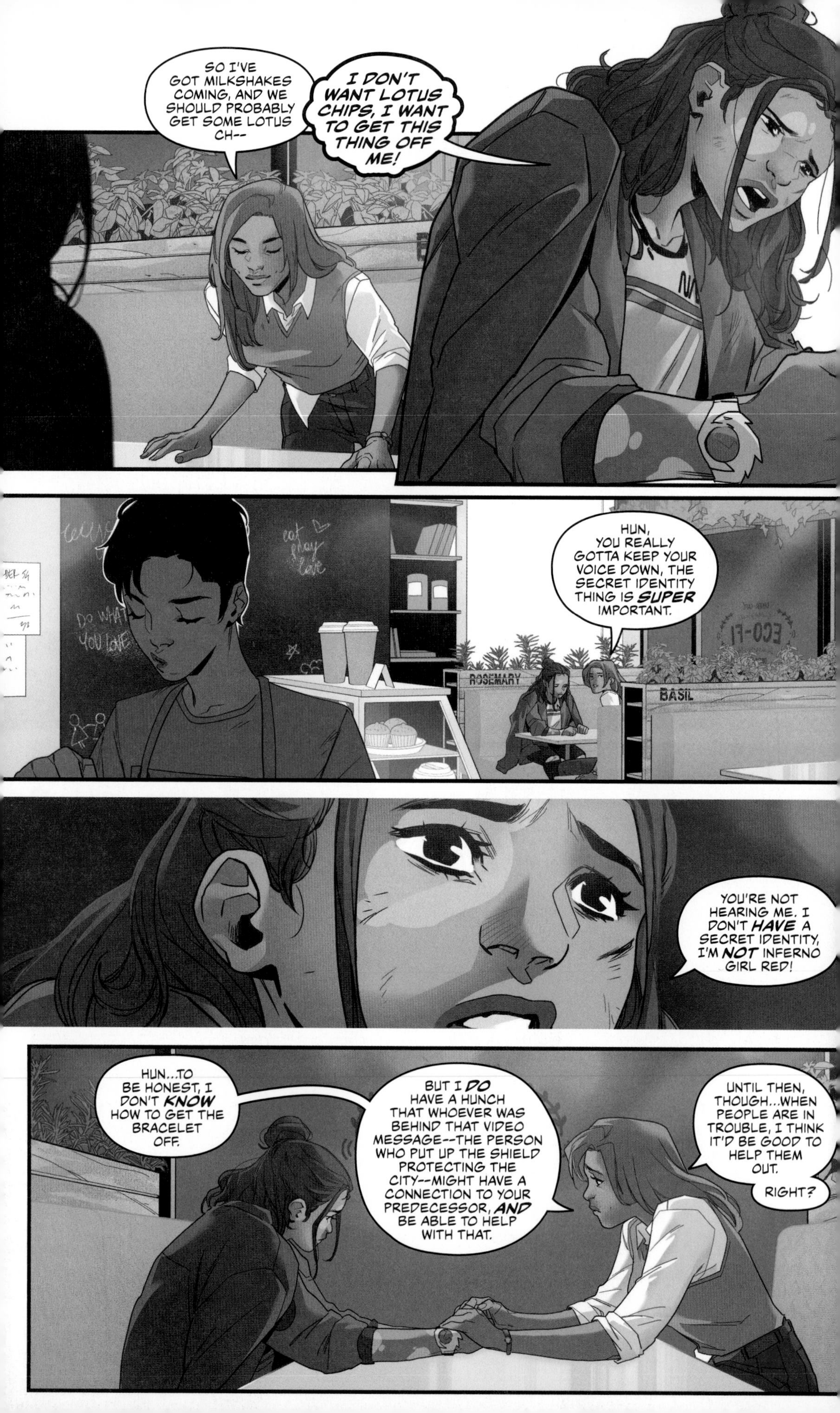
SO I'VE GOT MILKSHAKES COMING, AND WE SHOULD PROBABLY GET SOME LOTUS CH--
I DON'T WANT LOTUS CHIPS, I WANT TO GET THIS THING OFF ME!
HUN, YOU REALLY GOTTA KEEP YOUR VOICE DOWN, THE SECRET IDENTITY THING IS SUPER IMPORTANT.
ROSEMARY
BASIL
ECO-FI
YOU'RE NOT HEARING ME. I DON'T HAVE A SECRET IDENTITY, I'M NOT INFERNO GIRL RED!
HUN...TO BE HONEST, I DON'T KNOW HOW TO GET THE BRACELET OFF.
BUT I DO HAVE A HUNCH THAT WHOEVER WAS BEHIND THAT VIDEO MESSAGE--THE PERSON WHO PUT UP THE SHIELD PROTECTING THE CITY--MIGHT HAVE A CONNECTION TO YOUR PREDECESSOR, AND BE ABLE TO HELP WITH THAT.
UNTIL THEN, THOUGH...WHEN PEOPLE ARE IN TROUBLE, I THINK IT'D BE GOOD TO HELP THEM OUT.
RIGHT?

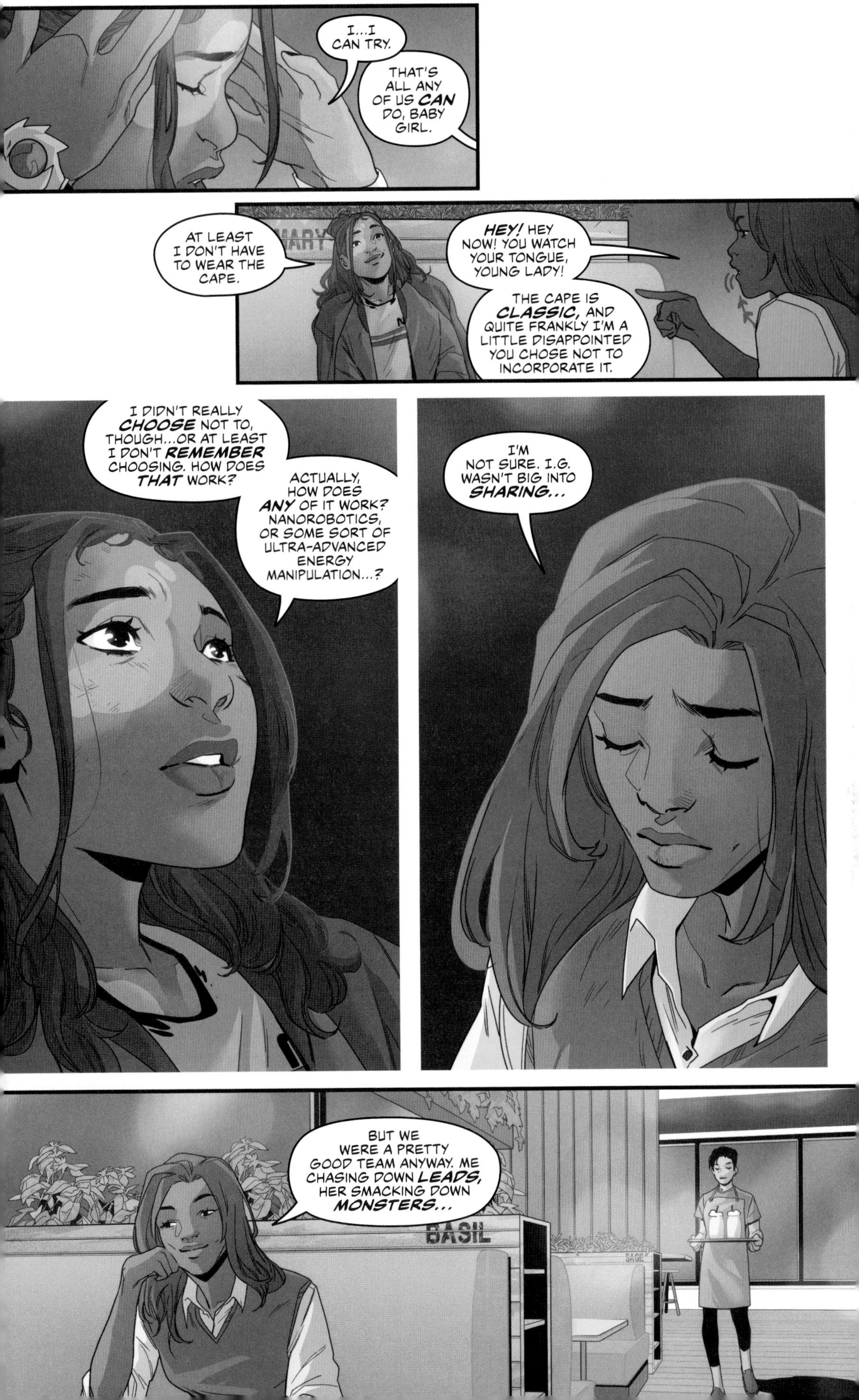

I...I CAN TRY.
THAT'S ALL ANY OF US CAN DO, BABY GIRL.
AT LEAST I DON'T HAVE TO WEAR THE CAPE.
HEY! HEY NOW! YOU WATCH YOUR TONGUE, YOUNG LADY!
THE CAPE IS CLASSIC, AND QUITE FRANKLY I'M A LITTLE DISAPPOINTED YOU CHOSE NOT TO INCORPORATE IT.
I DIDN'T REALLY CHOOSE NOT TO, THOUGH...OR AT LEAST I DON'T REMEMBER CHOOSING. HOW DOES THAT WORK?
ACTUALLY, HOW DOES ANY OF IT WORK? NANOROBOTICS, OR SOME SORT OF ULTRA-ADVANCED ENERGY MANIPULATION...?
I'M NOT SURE. I.G. WASN'T BIG INTO SHARING...
BUT WE WERE A PRETTY GOOD TEAM ANYWAY. ME CHASING DOWN LEADS, HER SMACKING DOWN MONSTERS...
BASIL

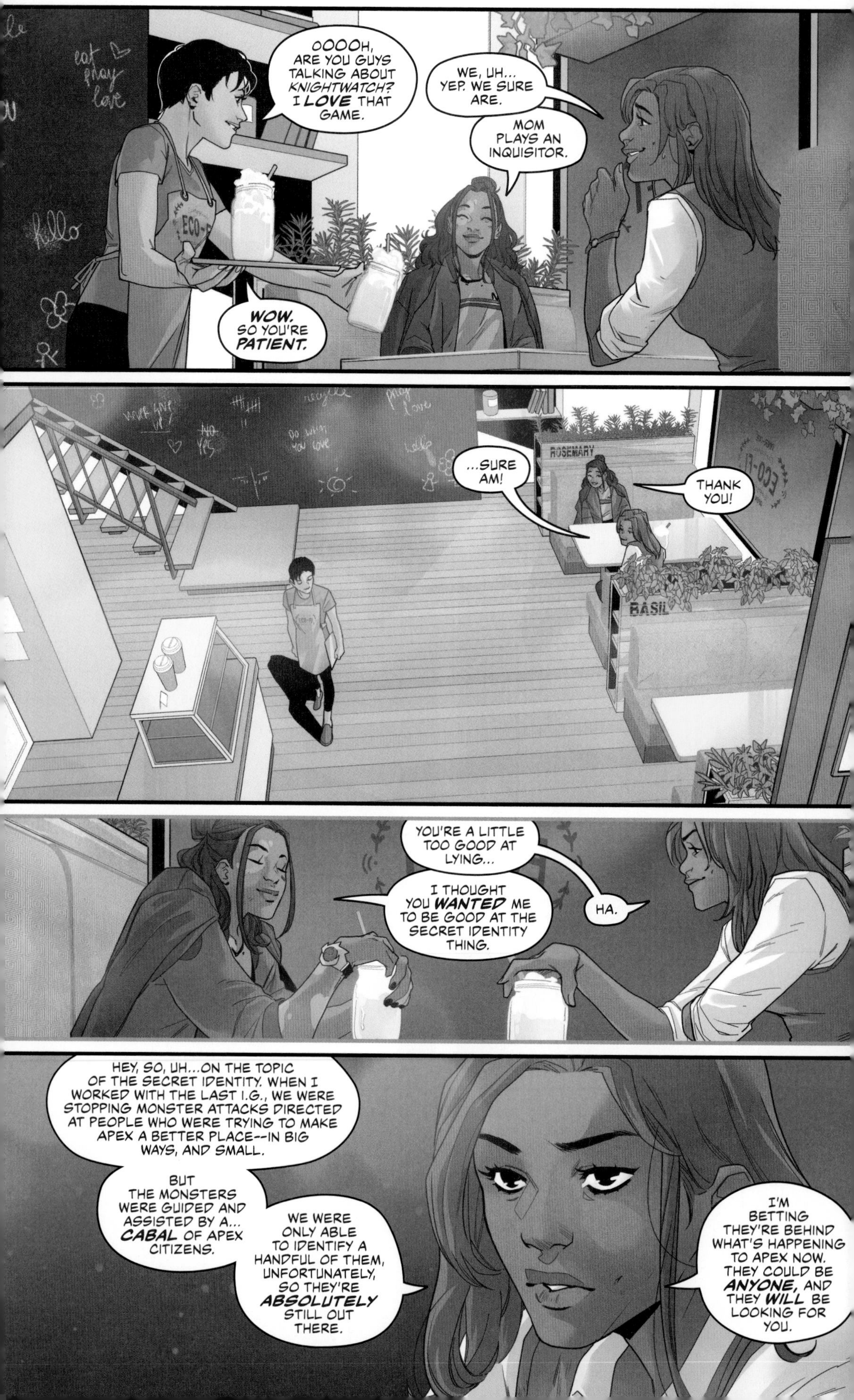
OOOOH, ARE YOU GUYS TALKING ABOUT KNIGHTWATCH? I LOVE THAT GAME.
WE, UH... YEP. WE SURE ARE.
MOM PLAYS AN INQUISITOR.
WOW. SO YOU'RE PATIENT.
ROSEMARY
...SURE AM!
THANK YOU!
BASIL
YOU'RE A LITTLE TOO GOOD AT LYING...
I THOUGHT YOU WANTED ME TO BE GOOD AT THE SECRET IDENTITY THING.
HA.
HEY, SO, UH...ON THE TOPIC OF THE SECRET IDENTITY. WHEN I WORKED WITH THE LAST I.G., WE WERE STOPPING MONSTER ATTACKS DIRECTED AT PEOPLE WHO WERE TRYING TO MAKE APEX A BETTER PLACE--IN BIG WAYS, AND SMALL.
BUT THE MONSTERS WERE GUIDED AND ASSISTED BY A... CABAL OF APEX CITIZENS.
WE WERE ONLY ABLE TO IDENTIFY A HANDFUL OF THEM, UNFORTUNATELY, SO THEY'RE ABSOLUTELY STILL OUT THERE.
I'M BETTING THEY'RE BEHIND WHAT'S HAPPENING TO APEX NOW. THEY COULD BE ANYONE, AND THEY WILL BE LOOKING FOR YOU.

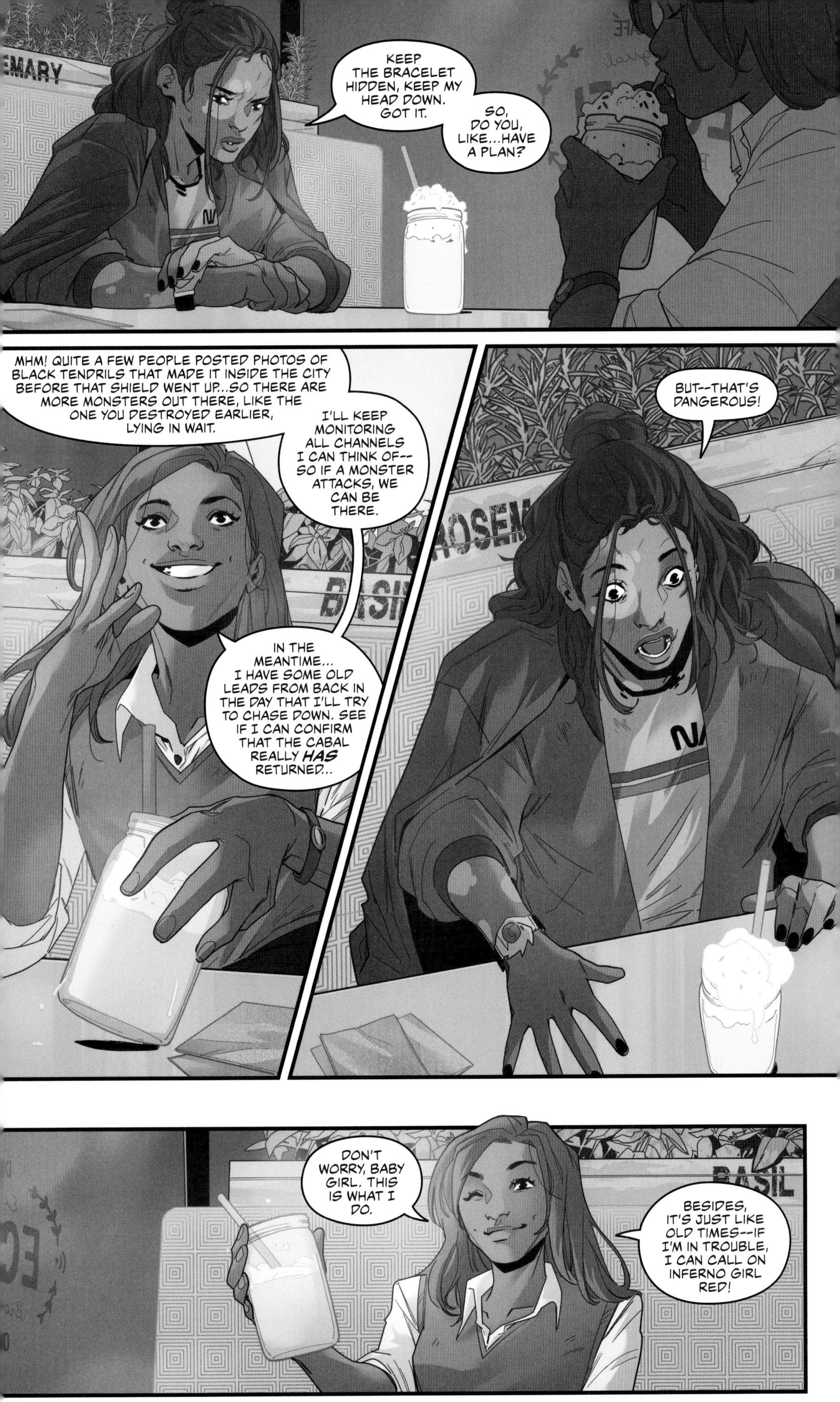
KEEP THE BRACELET HIDDEN, KEEP MY HEAD DOWN. GOT IT.
SO, DO YOU, LIKE...HAVE A PLAN?
MHM! QUITE A FEW PEOPLE POSTED PHOTOS OF BLACK TENDRILS THAT MADE IT INSIDE THE CITY BEFORE THAT SHIELD WENT UP...SO THERE ARE MORE MONSTERS OUT THERE, LIKE THE ONE YOU DESTROYED EARLIER, LYING IN WAIT.
I'LL KEEP MONITORING ALL CHANNELS I CAN THINK OF--SO IF A MONSTER ATTACKS, WE CAN BE THERE.
IN THE MEANTIME... I HAVE SOME OLD LEADS FROM BACK IN THE DAY THAT I'LL TRY TO CHASE DOWN. SEE IF I CAN CONFIRM THAT THE CABAL REALLY HAS RETURNED...
BUT--THAT'S DANGEROUS!
DON'T WORRY, BABY GIRL. THIS IS WHAT I DO.
BESIDES, IT'S JUST LIKE OLD TIMES--IF I'M IN TROUBLE, I CAN CALL ON INFERNO GIRL RED!

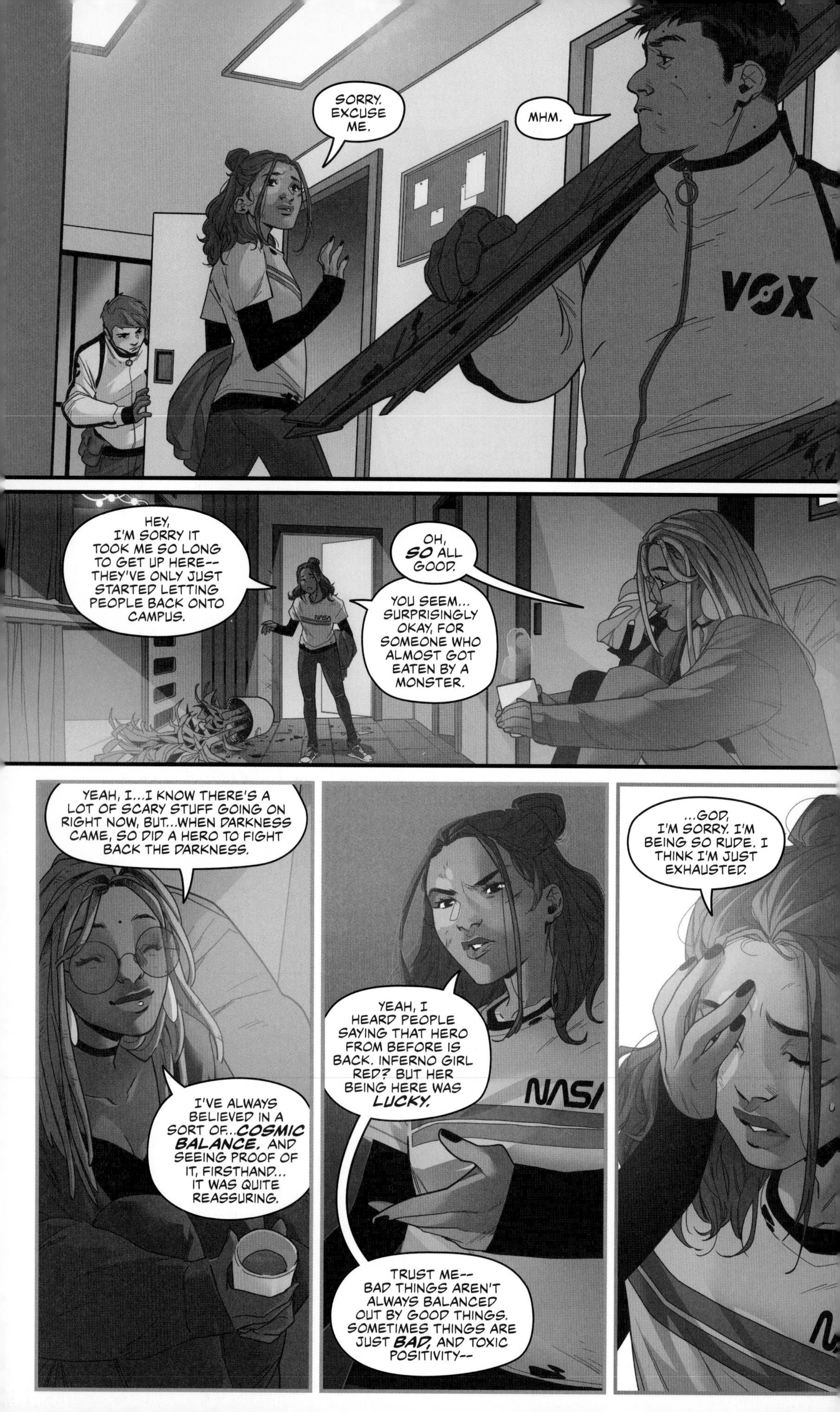
SORRY. EXCUSE ME.
MHM.
VOX
HEY, I'M SORRY IT TOOK ME SO LONG TO GET UP HERE-- THEY'VE ONLY JUST STARTED LETTING PEOPLE BACK ONTO CAMPUS.
OH, SO ALL GOOD.
YOU SEEM... SURPRISINGLY OKAY, FOR SOMEONE WHO ALMOST GOT EATEN BY A MONSTER.
YEAH, I...I KNOW THERE'S A LOT OF SCARY STUFF GOING ON RIGHT NOW, BUT...WHEN DARKNESS CAME, SO DID A HERO TO FIGHT BACK THE DARKNESS.
I'VE ALWAYS BELIEVED IN A SORT OF...COSMIC BALANCE. AND SEEING PROOF OF IT, FIRSTHAND... IT WAS QUITE REASSURING.
YEAH, I HEARD PEOPLE SAYING THAT HERO FROM BEFORE IS BACK. INFERNO GIRL RED? BUT HER BEING HERE WAS LUCKY.
TRUST ME-- BAD THINGS AREN'T ALWAYS BALANCED OUT BY GOOD THINGS. SOMETIMES THINGS ARE JUST BAD, AND TOXIC POSITIVITY--
...GOD, I'M SORRY. I'M BEING SO RUDE. I THINK I'M JUST EXHAUSTED.

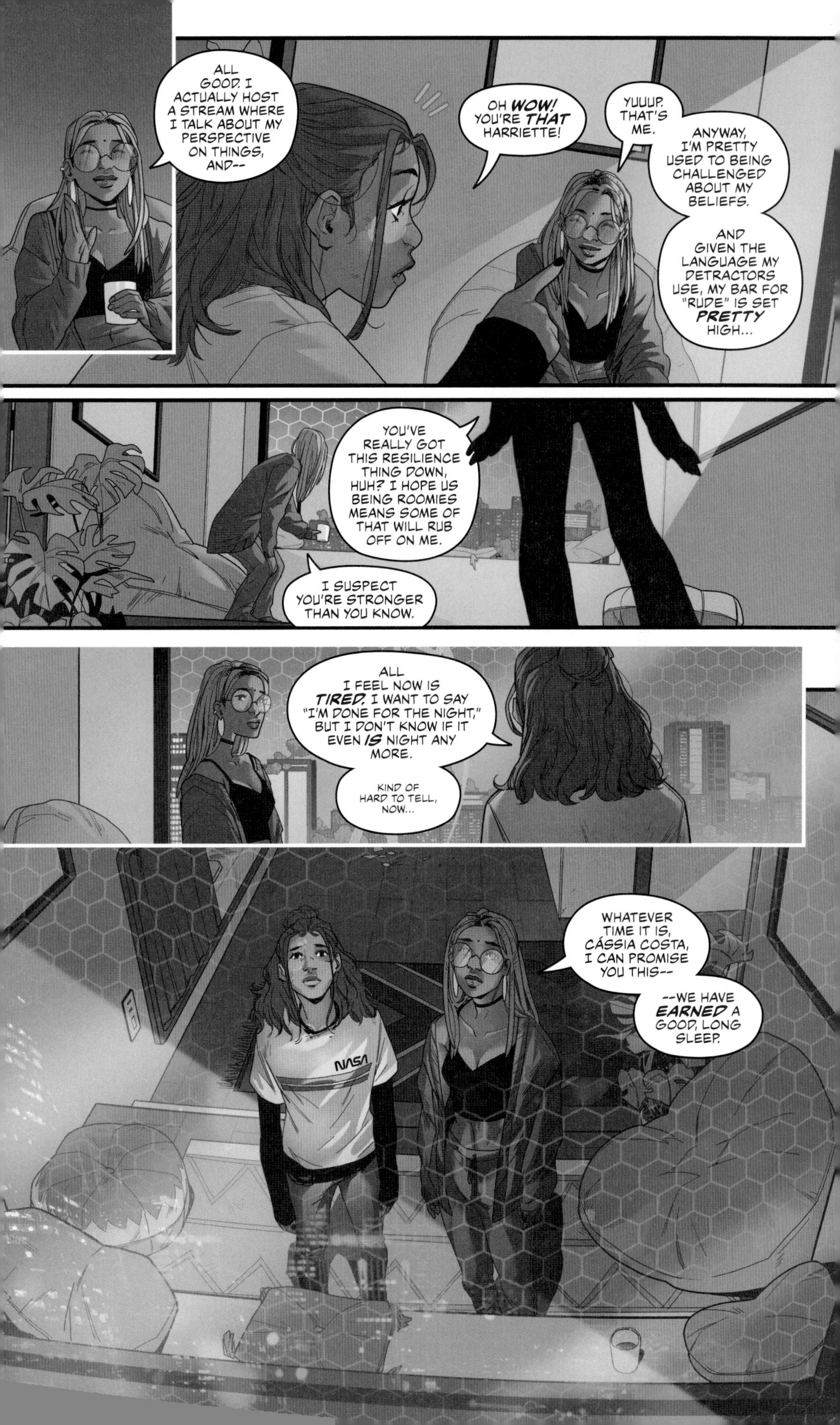
ALL GOOD. I ACTUALLY HOST A STREAM WHERE I TALK ABOUT MY PERSPECTIVE ON THINGS, AND--
OH WOW! YOU'RE THAT HARRIETTE!
YUUUP. THAT'S ME.
ANYWAY, I'M PRETTY USED TO BEING CHALLENGED ABOUT MY BELIEFS.
AND GIVEN THE LANGUAGE MY DETRACTORS USE, MY BAR FOR "RUDE" IS SET PRETTY HIGH...
YOU'VE REALLY GOT THIS RESILIENCE THING DOWN, HUH? I HOPE US BEING ROOMIES MEANS SOME OF THAT WILL RUB OFF ON ME.
I SUSPECT YOU'RE STRONGER THAN YOU KNOW.
ALL I FEEL NOW IS TIRED. I WANT TO SAY "I'M DONE FOR THE NIGHT," BUT I DON'T KNOW IF IT EVEN IS NIGHT ANY MORE.
KIND OF HARD TO TELL, NOW...
WHATEVER TIME IT IS, CÁSSIA COSTA, I CAN PROMISE YOU THIS--
--WE HAVE EARNED A GOOD, LONG SLEEP.
NASA

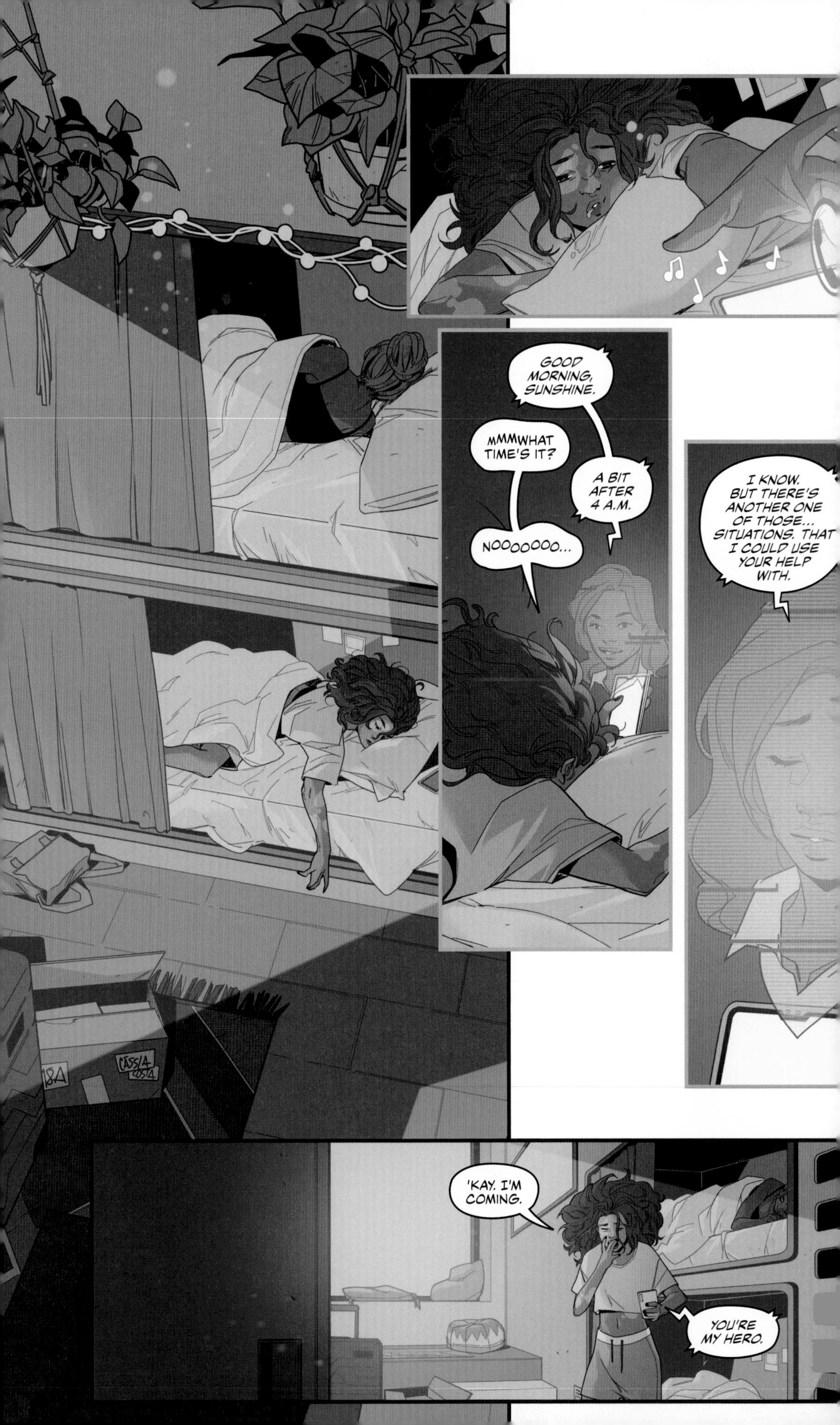
GOOD MORNING, SUNSHINE.
MMMWHAT TIME'S IT?
A BIT AFTER 4 A.M.
NOOOOOOO...
I KNOW. BUT THERE'S ANOTHER ONE OF THOSE... SITUATIONS. THAT I COULD USE YOUR HELP WITH.
'KAY. I'M COMING.
YOU'RE MY HERO.

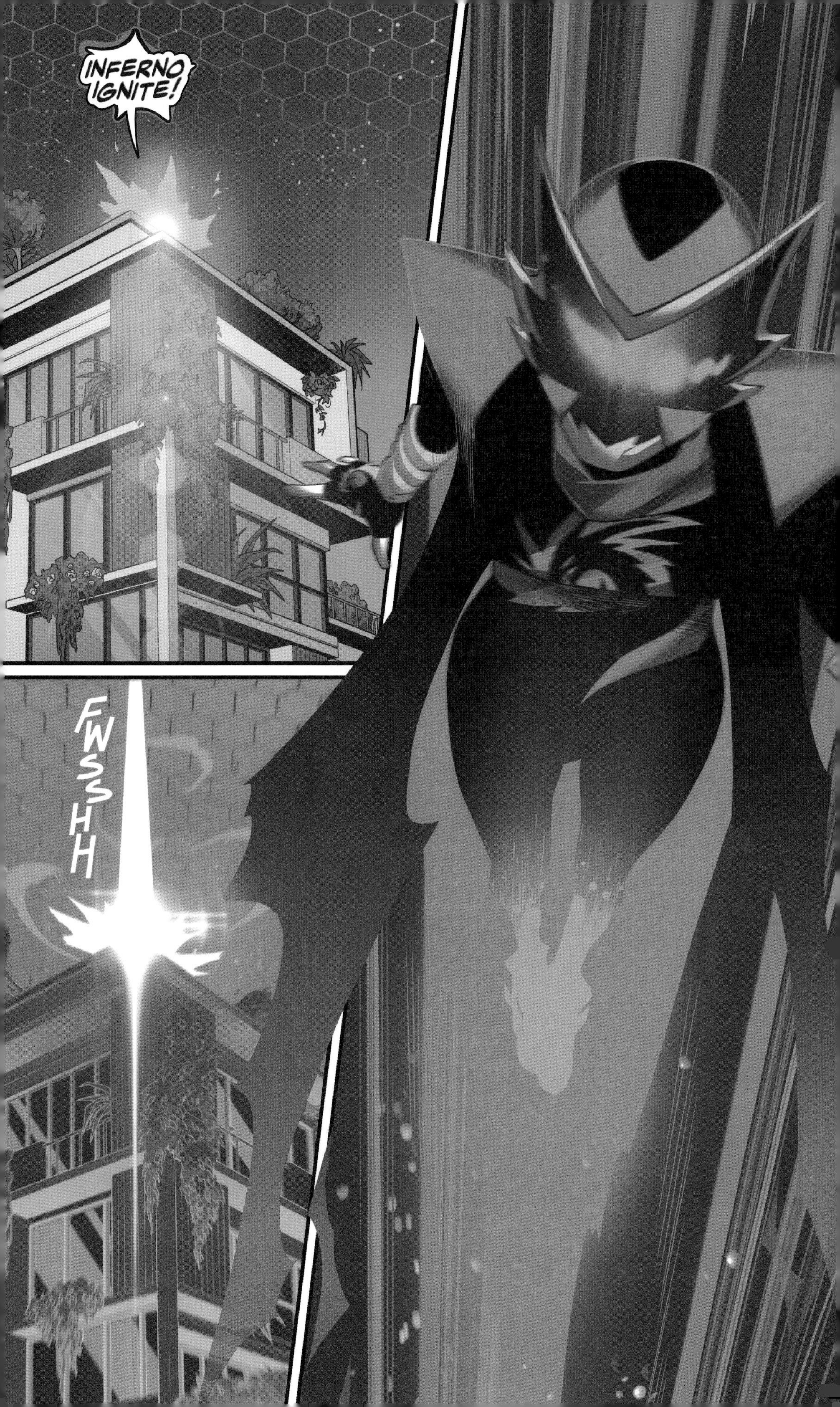
INFERNO IGNITE!
FWSSHH

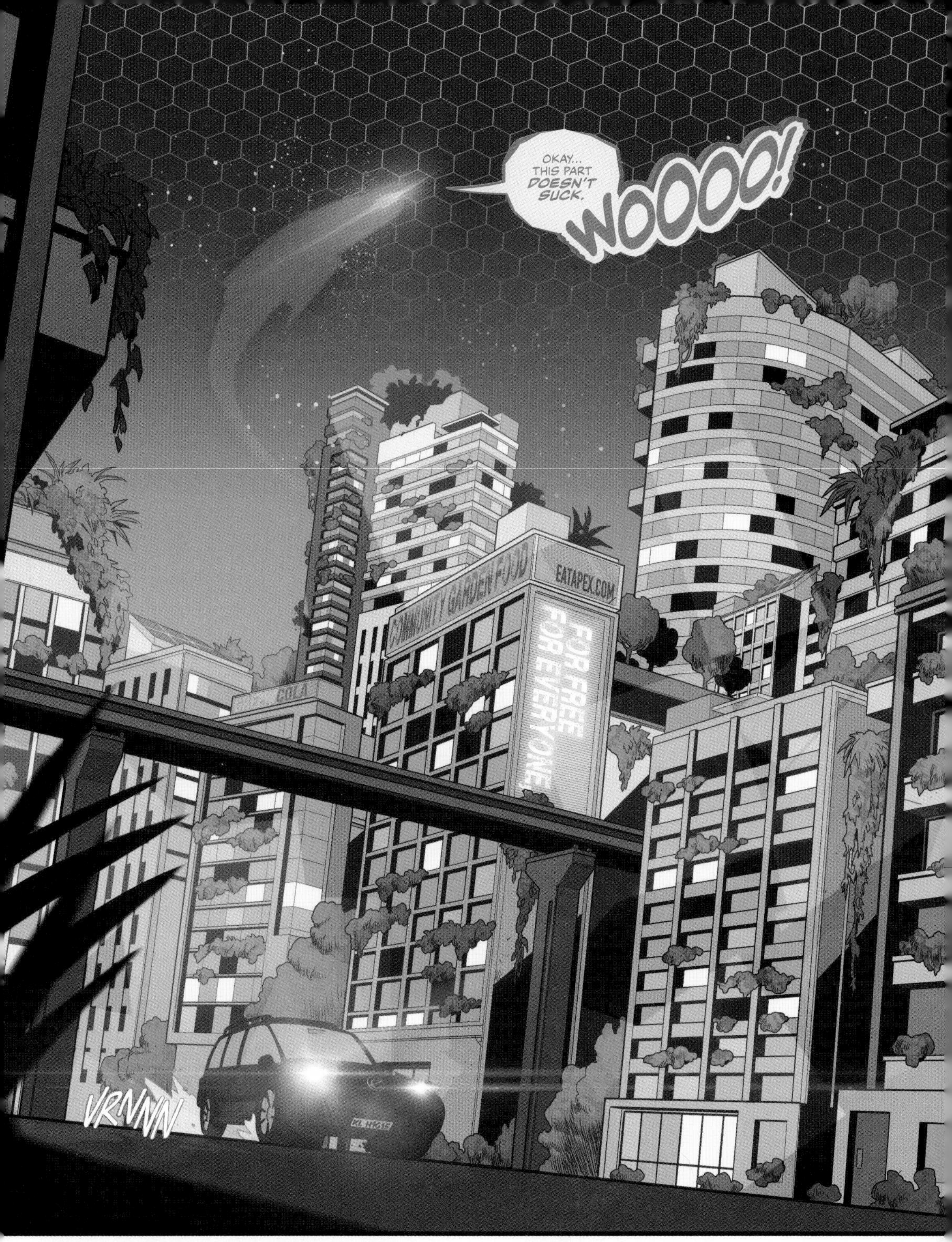
OKAY... THIS PART DOESN'T SUCK.
WOOOO!
COMMUNITY GARDEN FOOD
EATAPEX.COM
FOR FREE FOR EVERYONE
COLA
VRNNN

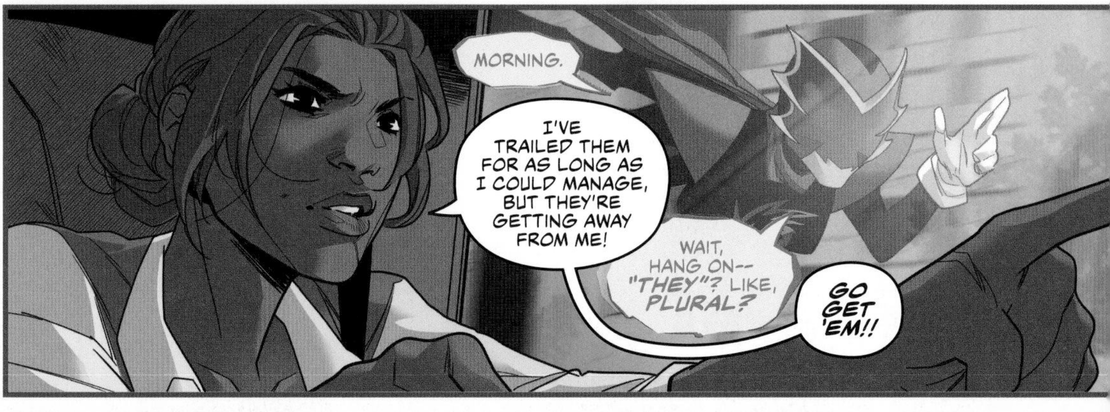
MORNING.
I'VE TRAILED THEM FOR AS LONG AS I COULD MANAGE, BUT THEY'RE GETTING AWAY FROM ME!
WAIT, HANG ON-- "THEY"? LIKE, PLURAL?
GO GET 'EM!!

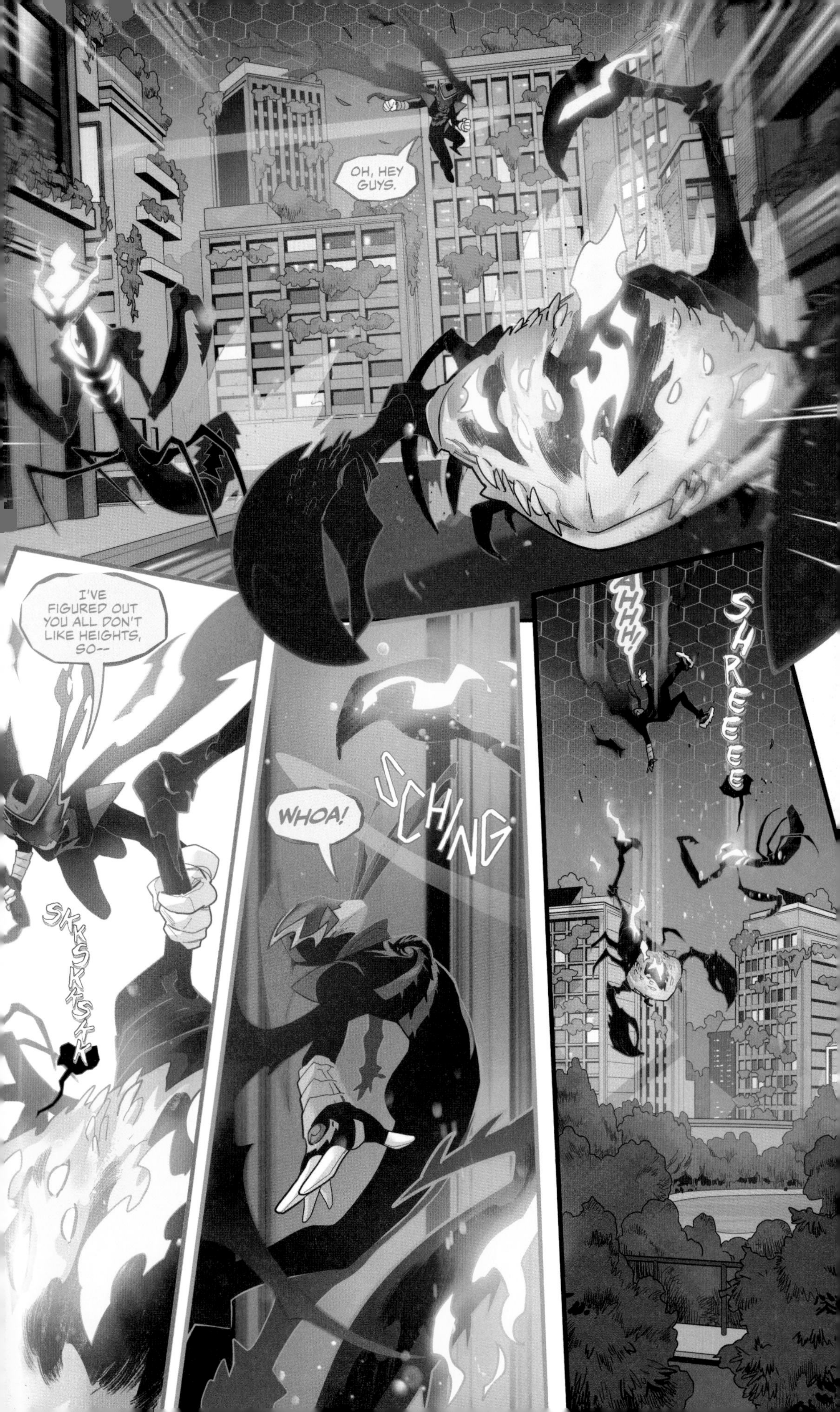
OH, HEY GUYS.
I'VE FIGURED OUT YOU ALL DON'T LIKE HEIGHTS, SO--
SKKSKKSKK
WHOA!
SCHING
AHHH!
SHREEEE

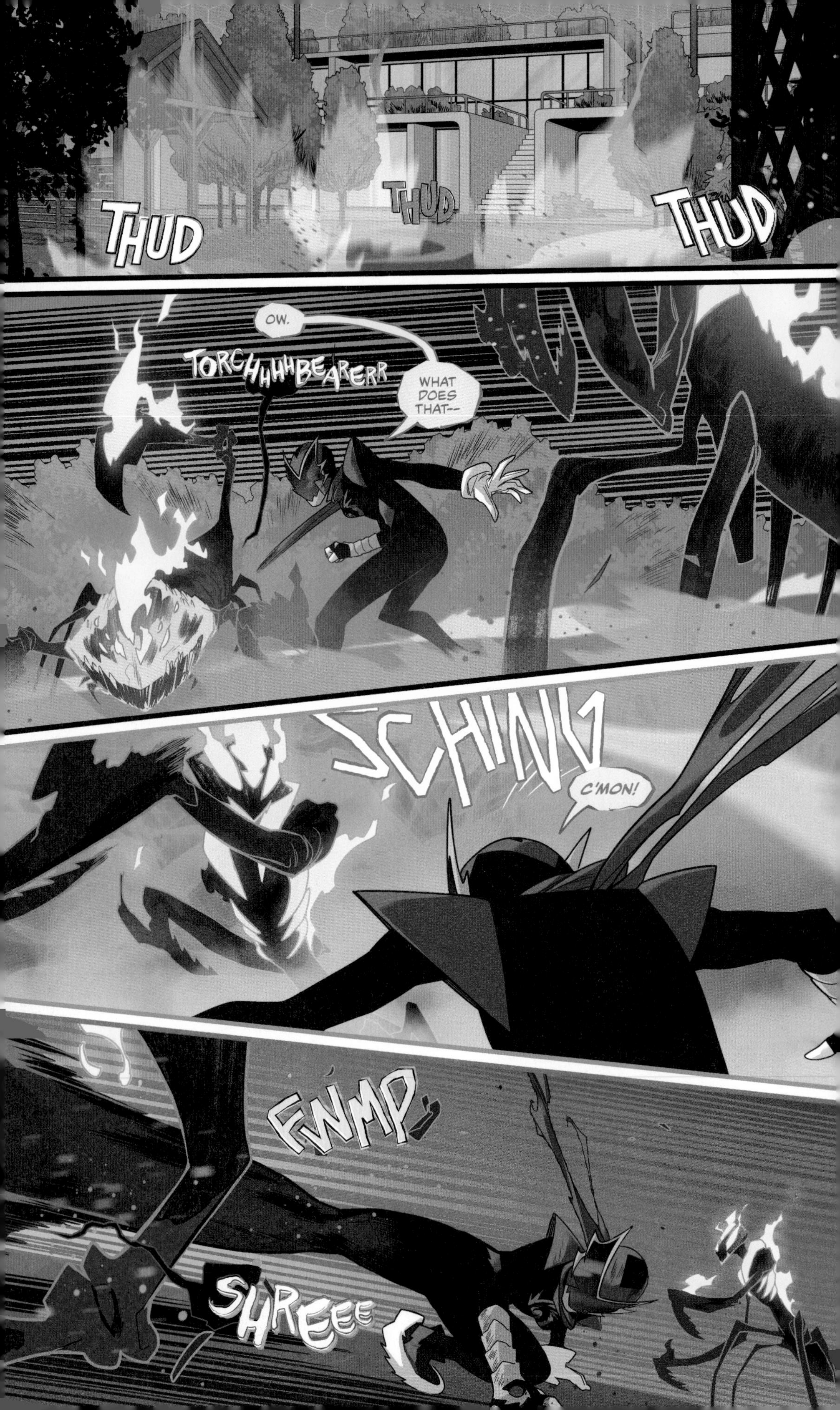
THUD
THUD
THUD
TORCHHHHBEARERR
OW.
WHAT DOES THAT--
SCHING
C'MON!
FWMP
SHREEEE

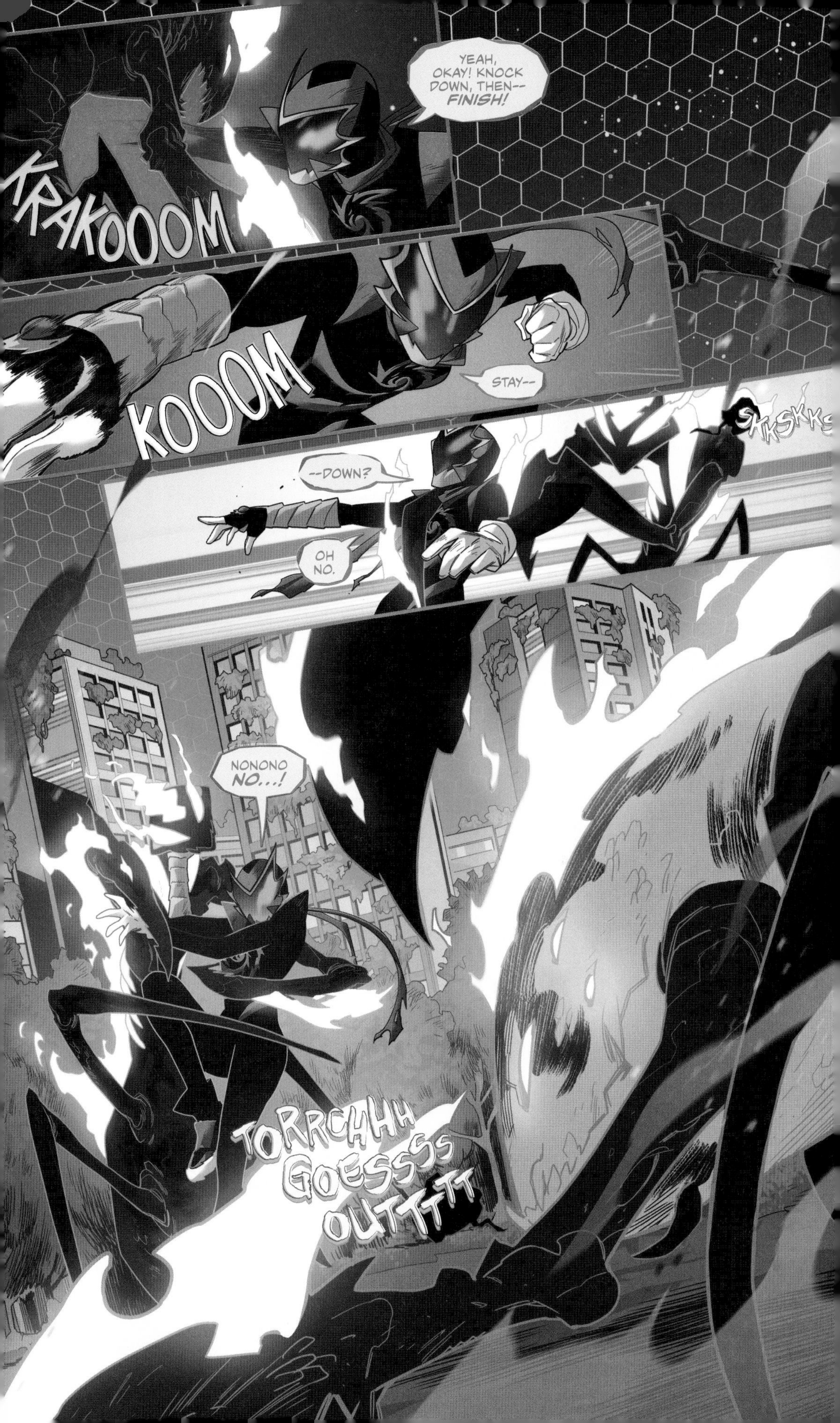
YEAH, OKAY! KNOCK DOWN, THEN-- FINISH!
KRAKOOOM
KOOOM
STAY--
SKKSKKS
--DOWN?
OH NO.
NONONO NO...!
TORRCHHH GOESSSSS OUTTTTT

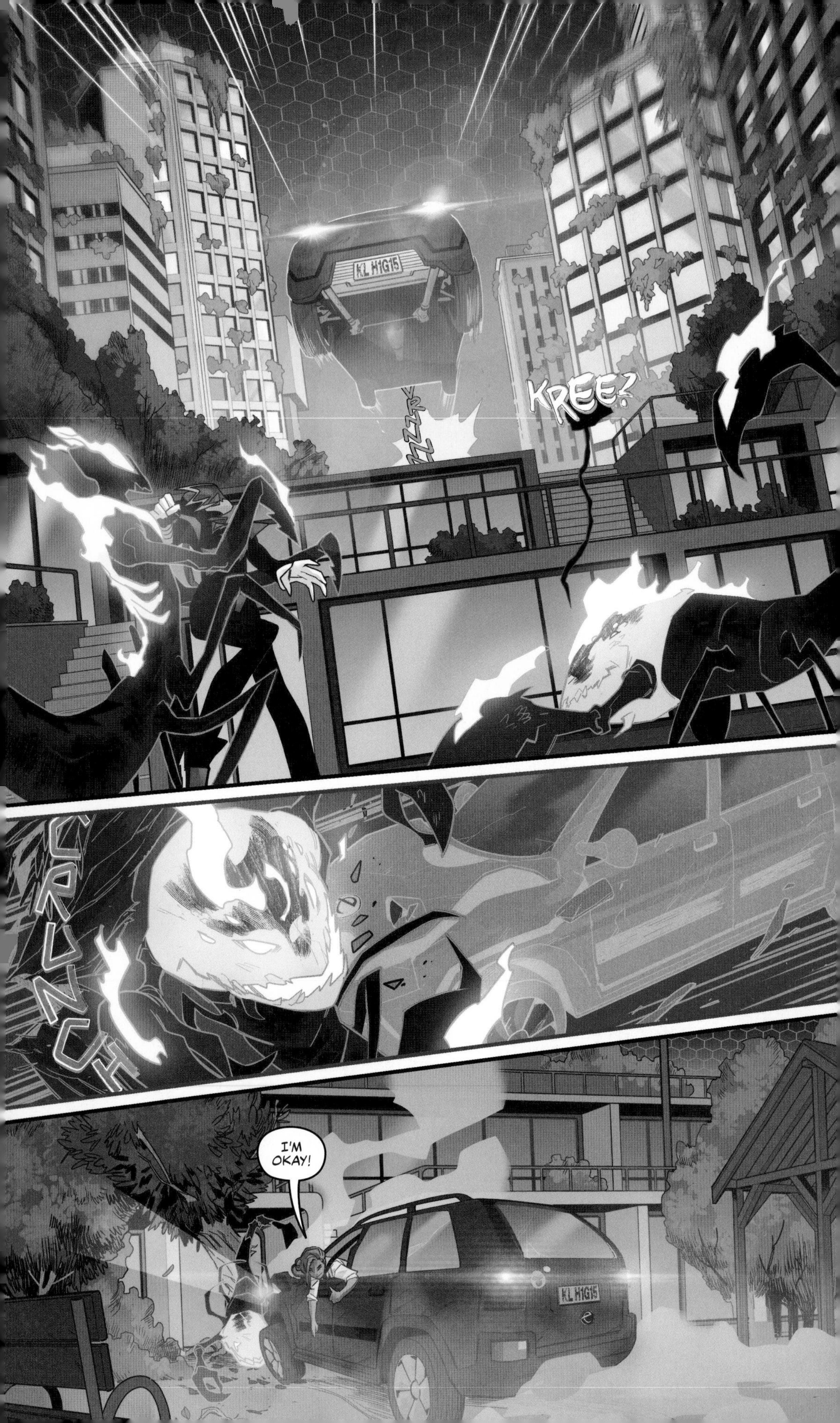

KL H1G15
VRNNN
KREE?
CRUNCH
I'M OKAY!
KL H1G15

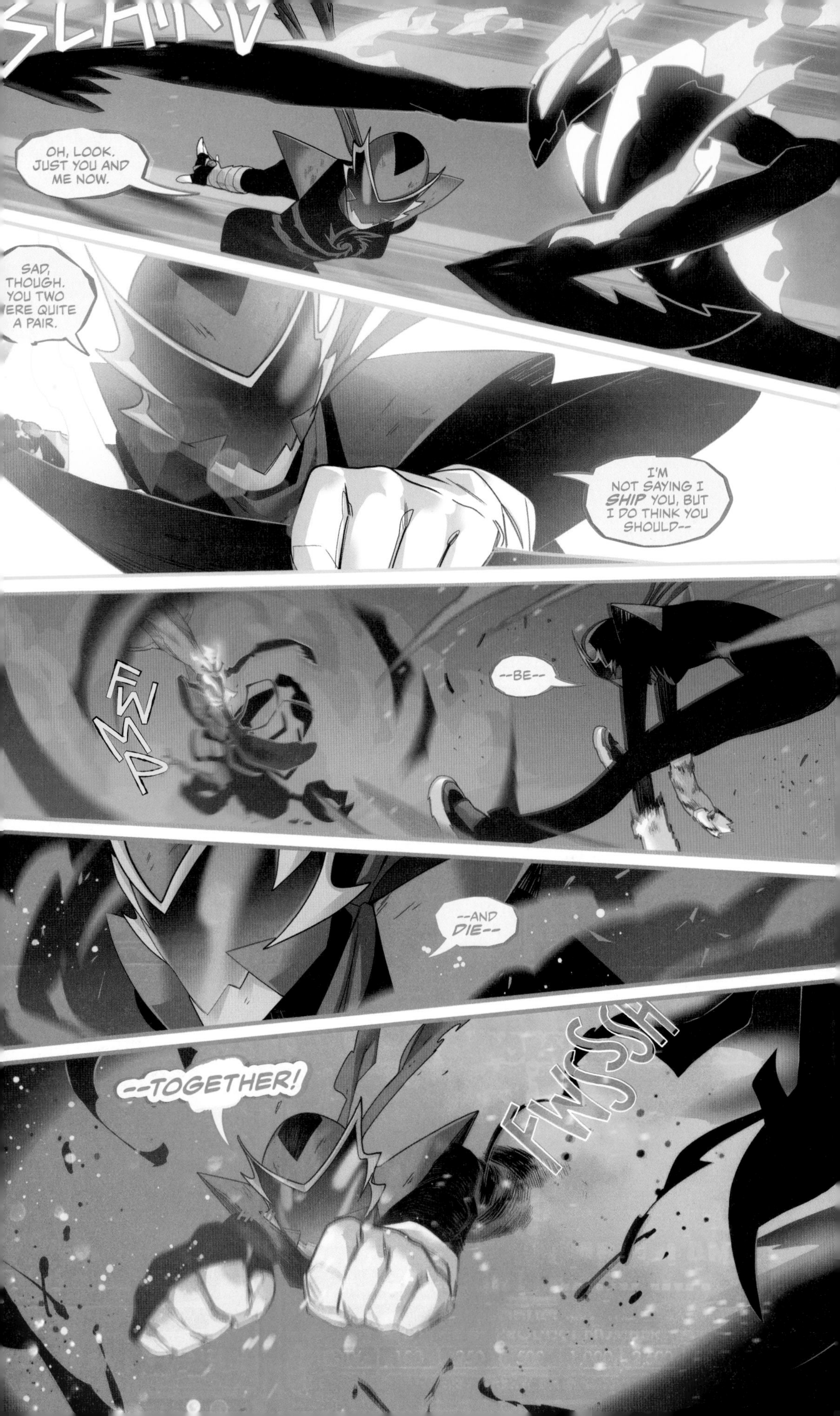
SCHING
OH, LOOK. JUST YOU AND ME NOW.
SAD, THOUGH. YOU TWO ERE QUITE A PAIR.
I'M NOT SAYING I SHIP YOU, BUT I DO THINK YOU SHOULD--
FWMP
--BE--
--AND DIE--
--TOGETHER!
FWSSH

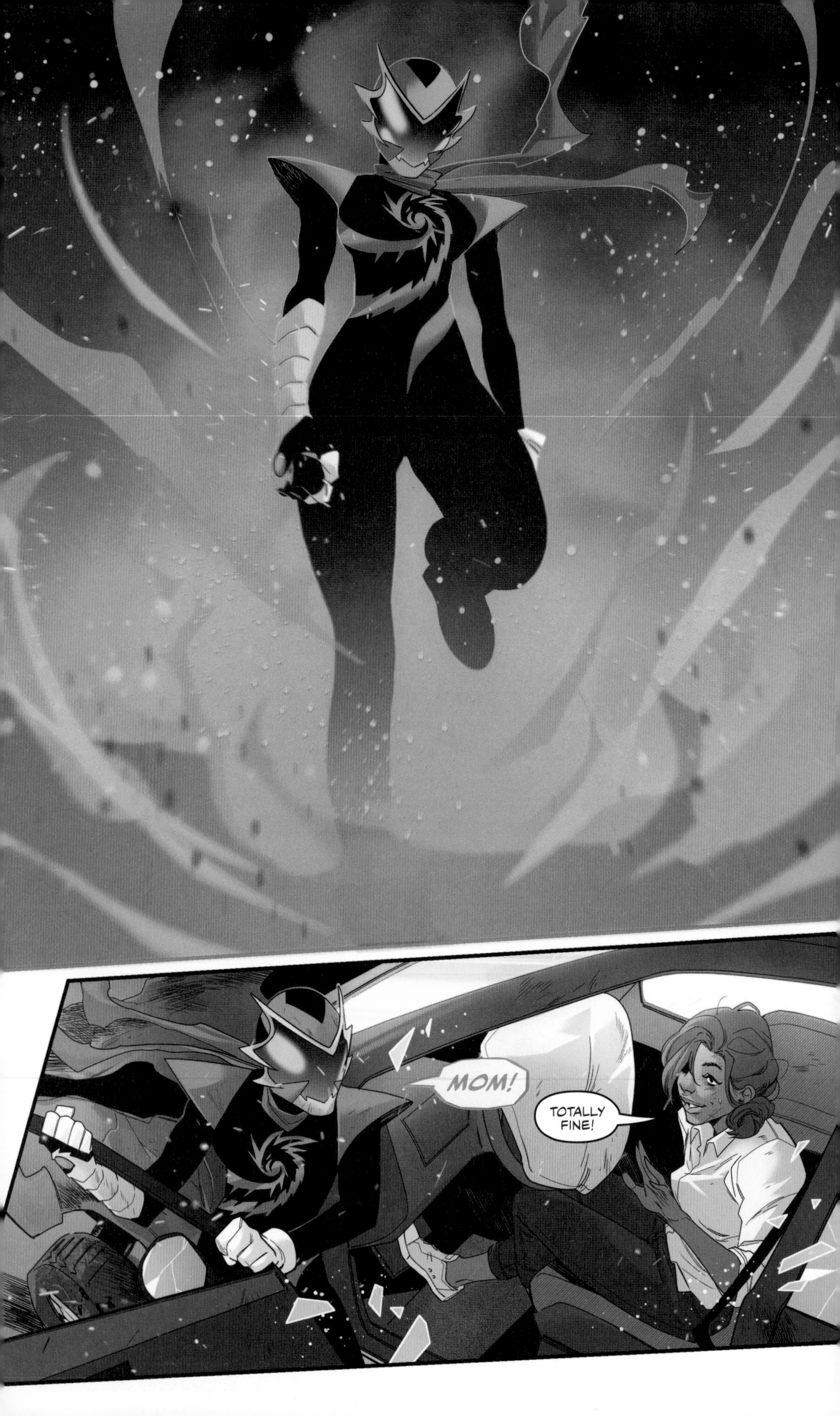
MOM!
TOTALLY FINE!

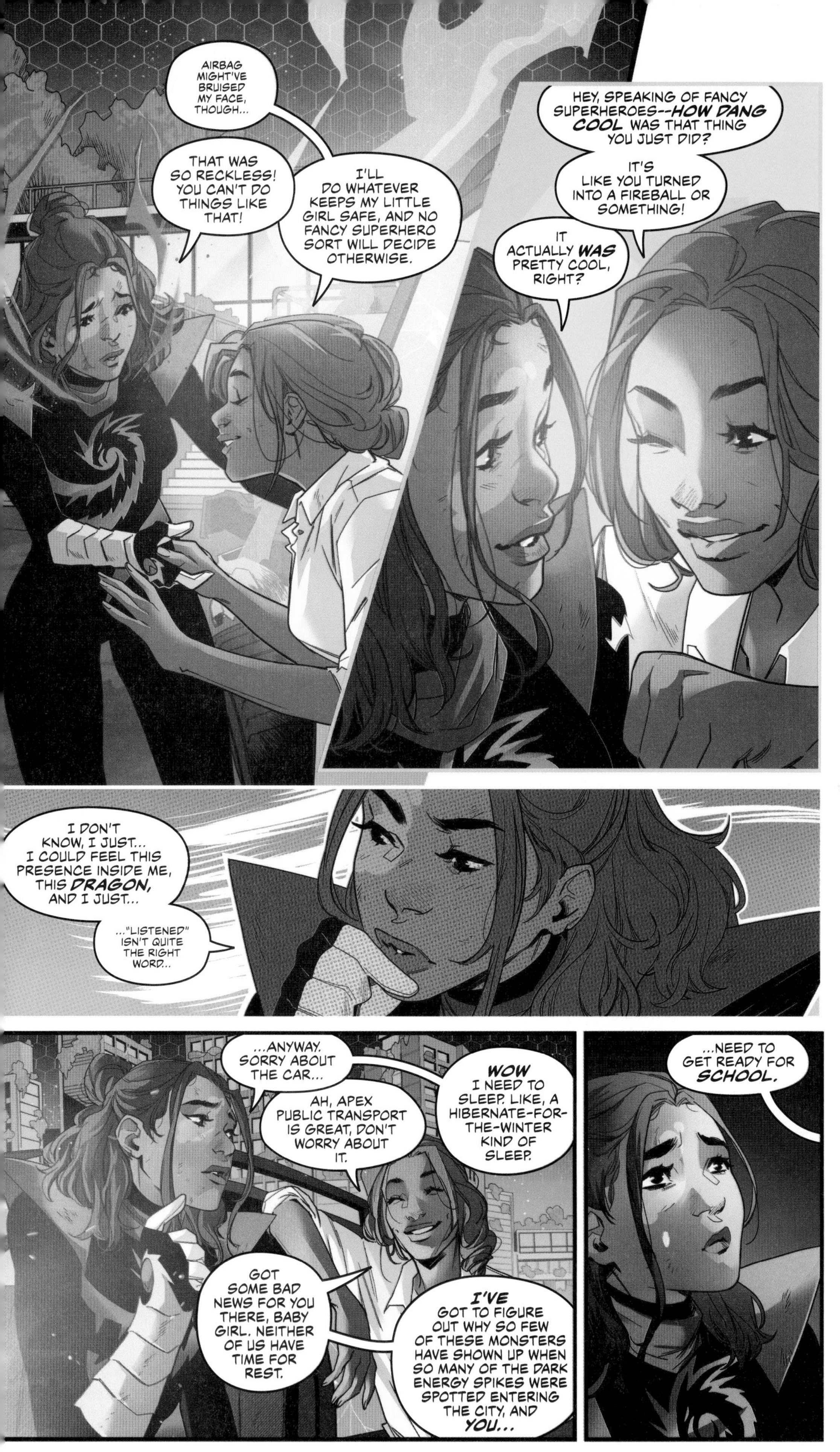
AIRBAG MIGHT'VE BRUISED MY FACE, THOUGH...
THAT WAS SO RECKLESS! YOU CAN'T DO THINGS LIKE THAT!
I'LL DO WHATEVER KEEPS MY LITTLE GIRL SAFE, AND NO FANCY SUPERHERO SORT WILL DECIDE OTHERWISE.
HEY, SPEAKING OF FANCY SUPERHEROES--**HOW DANG COOL** WAS THAT THING YOU JUST DID?
IT'S LIKE YOU TURNED INTO A FIREBALL OR SOMETHING!
IT ACTUALLY **WAS** PRETTY COOL, RIGHT?
I DON'T KNOW, I JUST... I COULD FEEL THIS PRESENCE INSIDE ME, THIS **DRAGON,** AND I JUST...
..."LISTENED" ISN'T QUITE THE RIGHT WORD...
...ANYWAY. SORRY ABOUT THE CAR...
AH, APEX PUBLIC TRANSPORT IS GREAT, DON'T WORRY ABOUT IT.
WOW I NEED TO SLEEP. LIKE, A HIBERNATE-FOR-THE-WINTER KIND OF SLEEP.
GOT SOME BAD NEWS FOR YOU THERE, BABY GIRL. NEITHER OF US HAVE TIME FOR REST.
I'VE GOT TO FIGURE OUT WHY SO FEW OF THESE MONSTERS HAVE SHOWN UP WHEN SO MANY OF THE DARK ENERGY SPIKES WERE SPOTTED ENTERING THE CITY, AND **YOU...**
...NEED TO GET READY FOR **SCHOOL.**

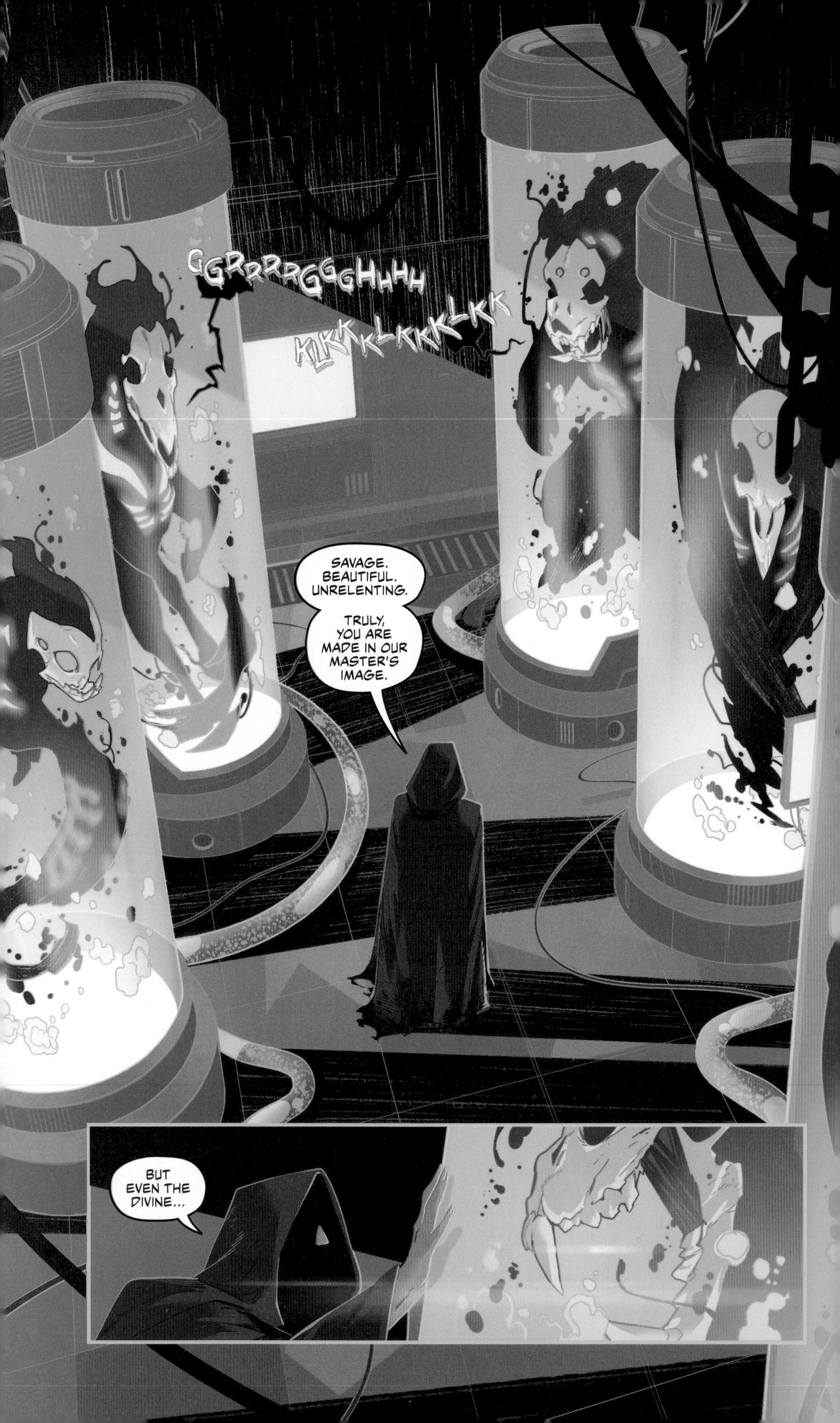
GGRRRRGGGHHHH
KLKKKLKKKLKK
SAVAGE. BEAUTIFUL. UNRELENTING.
TRULY, YOU ARE MADE IN OUR MASTER'S IMAGE.
BUT EVEN THE DIVINE...

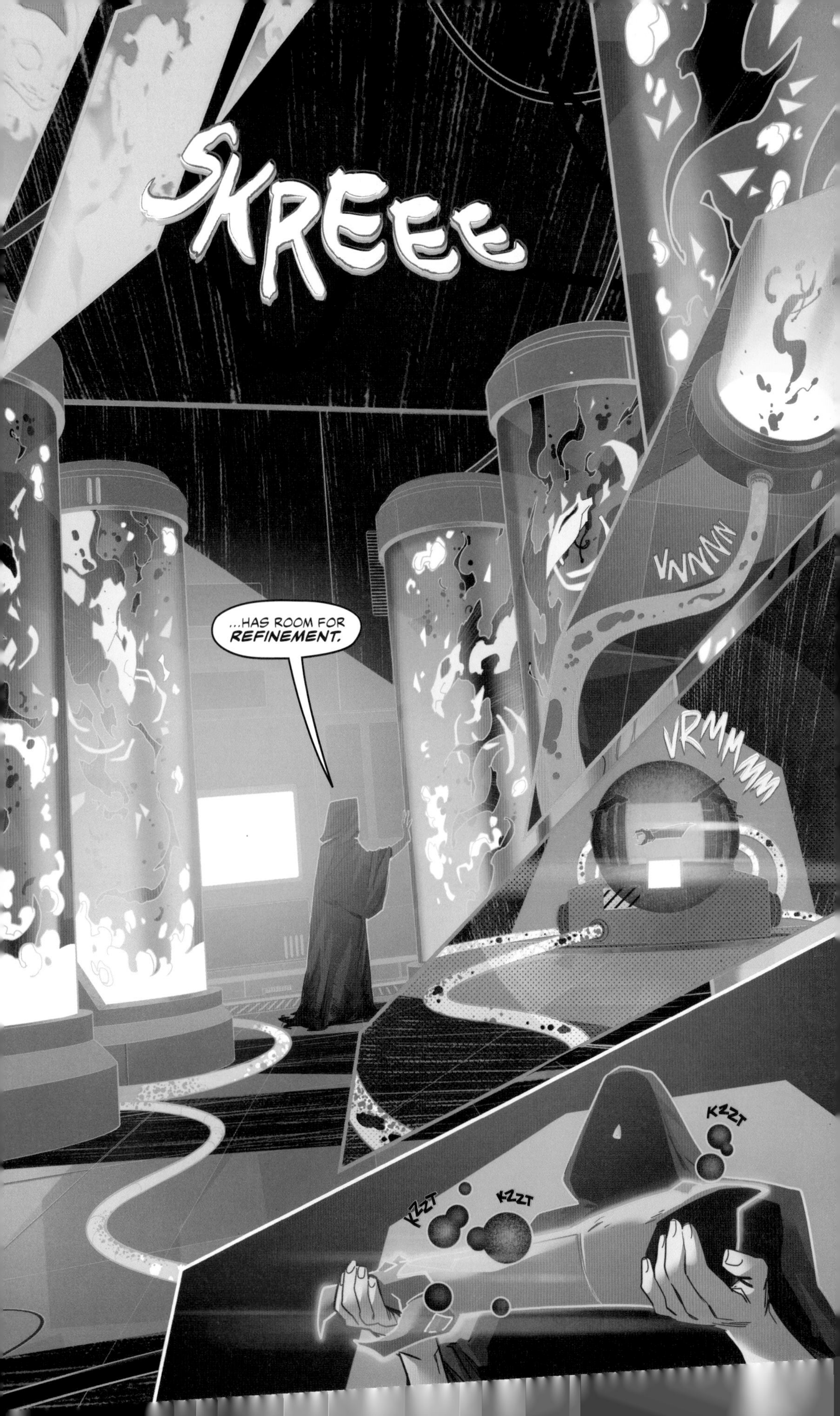
SKREEE
...HAS ROOM FOR REFINEMENT.
VNNNN
VRMMMM
KZZT
KZZT
KZZT

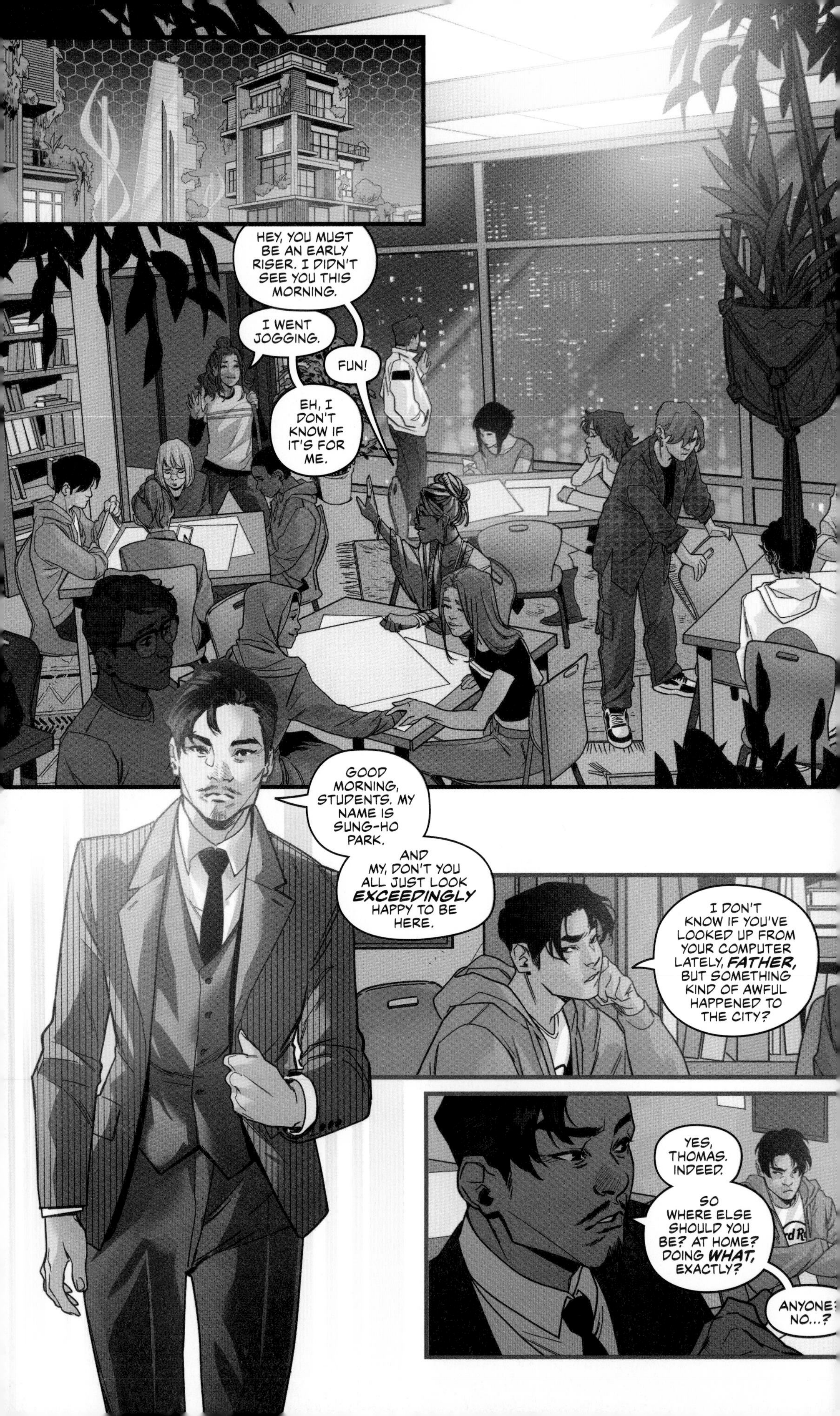
HEY, YOU MUST BE AN EARLY RISER. I DIDN'T SEE YOU THIS MORNING.
I WENT JOGGING.
FUN!
EH, I DON'T KNOW IF IT'S FOR ME.
GOOD MORNING, STUDENTS. MY NAME IS SUNG-HO PARK.
AND MY, DON'T YOU ALL JUST LOOK ***EXCEEDINGLY*** HAPPY TO BE HERE.
I DON'T KNOW IF YOU'VE LOOKED UP FROM YOUR COMPUTER LATELY, ***FATHER,*** BUT SOMETHING KIND OF AWFUL HAPPENED TO THE CITY?
YES, THOMAS. INDEED.
SO WHERE ELSE SHOULD YOU BE? AT HOME? DOING ***WHAT,*** EXACTLY?
ANYONE? NO...?

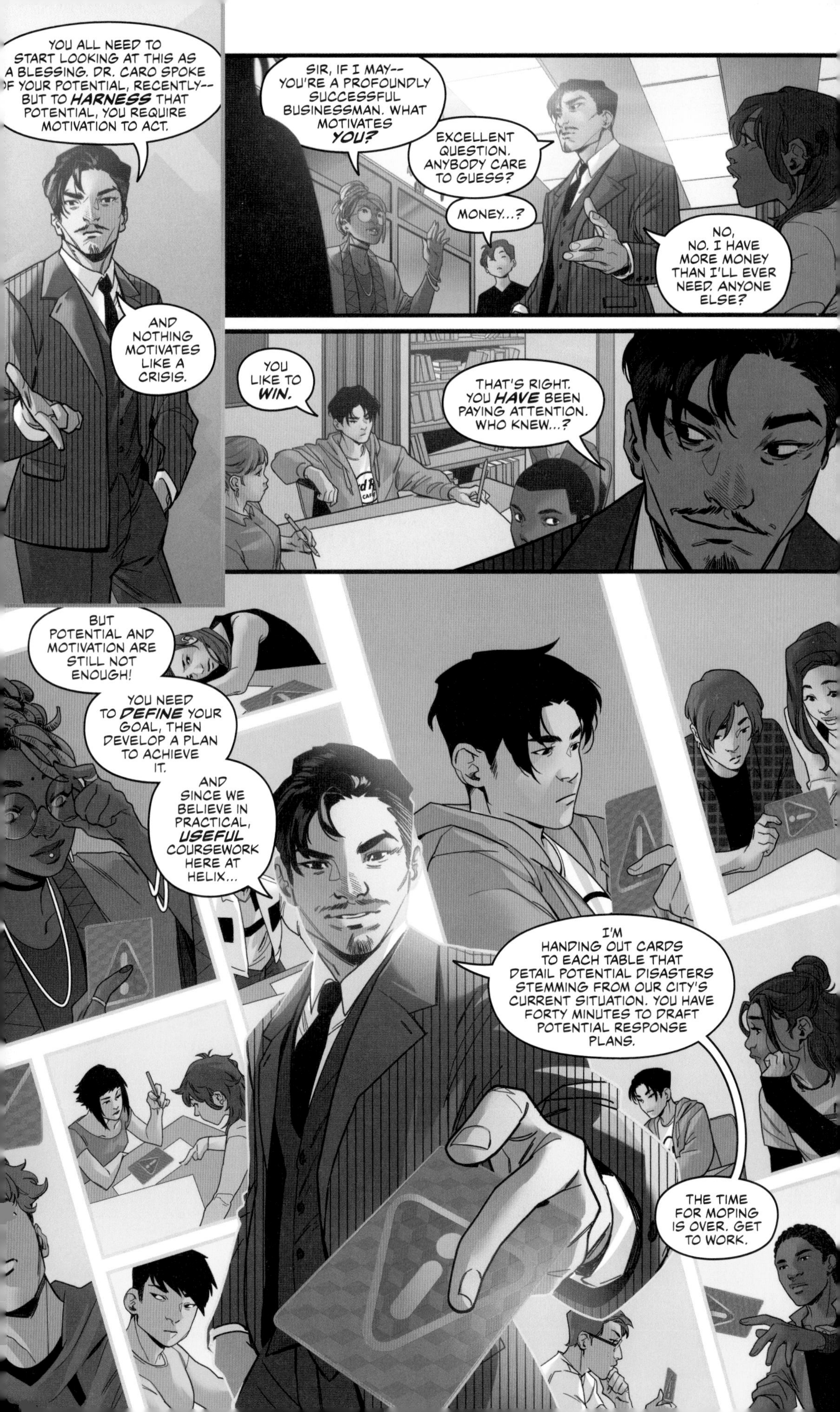

YOU ALL NEED TO START LOOKING AT THIS AS A BLESSING. DR. CARO SPOKE OF YOUR POTENTIAL, RECENTLY-- BUT TO HARNESS THAT POTENTIAL, YOU REQUIRE MOTIVATION TO ACT.
AND NOTHING MOTIVATES LIKE A CRISIS.
SIR, IF I MAY-- YOU'RE A PROFOUNDLY SUCCESSFUL BUSINESSMAN. WHAT MOTIVATES YOU?
EXCELLENT QUESTION. ANYBODY CARE TO GUESS?
MONEY...?
NO, NO. I HAVE MORE MONEY THAN I'LL EVER NEED. ANYONE ELSE?
YOU LIKE TO WIN.
THAT'S RIGHT. YOU HAVE BEEN PAYING ATTENTION. WHO KNEW...?
BUT POTENTIAL AND MOTIVATION ARE STILL NOT ENOUGH!
YOU NEED TO DEFINE YOUR GOAL, THEN DEVELOP A PLAN TO ACHIEVE IT.
AND SINCE WE BELIEVE IN PRACTICAL, USEFUL COURSEWORK HERE AT HELIX...
I'M HANDING OUT CARDS TO EACH TABLE THAT DETAIL POTENTIAL DISASTERS STEMMING FROM OUR CITY'S CURRENT SITUATION. YOU HAVE FORTY MINUTES TO DRAFT POTENTIAL RESPONSE PLANS.
THE TIME FOR MOPING IS OVER. GET TO WORK.

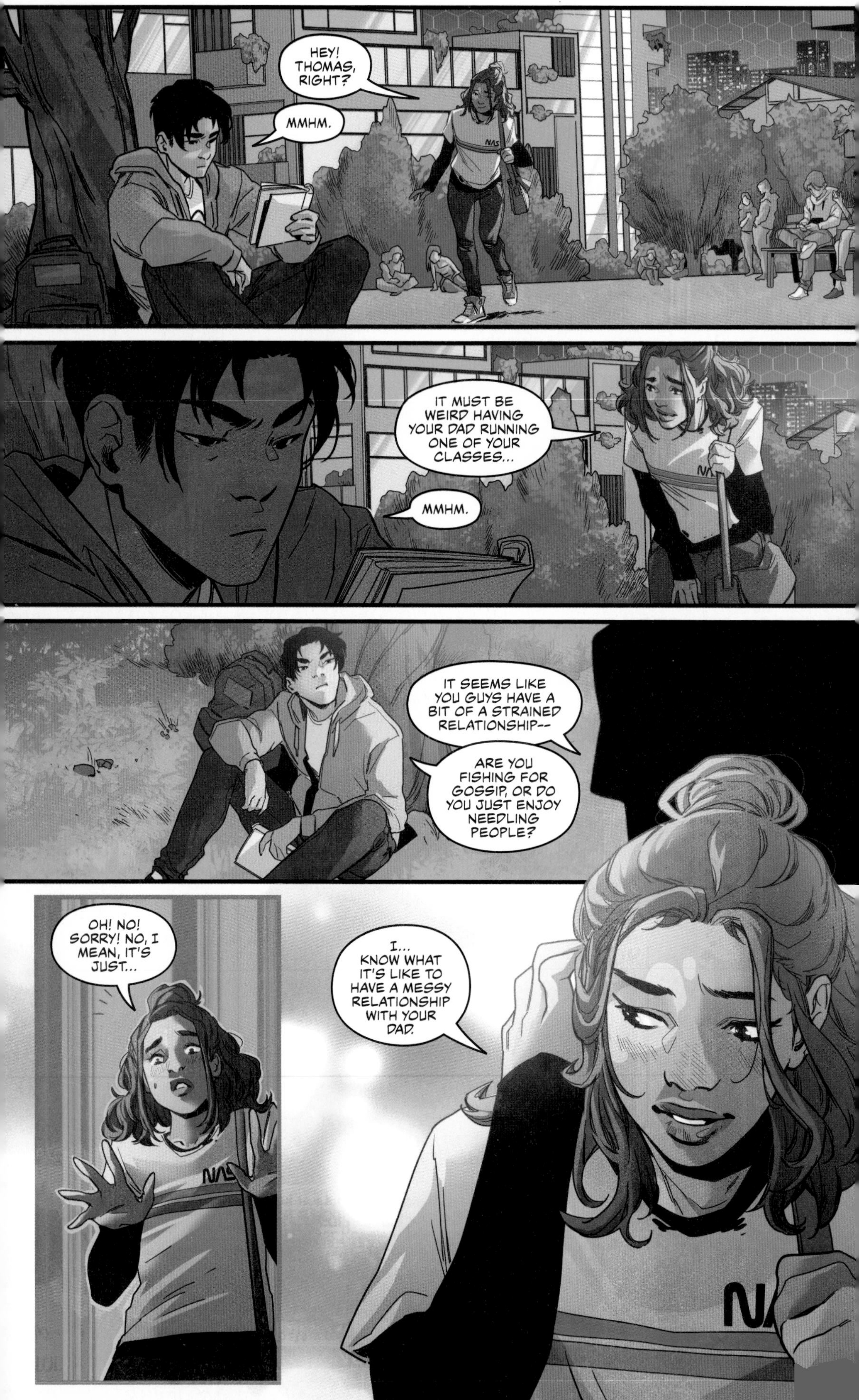
HEY! THOMAS, RIGHT?
MMHM.
IT MUST BE WEIRD HAVING YOUR DAD RUNNING ONE OF YOUR CLASSES...
MMHM.
IT SEEMS LIKE YOU GUYS HAVE A BIT OF A STRAINED RELATIONSHIP--
ARE YOU FISHING FOR GOSSIP, OR DO YOU JUST ENJOY NEEDLING PEOPLE?
OH! NO! SORRY! NO, I MEAN, IT'S JUST...
I... KNOW WHAT IT'S LIKE TO HAVE A MESSY RELATIONSHIP WITH YOUR DAD.

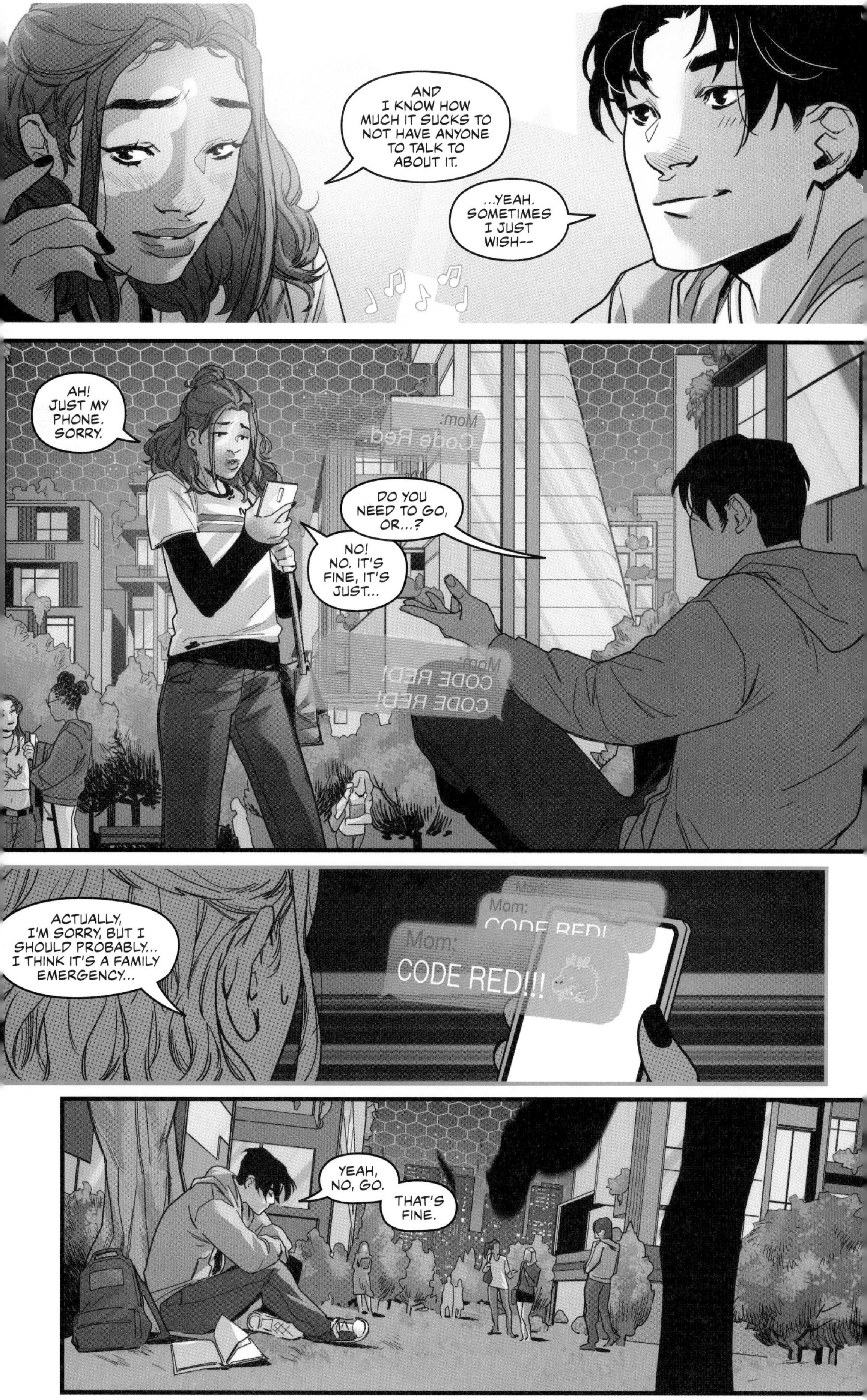
AND I KNOW HOW MUCH IT SUCKS TO NOT HAVE ANYONE TO TALK TO ABOUT IT.
...YEAH. SOMETIMES I JUST WISH--
AH! JUST MY PHONE. SORRY.
Mom: Code Red.
DO YOU NEED TO GO, OR...?
NO! NO. IT'S FINE, IT'S JUST...
Mom: CODE RED! CODE RED!
ACTUALLY, I'M SORRY, BUT I SHOULD PROBABLY... I THINK IT'S A FAMILY EMERGENCY...
Mom: CODE RED!!!
YEAH, NO, GO.
THAT'S FINE.

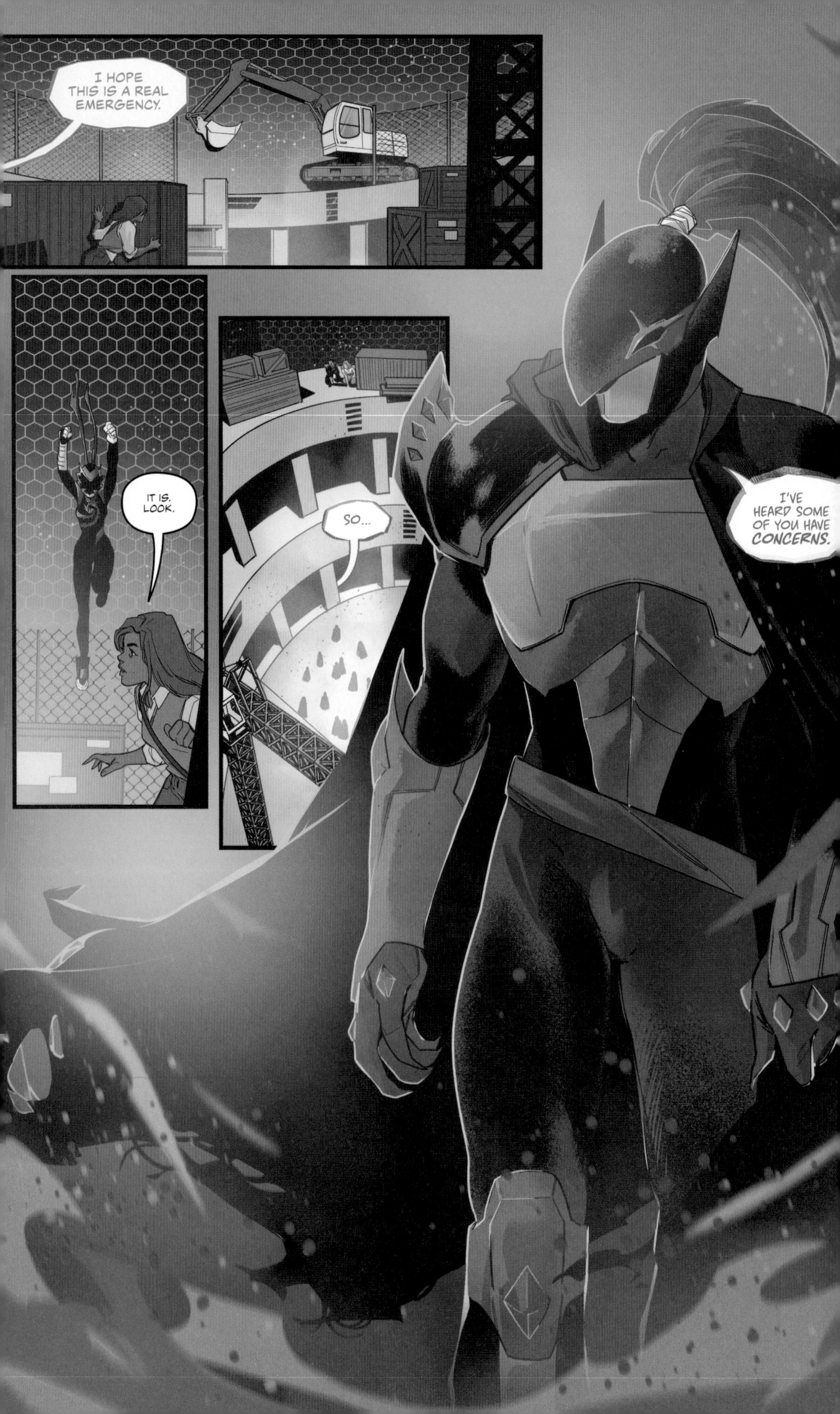
I HOPE THIS IS A REAL EMERGENCY.
IT IS. LOOK.
SO...
I'VE HEARD SOME OF YOU HAVE CONCERNS.

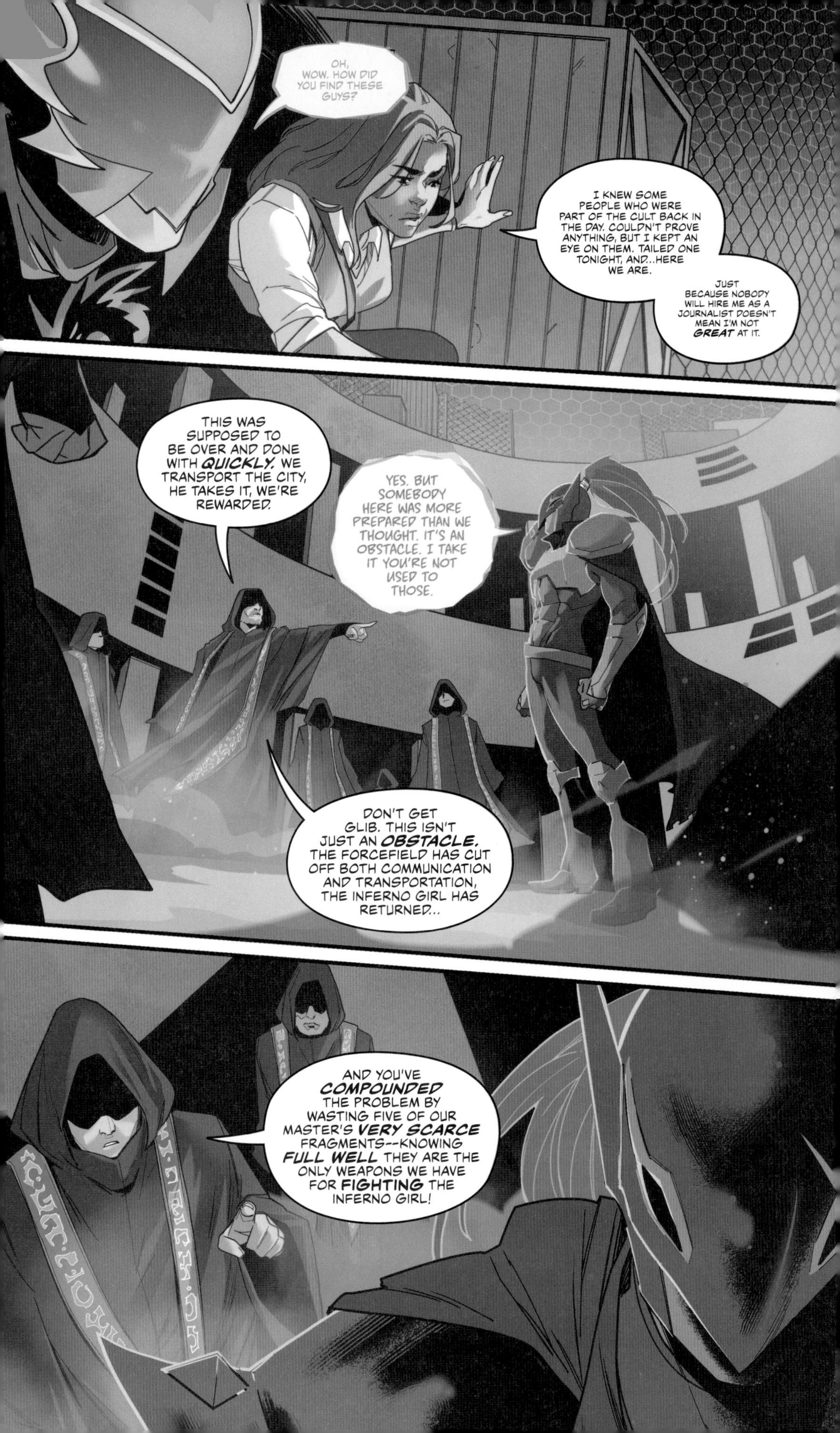
OH, WOW. HOW DID YOU FIND THESE GUYS?
I KNEW SOME PEOPLE WHO WERE PART OF THE CULT BACK IN THE DAY. COULDN'T PROVE ANYTHING, BUT I KEPT AN EYE ON THEM. TAILED ONE TONIGHT, AND...HERE WE ARE.
JUST BECAUSE NOBODY WILL HIRE ME AS A JOURNALIST DOESN'T MEAN I'M NOT GREAT AT IT.
THIS WAS SUPPOSED TO BE OVER AND DONE WITH QUICKLY. WE TRANSPORT THE CITY, HE TAKES IT, WE'RE REWARDED.
YES. BUT SOMEBODY HERE WAS MORE PREPARED THAN WE THOUGHT. IT'S AN OBSTACLE. I TAKE IT YOU'RE NOT USED TO THOSE.
DON'T GET GLIB. THIS ISN'T JUST AN OBSTACLE. THE FORCEFIELD HAS CUT OFF BOTH COMMUNICATION AND TRANSPORTATION, THE INFERNO GIRL HAS RETURNED...
AND YOU'VE COMPOUNDED THE PROBLEM BY WASTING FIVE OF OUR MASTER'S VERY SCARCE FRAGMENTS--KNOWING FULL WELL THEY ARE THE ONLY WEAPONS WE HAVE FOR FIGHTING THE INFERNO GIRL!

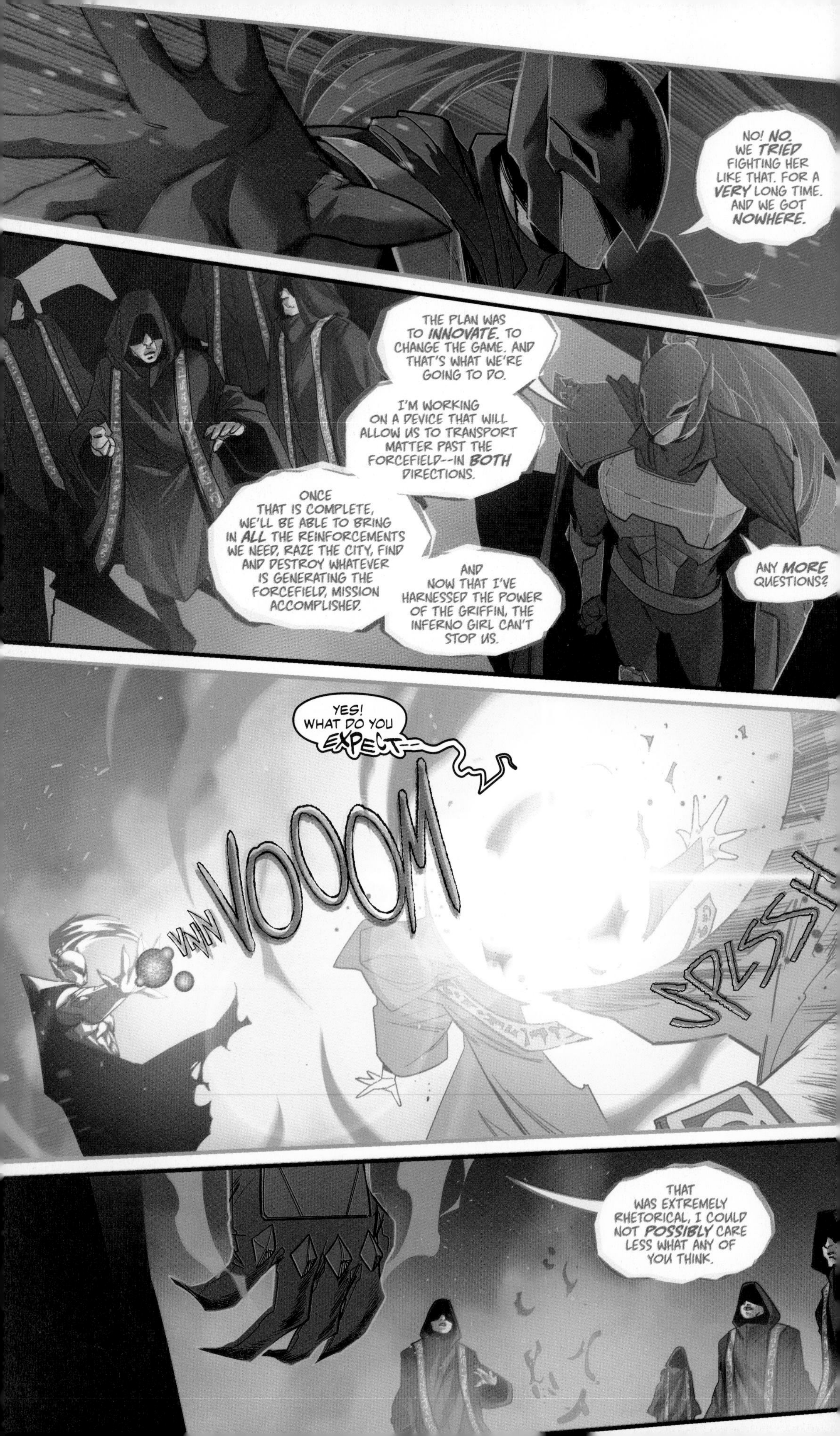
NO! NO. WE TRIED FIGHTING HER LIKE THAT. FOR A VERY LONG TIME. AND WE GOT NOWHERE.
THE PLAN WAS TO INNOVATE. TO CHANGE THE GAME. AND THAT'S WHAT WE'RE GOING TO DO.
I'M WORKING ON A DEVICE THAT WILL ALLOW US TO TRANSPORT MATTER PAST THE FORCEFIELD--IN BOTH DIRECTIONS.
ONCE THAT IS COMPLETE, WE'LL BE ABLE TO BRING IN ALL THE REINFORCEMENTS WE NEED, RAZE THE CITY, FIND AND DESTROY WHATEVER IS GENERATING THE FORCEFIELD, MISSION ACCOMPLISHED.
AND NOW THAT I'VE HARNESSED THE POWER OF THE GRIFFIN, THE INFERNO GIRL CAN'T STOP US.
ANY MORE QUESTIONS?
YES! WHAT DO YOU EXPECT--
VNN VOOOM
SPLSSH
THAT WAS EXTREMELY RHETORICAL, I COULD NOT POSSIBLY CARE LESS WHAT ANY OF YOU THINK.

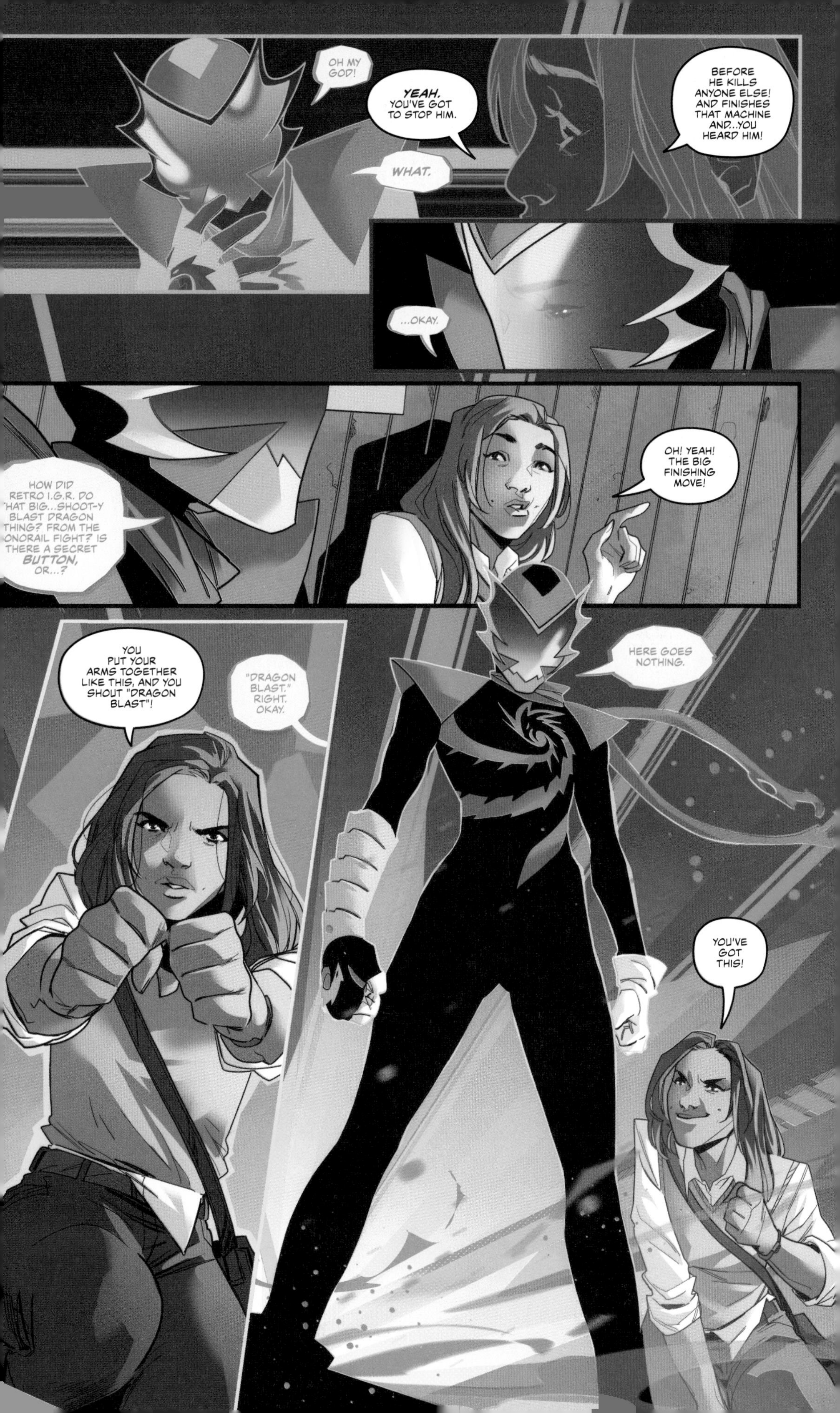
OH MY GOD!
YEAH. YOU'VE GOT TO STOP HIM.
WHAT.
BEFORE HE KILLS ANYONE ELSE! AND FINISHES THAT MACHINE AND...YOU HEARD HIM!
...OKAY.
HOW DID RETRO I.G.R. DO THAT BIG...SHOOT-Y BLAST DRAGON THING? FROM THE MONORAIL FIGHT? IS THERE A SECRET BUTTON, OR...?
OH! YEAH! THE BIG FINISHING MOVE!
YOU PUT YOUR ARMS TOGETHER LIKE THIS, AND YOU SHOUT "DRAGON BLAST"!
"DRAGON BLAST." RIGHT. OKAY.
HERE GOES NOTHING.
YOU'VE GOT THIS!

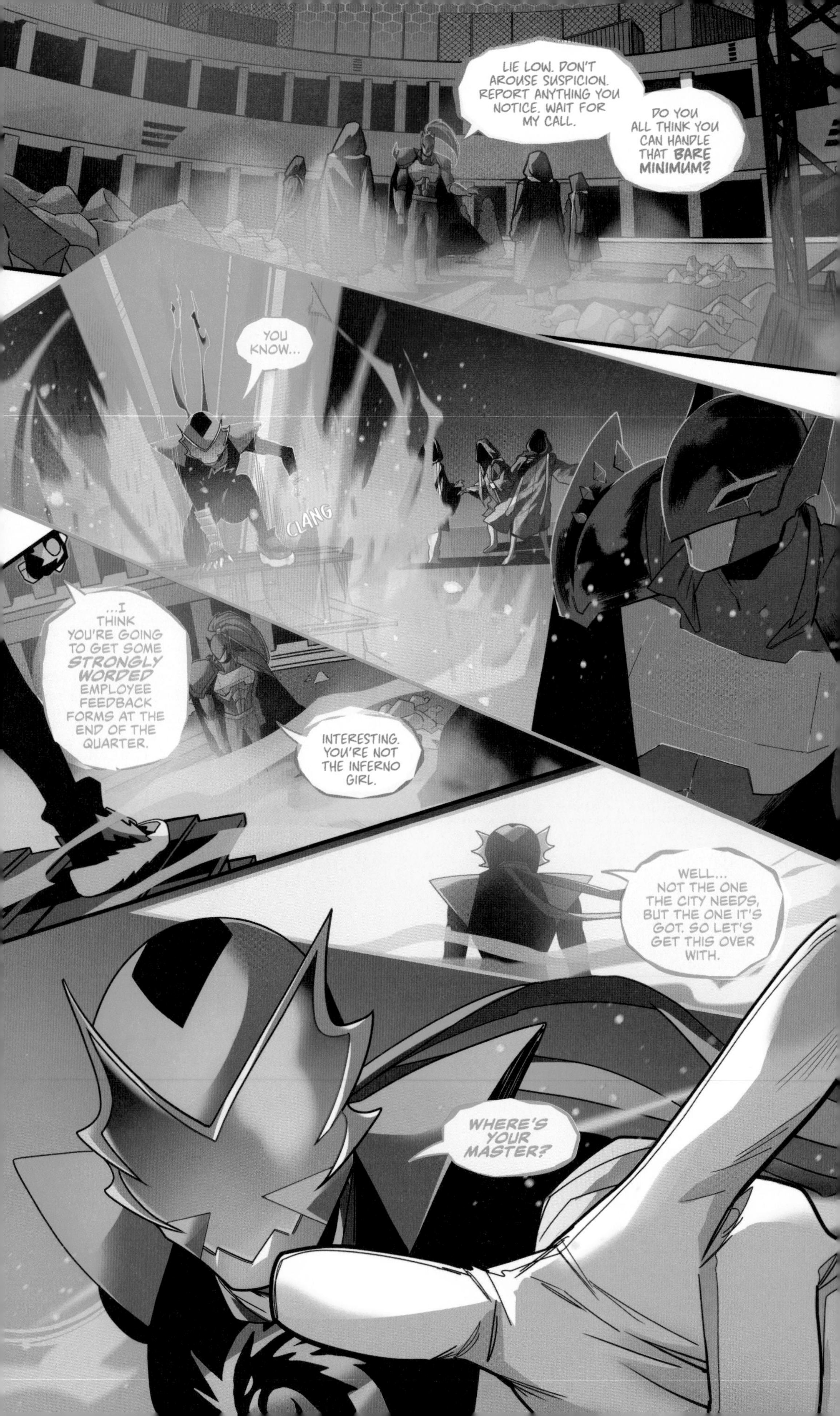
LIE LOW. DON'T AROUSE SUSPICION. REPORT ANYTHING YOU NOTICE. WAIT FOR MY CALL.
DO YOU ALL THINK YOU CAN HANDLE THAT **BARE MINIMUM?**
YOU KNOW...
CLANG
...I THINK YOU'RE GOING TO GET SOME ***STRONGLY WORDED*** EMPLOYEE FEEDBACK FORMS AT THE END OF THE QUARTER.
INTERESTING. YOU'RE NOT THE INFERNO GIRL.
WELL... NOT THE ONE THE CITY NEEDS, BUT THE ONE IT'S GOT. SO LET'S GET THIS OVER WITH.
WHERE'S YOUR MASTER?

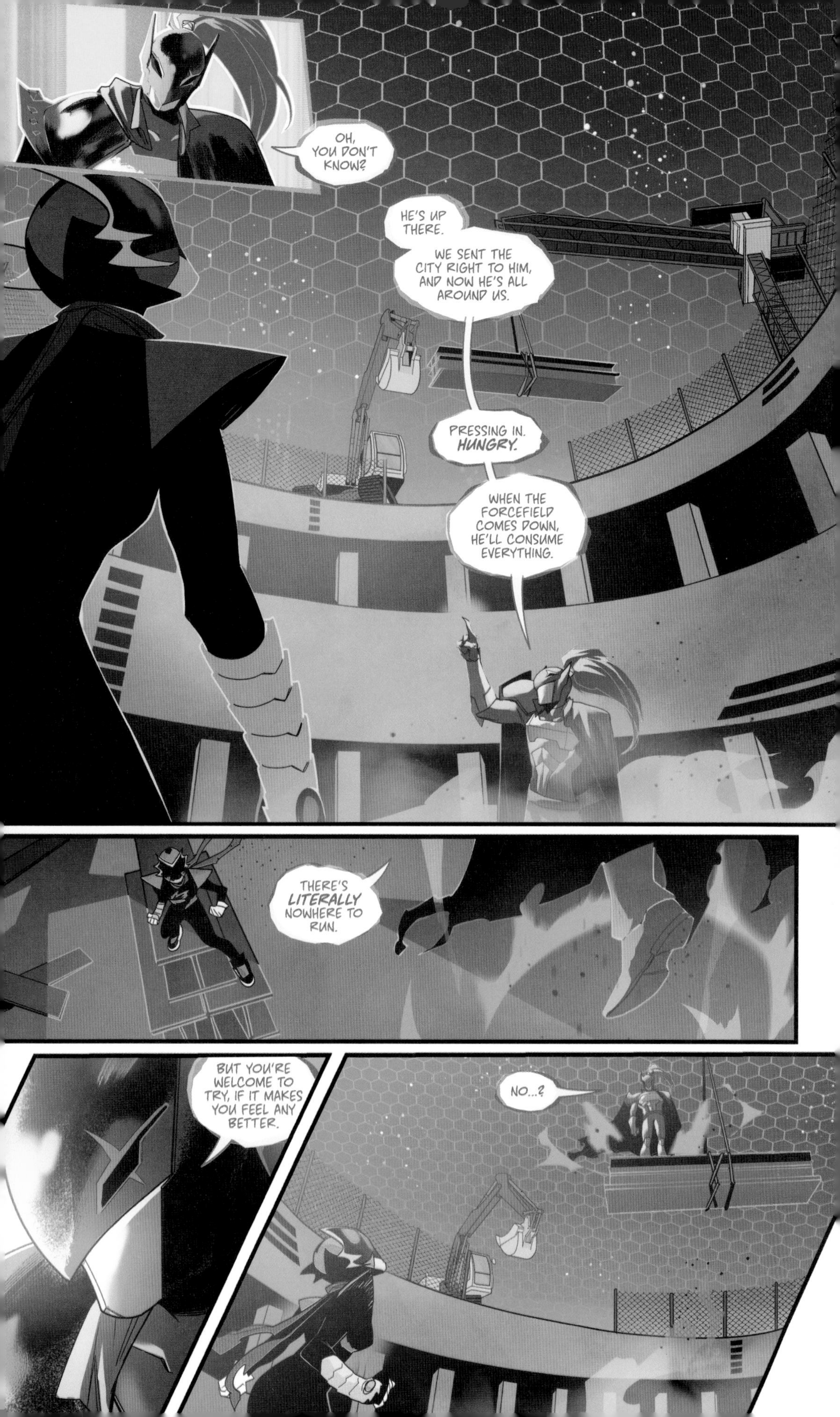
OH, YOU DON'T KNOW?
HE'S UP THERE.
WE SENT THE CITY RIGHT TO HIM, AND NOW HE'S ALL AROUND US.
PRESSING IN. HUNGRY.
WHEN THE FORCEFIELD COMES DOWN, HE'LL CONSUME EVERYTHING.
THERE'S LITERALLY NOWHERE TO RUN.
BUT YOU'RE WELCOME TO TRY, IF IT MAKES YOU FEEL ANY BETTER.
NO...?

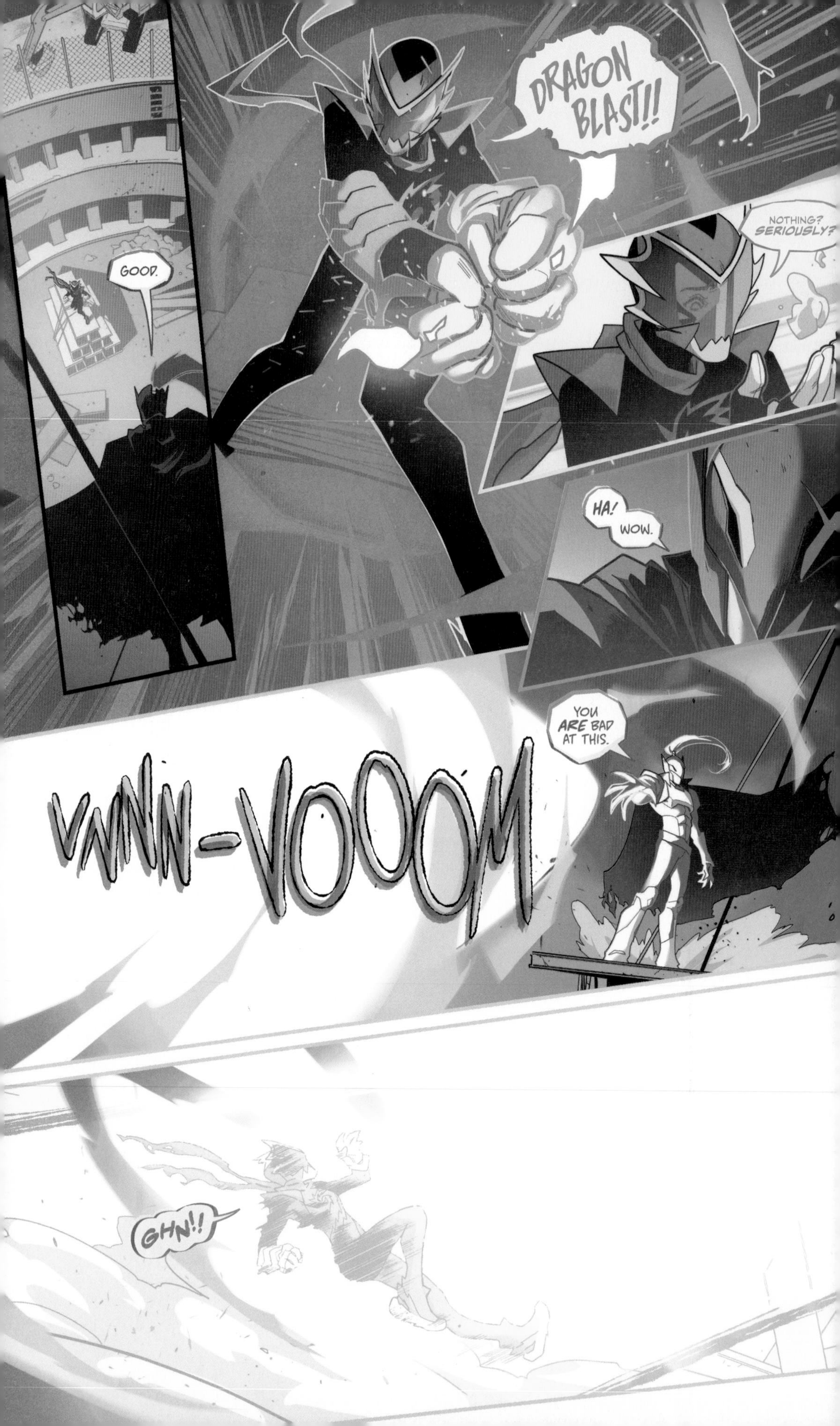
DRAGON BLAST!!
GOOD.
NOTHING? SERIOUSLY?
HA! WOW.
YOU ARE BAD AT THIS.
VWNN-VOOOM
GHN!!

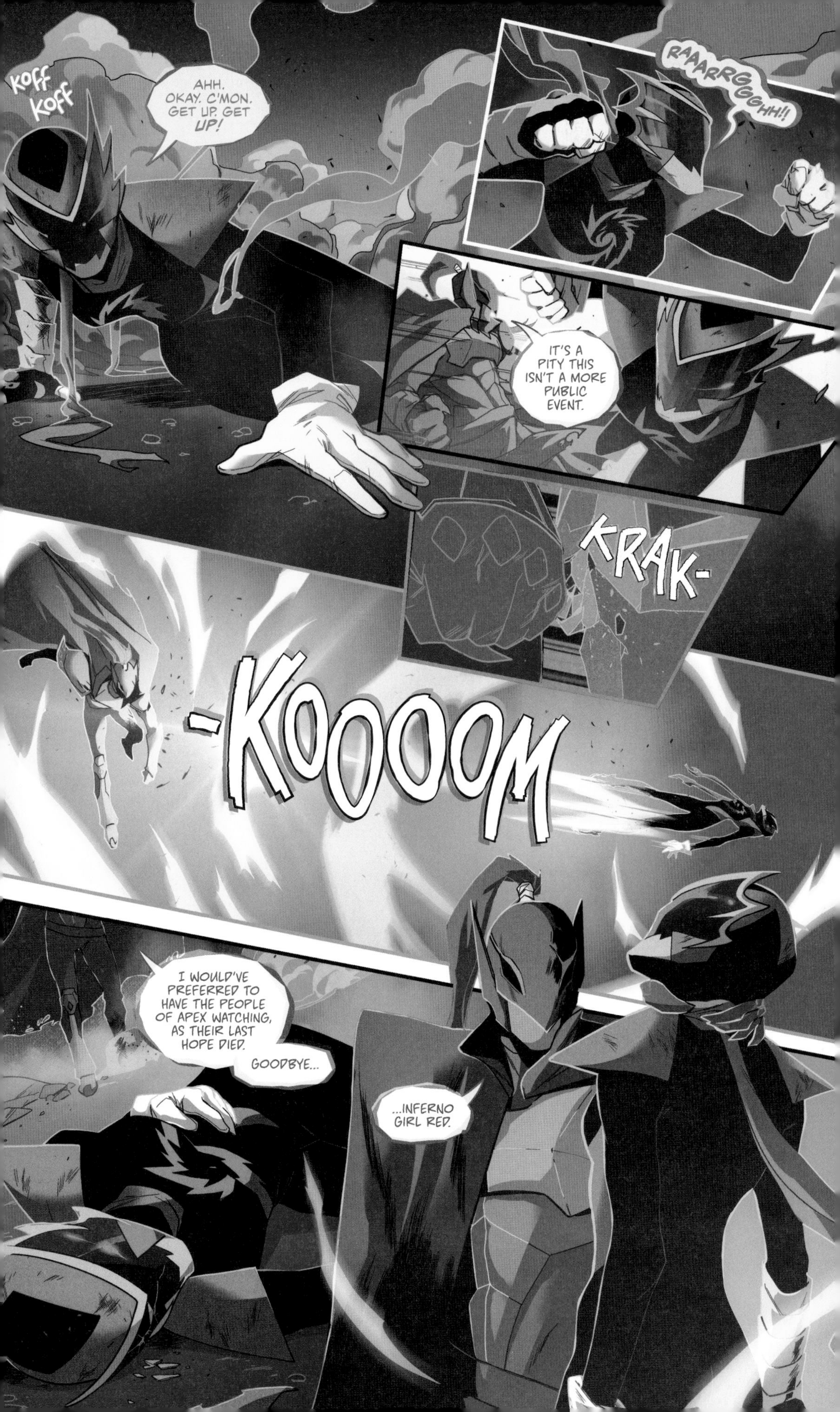
KOFF KOFF
AHH. OKAY. C'MON. GET UP. GET UP!
RAAARRGGGHH!!
IT'S A PITY THIS ISN'T A MORE PUBLIC EVENT.
KRAK-
-KOOOOM
I WOULD'VE PREFERRED TO HAVE THE PEOPLE OF APEX WATCHING, AS THEIR LAST HOPE DIED.
GOODBYE...
...INFERNO GIRL RED.

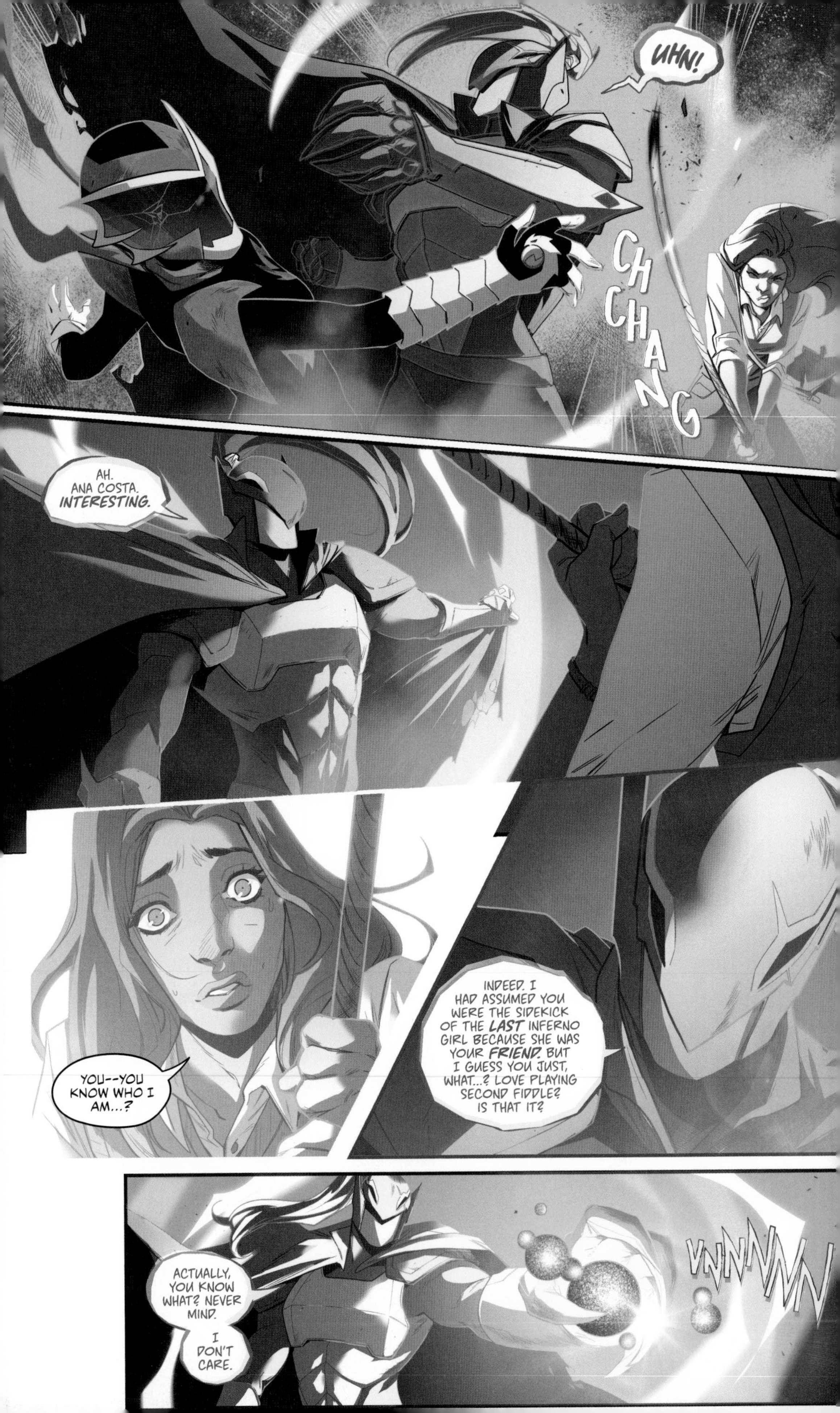
UHN!
CHCHANG
AH. ANA COSTA. **INTERESTING.**
YOU--YOU KNOW WHO I AM...?
INDEED. I HAD ASSUMED YOU WERE THE SIDEKICK OF THE ***LAST*** INFERNO GIRL BECAUSE SHE WAS YOUR ***FRIEND.*** BUT I GUESS YOU JUST, WHAT...? LOVE PLAYING SECOND FIDDLE? IS THAT IT?
VNNNNNN
ACTUALLY, YOU KNOW WHAT? NEVER MIND.
I DON'T CARE.

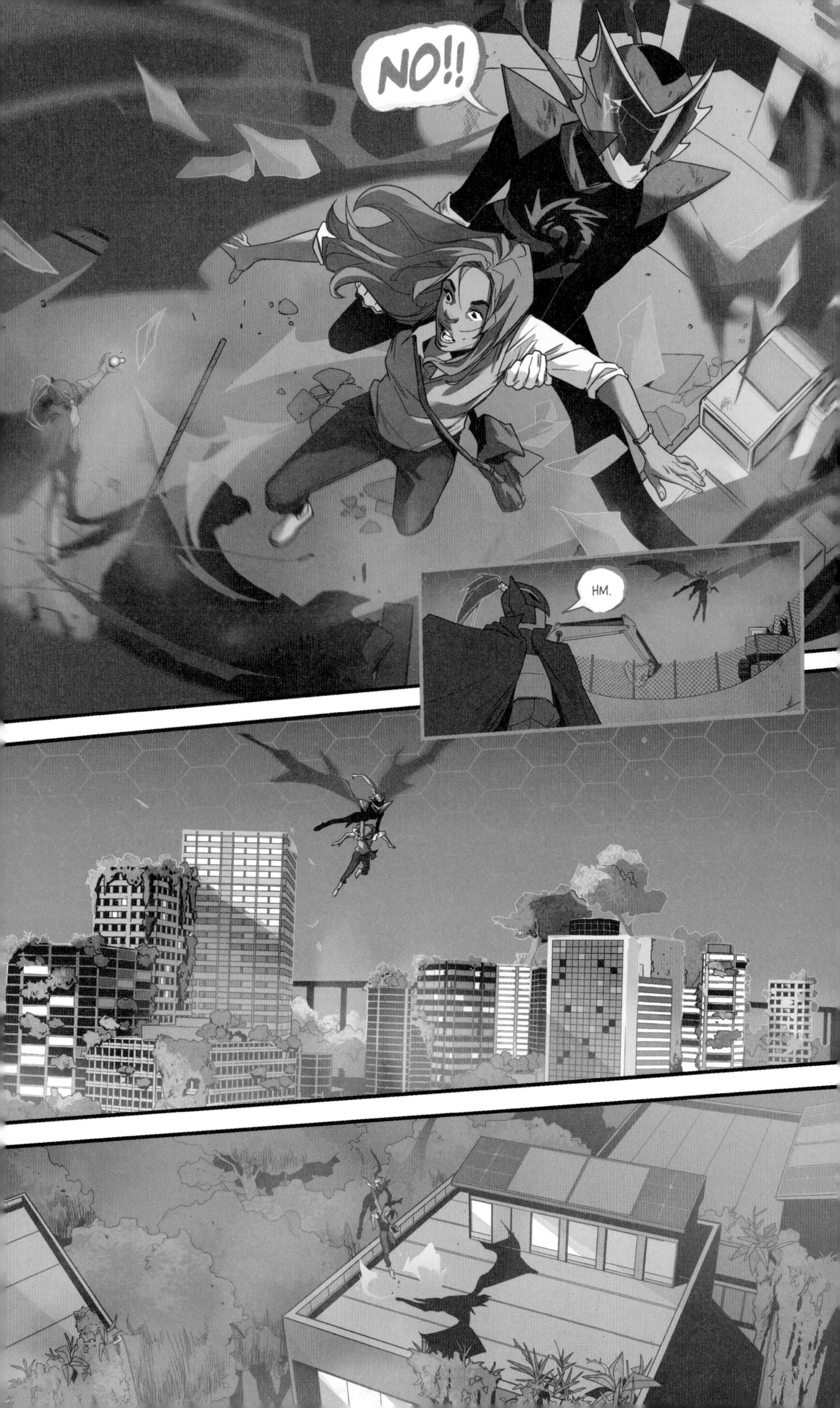
NO!!
HM.

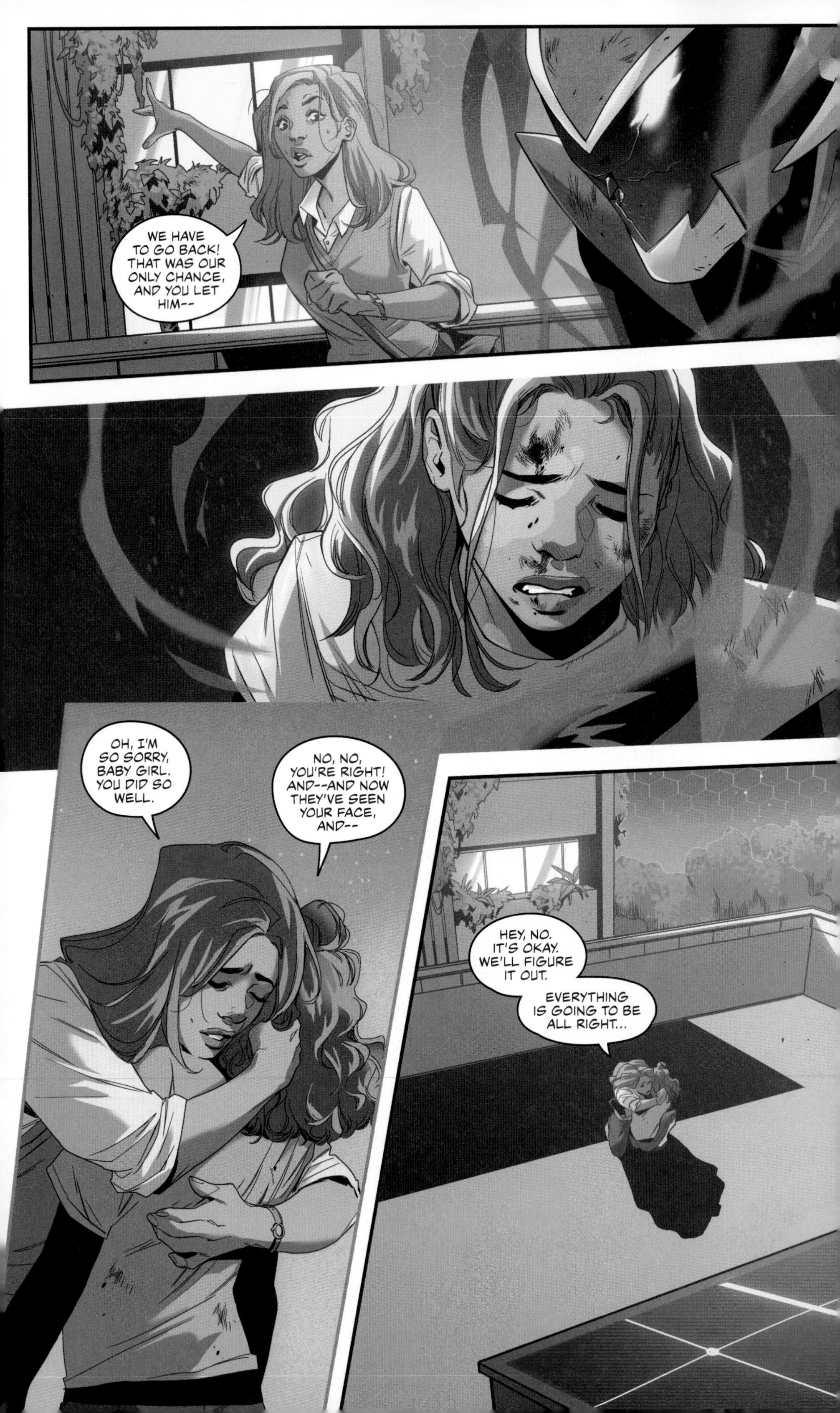
WE HAVE TO GO BACK! THAT WAS OUR ONLY CHANCE, AND YOU LET HIM--
OH, I'M SO SORRY, BABY GIRL. YOU DID SO WELL.
NO, NO, YOU'RE RIGHT! AND--AND NOW THEY'VE SEEN YOUR FACE, AND--
HEY, NO. IT'S OKAY. WE'LL FIGURE IT OUT.
EVERYTHING IS GOING TO BE ALL RIGHT...

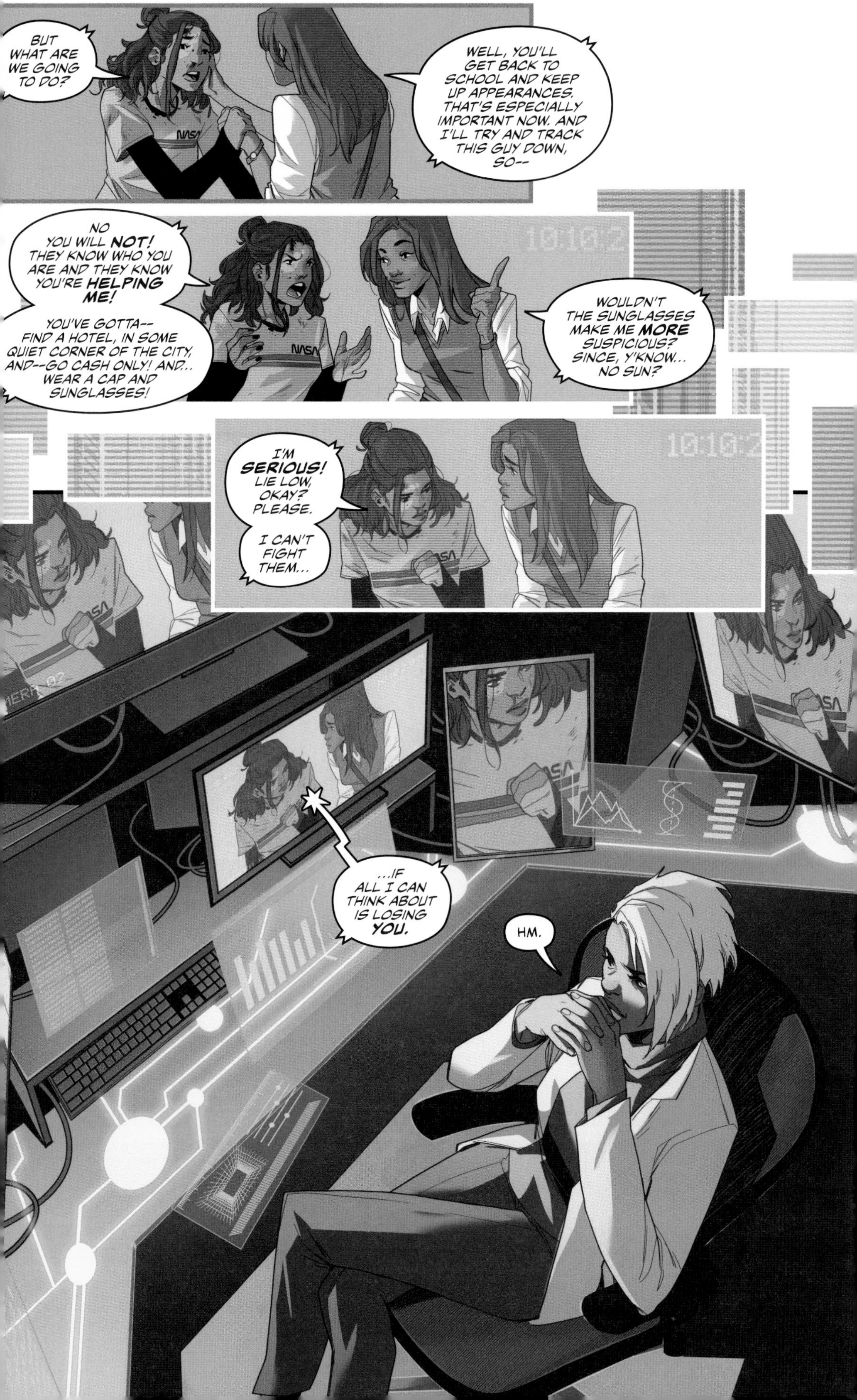
BUT WHAT ARE WE GOING TO DO?
WELL, YOU'LL GET BACK TO SCHOOL AND KEEP UP APPEARANCES. THAT'S ESPECIALLY IMPORTANT NOW. AND I'LL TRY AND TRACK THIS GUY DOWN, SO--
NO YOU WILL NOT! THEY KNOW WHO YOU ARE AND THEY KNOW YOU'RE HELPING ME!
YOU'VE GOTTA-- FIND A HOTEL, IN SOME QUIET CORNER OF THE CITY, AND--GO CASH ONLY! AND... WEAR A CAP AND SUNGLASSES!
WOULDN'T THE SUNGLASSES MAKE ME MORE SUSPICIOUS? SINCE, Y'KNOW... NO SUN?
I'M SERIOUS! LIE LOW, OKAY? PLEASE.
I CAN'T FIGHT THEM...
...IF ALL I CAN THINK ABOUT IS LOSING YOU.
HM.

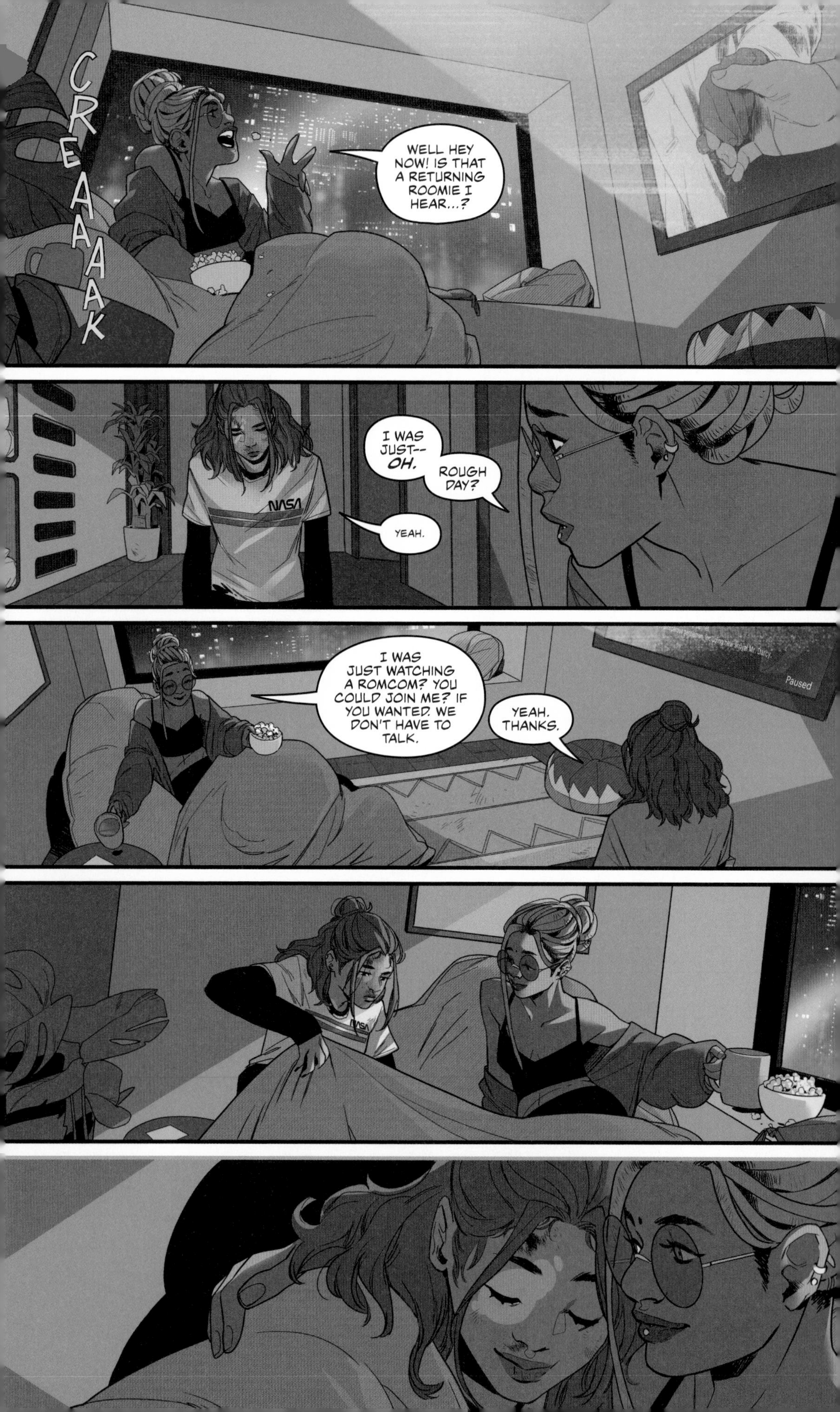

CREAAAAK
WELL HEY NOW! IS THAT A RETURNING ROOMIE I HEAR...?
I WAS JUST-- OH.
ROUGH DAY?
YEAH.
Paused
I WAS JUST WATCHING A ROMCOM? YOU COULD JOIN ME? IF YOU WANTED. WE DON'T HAVE TO TALK.
YEAH. THANKS.

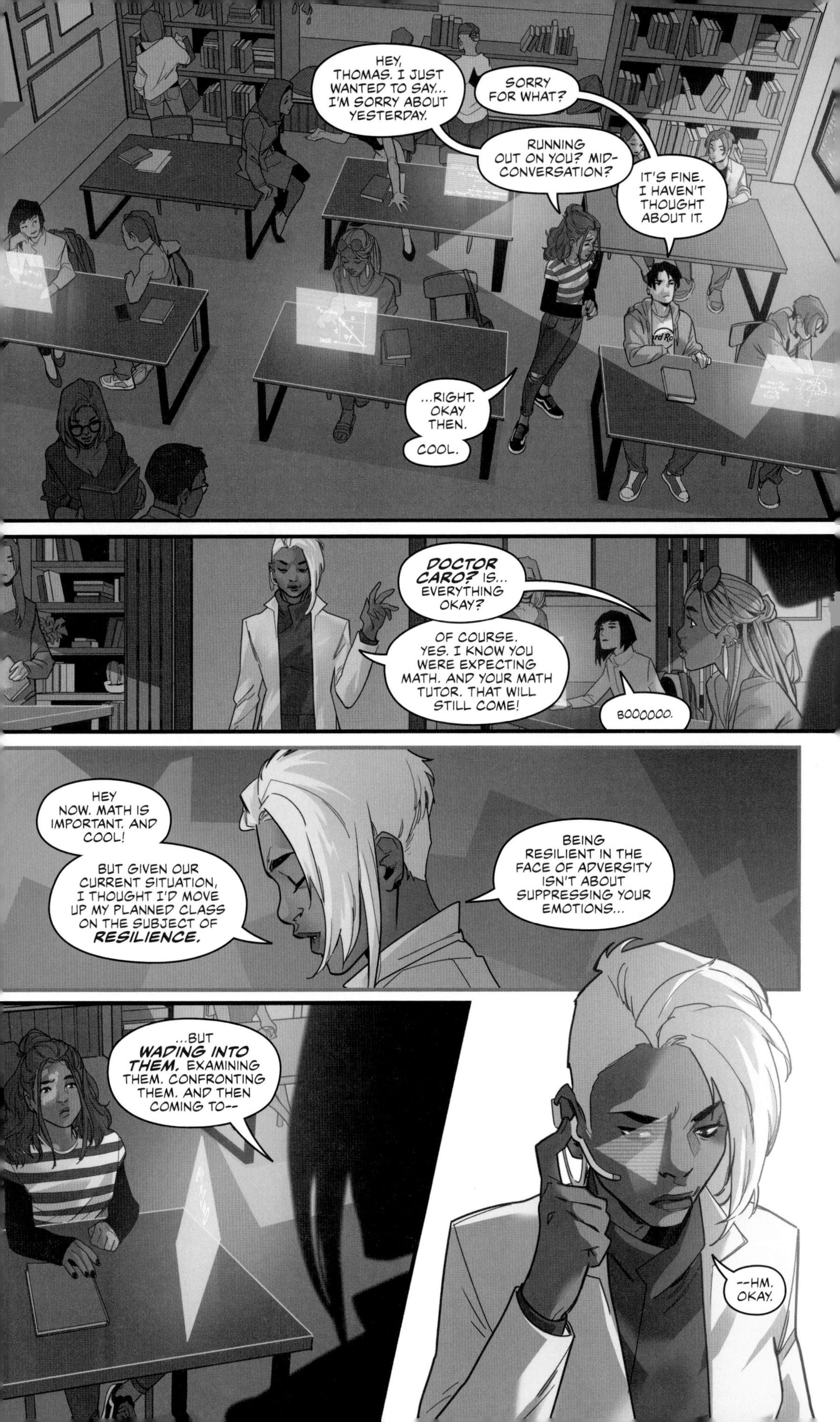
HEY, THOMAS. I JUST WANTED TO SAY... I'M SORRY ABOUT YESTERDAY.
SORRY FOR WHAT?
RUNNING OUT ON YOU? MID-CONVERSATION?
IT'S FINE. I HAVEN'T THOUGHT ABOUT IT.
...RIGHT. OKAY THEN.
COOL.
DOCTOR CARO? IS... EVERYTHING OKAY?
OF COURSE. YES. I KNOW YOU WERE EXPECTING MATH. AND YOUR MATH TUTOR. THAT WILL STILL COME!
BOOOOOO.
HEY NOW. MATH IS IMPORTANT. AND COOL!
BUT GIVEN OUR CURRENT SITUATION, I THOUGHT I'D MOVE UP MY PLANNED CLASS ON THE SUBJECT OF RESILIENCE.
BEING RESILIENT IN THE FACE OF ADVERSITY ISN'T ABOUT SUPPRESSING YOUR EMOTIONS...
...BUT WADING INTO THEM. EXAMINING THEM. CONFRONTING THEM. AND THEN COMING TO--
--HM. OKAY.

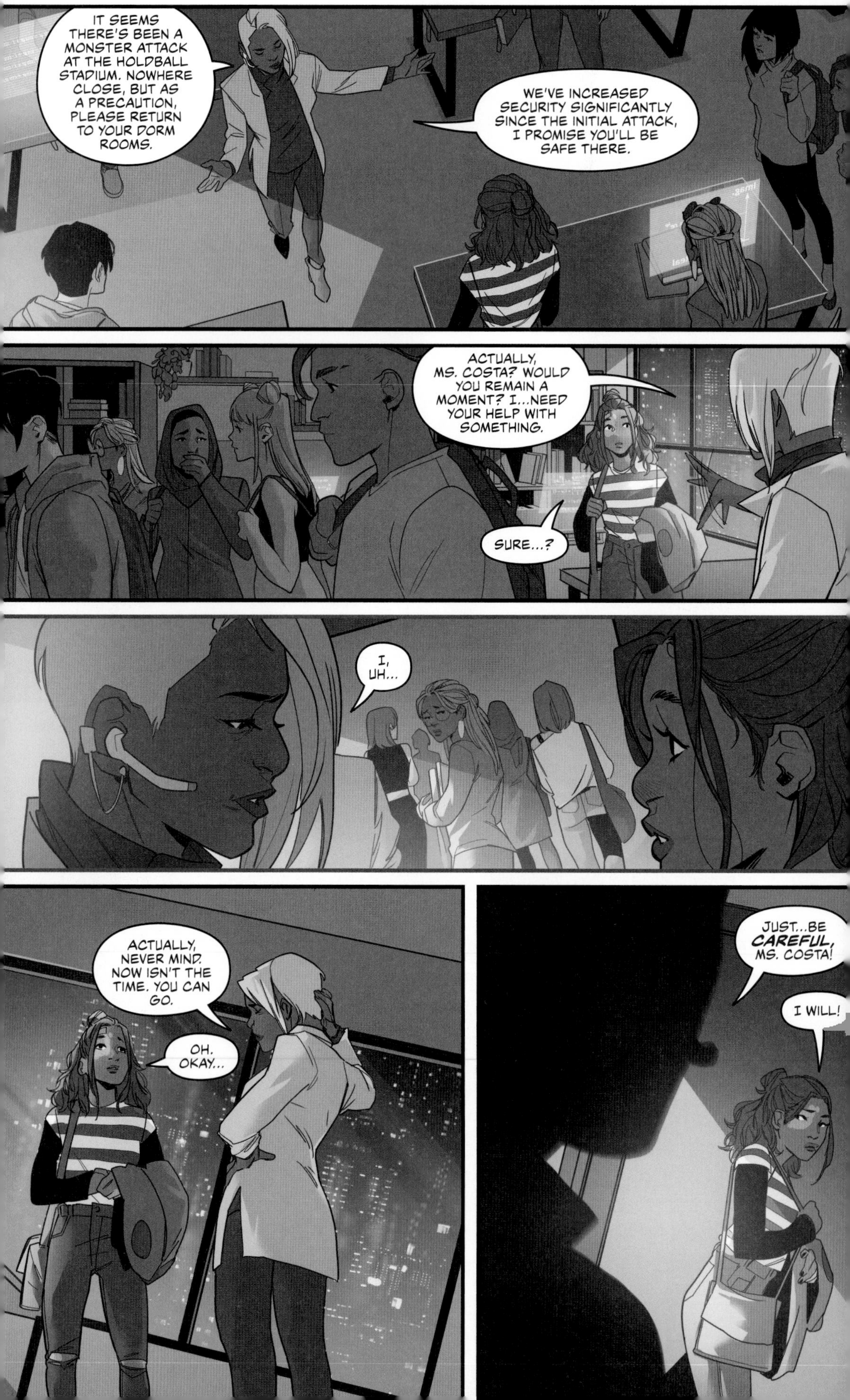
IT SEEMS THERE'S BEEN A MONSTER ATTACK AT THE HOLDBALL STADIUM. NOWHERE CLOSE, BUT AS A PRECAUTION, PLEASE RETURN TO YOUR DORM ROOMS.
WE'VE INCREASED SECURITY SIGNIFICANTLY SINCE THE INITIAL ATTACK, I PROMISE YOU'LL BE SAFE THERE.
ACTUALLY, MS. COSTA? WOULD YOU REMAIN A MOMENT? I...NEED YOUR HELP WITH SOMETHING.
SURE...?
I, UH...
ACTUALLY, NEVER MIND. NOW ISN'T THE TIME. YOU CAN GO.
OH. OKAY...
JUST...BE CAREFUL, MS. COSTA!
I WILL!

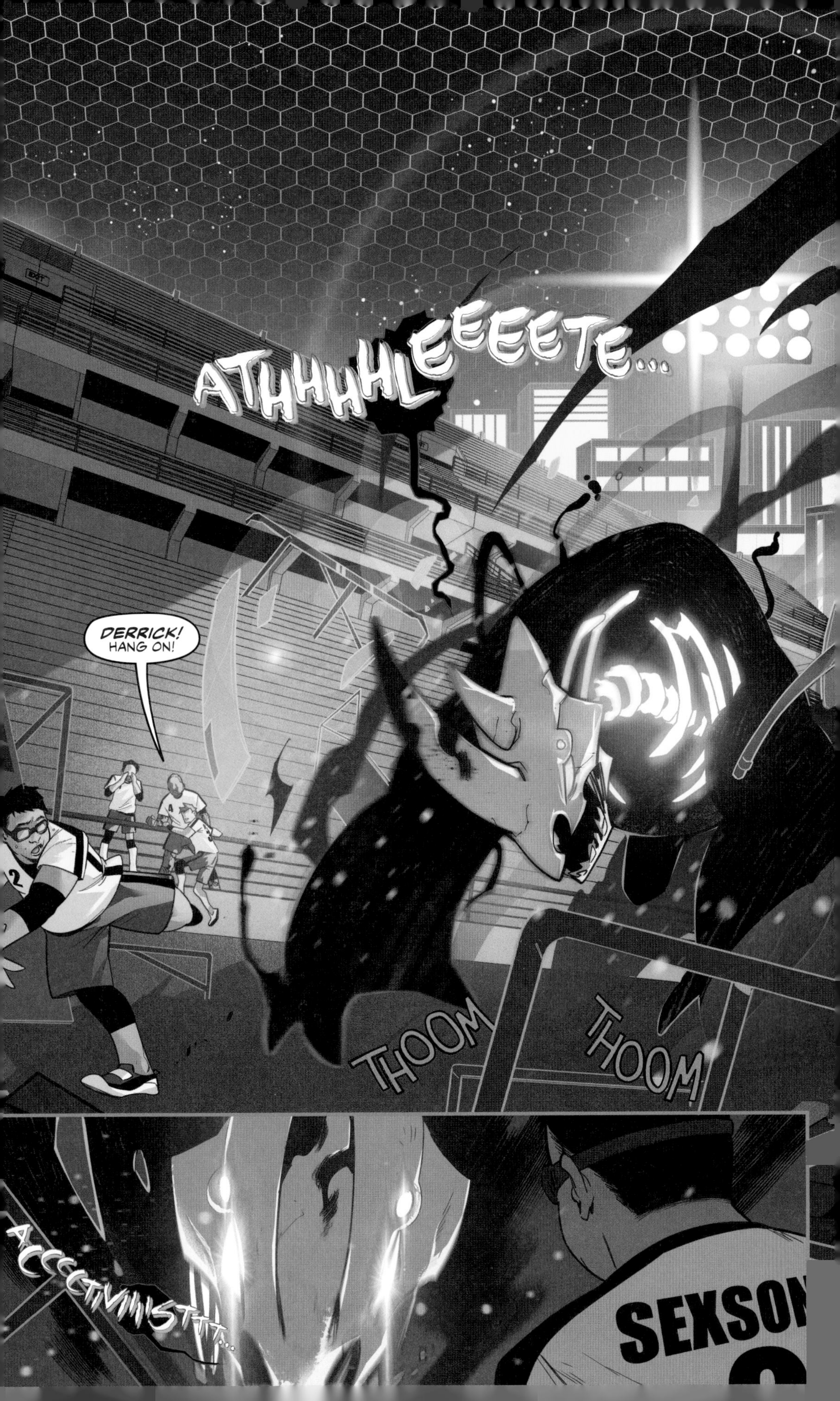
ATHHHHLEEEEETE...
DERRICK! HANG ON!
THOOM
THOOM
ACCCCTIVIIIISTTTT...
SEXSON

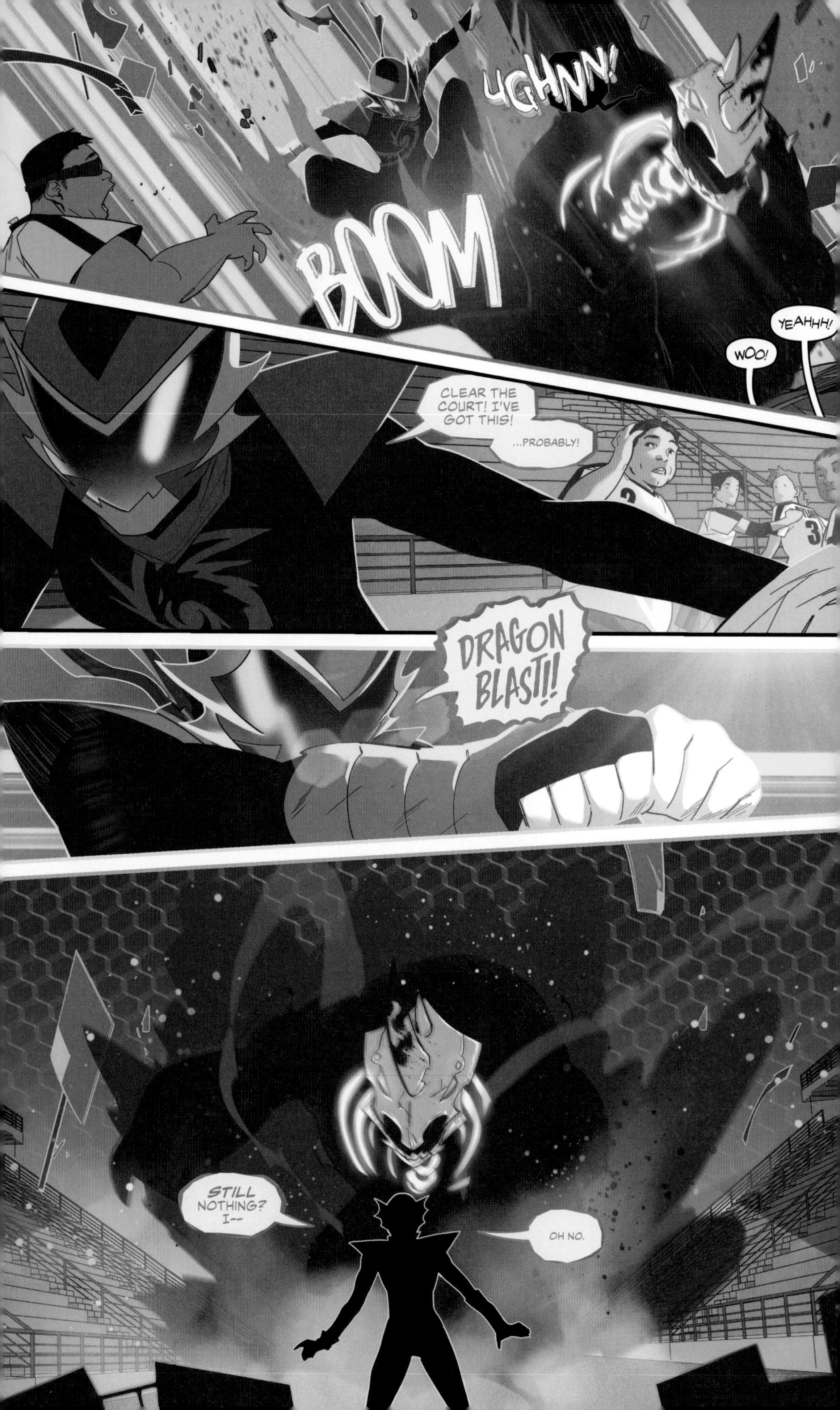
UGHNN!
BOOM
YEAHHH!
WOO!
CLEAR THE COURT! I'VE GOT THIS!
...PROBABLY!
DRAGON BLAST!!
STILL NOTHING? I--
OH NO.

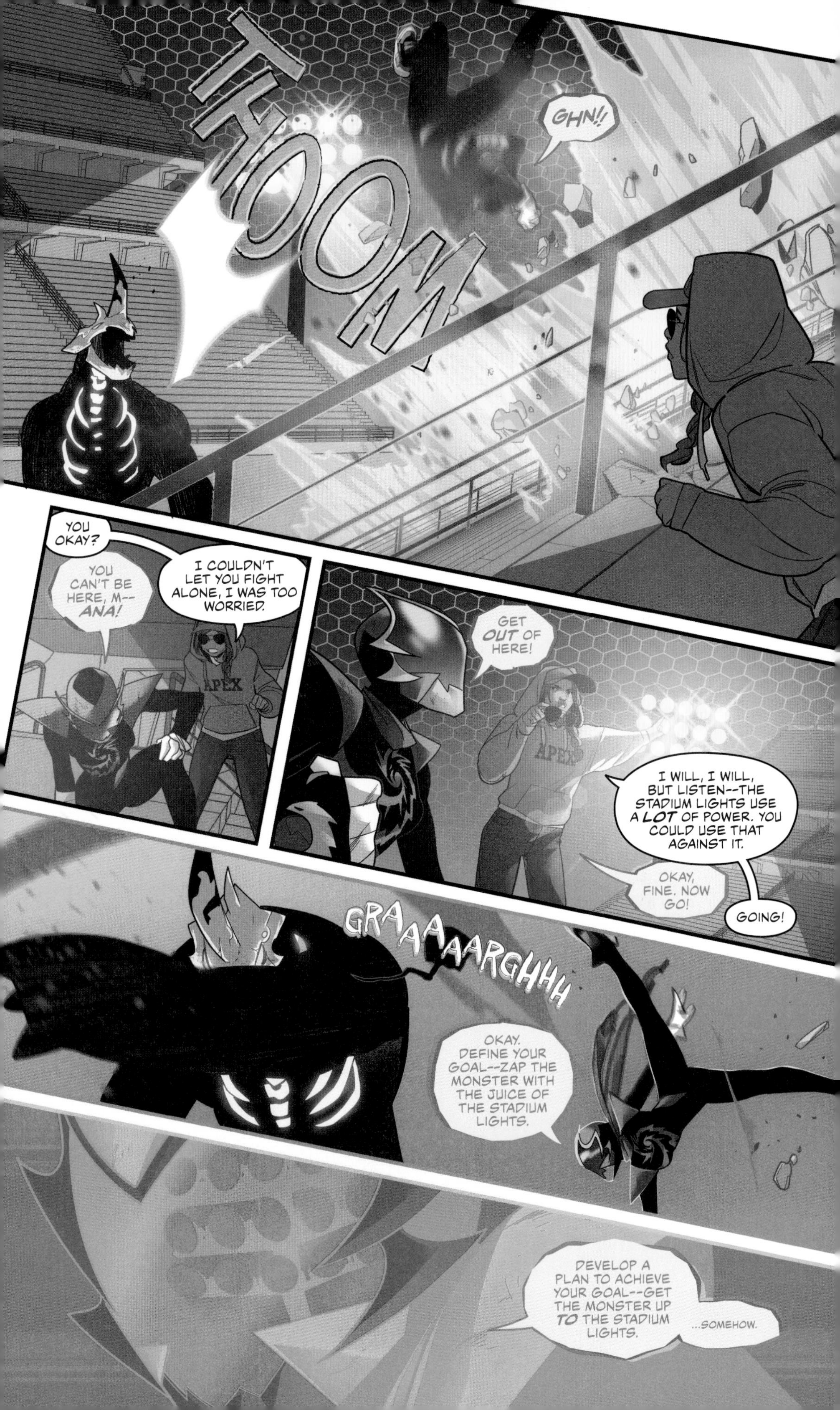
THOOM
GHN!!
YOU OKAY?
YOU CAN'T BE HERE, M--ANA!
I COULDN'T LET YOU FIGHT ALONE, I WAS TOO WORRIED.
APEX
GET OUT OF HERE!
APEX
I WILL, I WILL, BUT LISTEN--THE STADIUM LIGHTS USE A LOT OF POWER. YOU COULD USE THAT AGAINST IT.
OKAY, FINE. NOW GO!
GOING!
GRAAAAARGHHH
OKAY. DEFINE YOUR GOAL--ZAP THE MONSTER WITH THE JUICE OF THE STADIUM LIGHTS.
DEVELOP A PLAN TO ACHIEVE YOUR GOAL--GET THE MONSTER UP TO THE STADIUM LIGHTS.
...SOMEHOW.

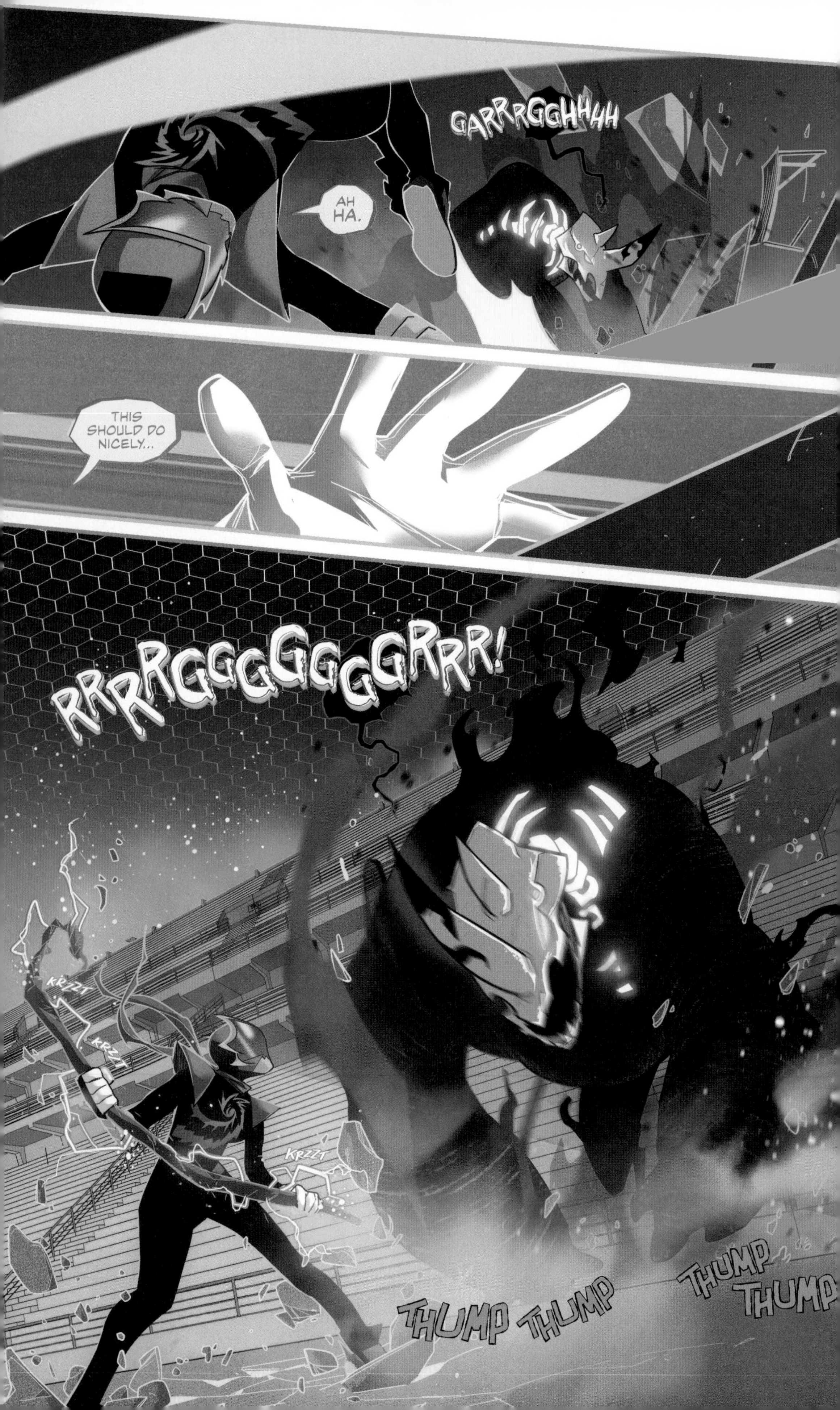
GARRRGGHHHH
AH HA.
THIS SHOULD DO NICELY...
RRRRGGGGGGRRR!
KRZZT
KRZZT
KRZZT
THUMP THUMP
THUMP THUMP

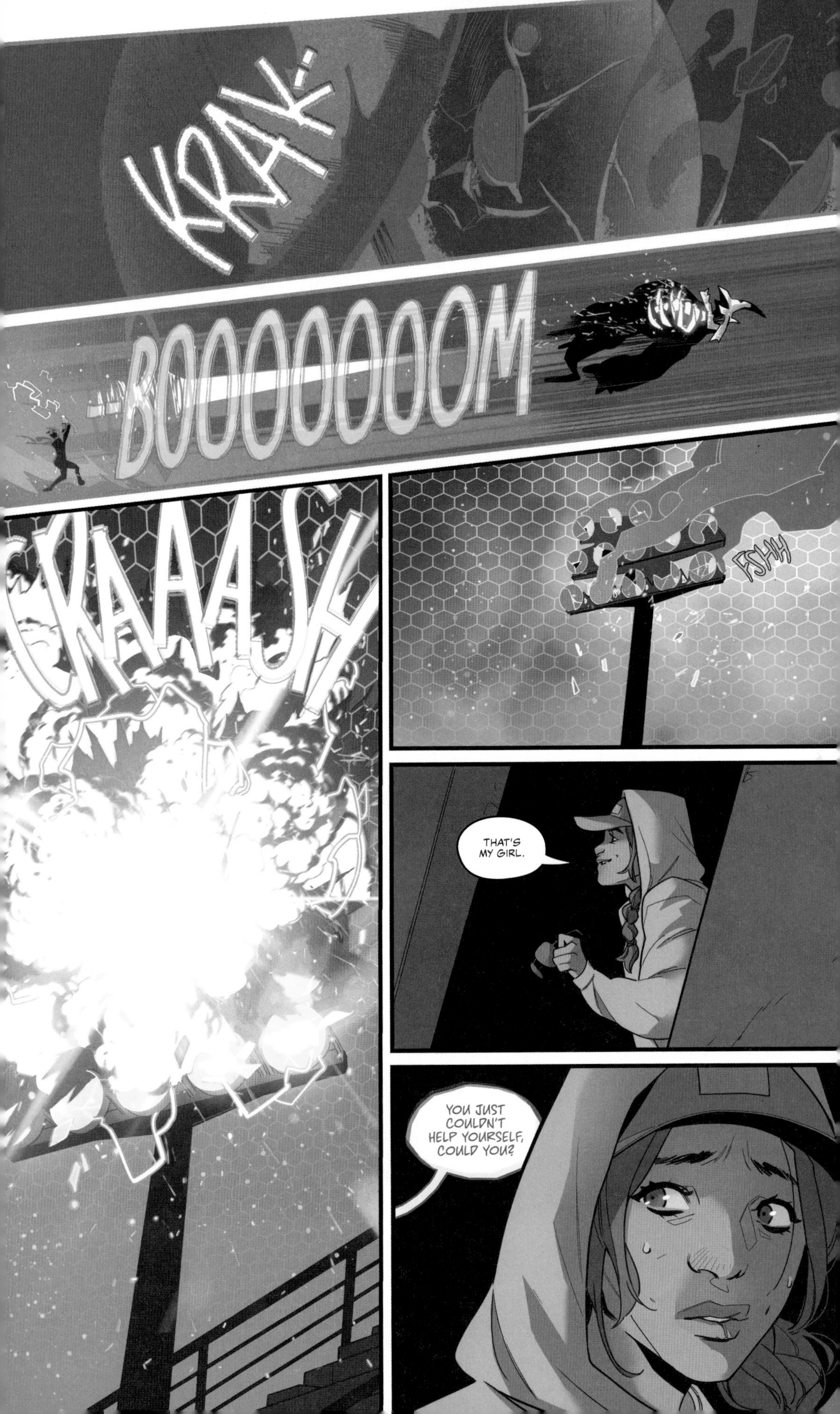
KRAK-
BOOOOOOOM
KRAAASH
FSHH
THAT'S MY GIRL.
YOU JUST COULDN'T HELP YOURSELF, COULD YOU?

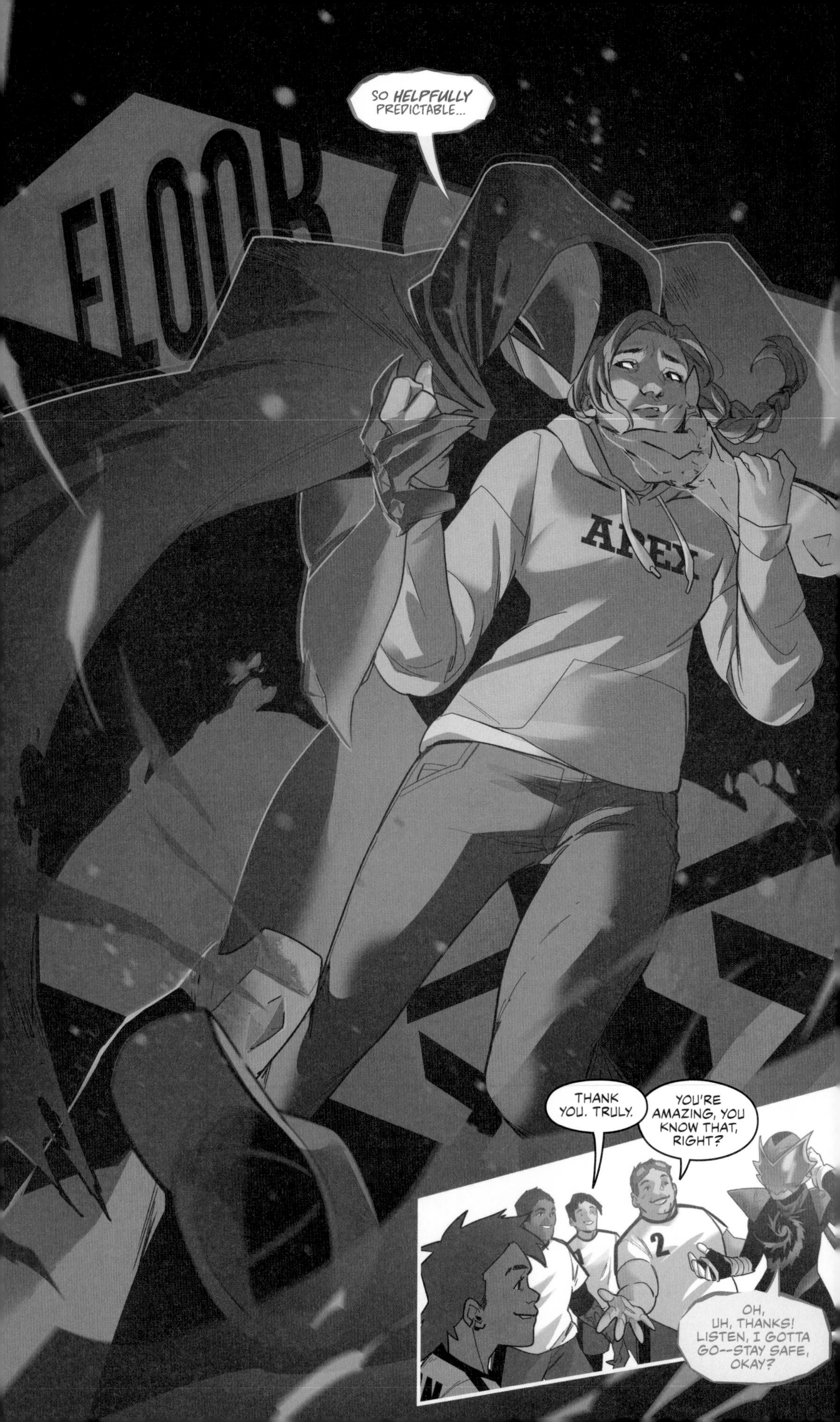
SO *HELPFULLY* PREDICTABLE...
FLOOR 7
APEX
THANK YOU. TRULY.
YOU'RE AMAZING, YOU KNOW THAT, RIGHT?
OH, UH, THANKS! LISTEN, I GOTTA GO--STAY SAFE, OKAY?

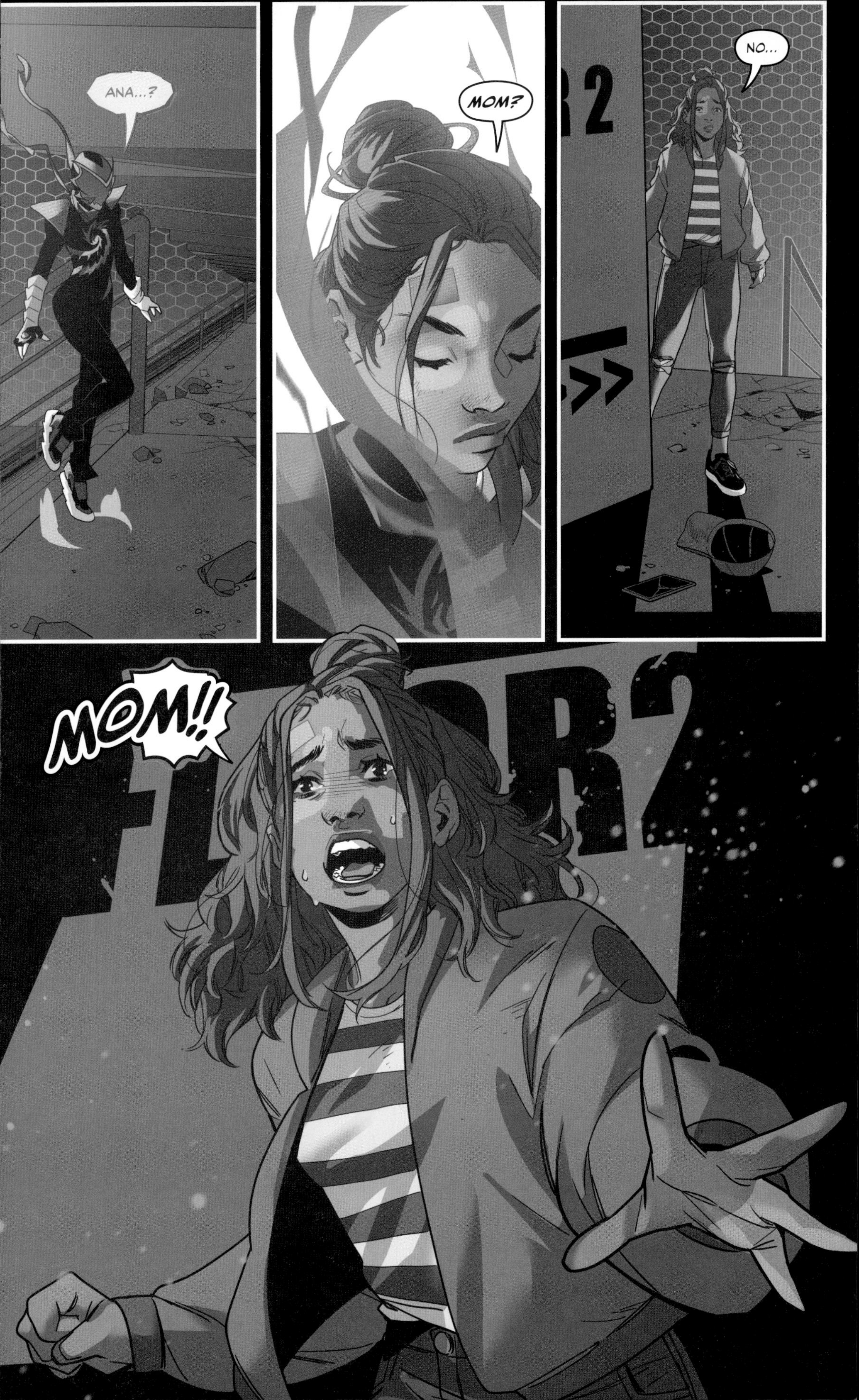
ANA...?
MOM?
NO...
MOM!!

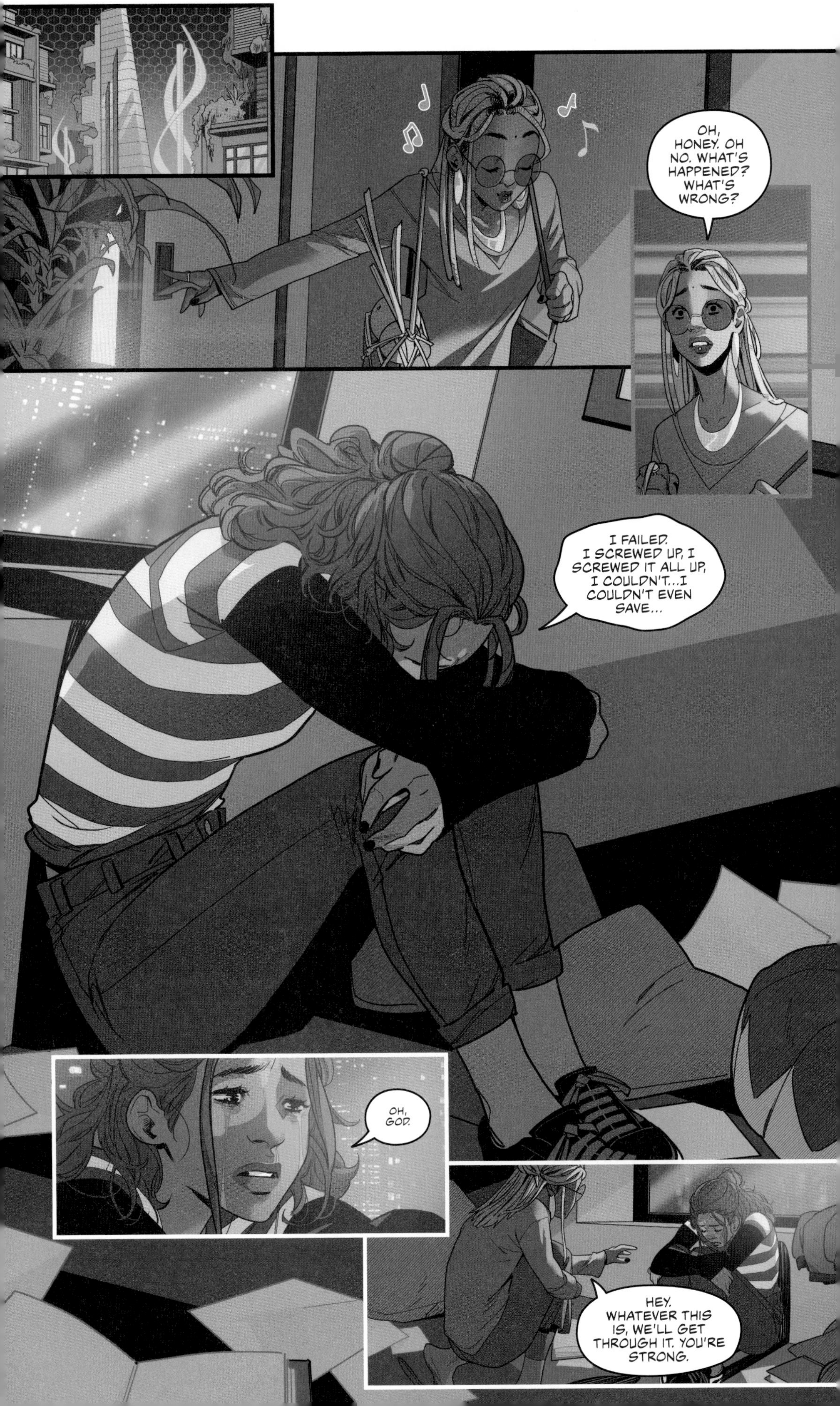
OH, HONEY. OH NO. WHAT'S HAPPENED? WHAT'S WRONG?
I FAILED. I SCREWED UP, I SCREWED IT ALL UP, I COULDN'T...I COULDN'T EVEN SAVE...
OH, GOD.
HEY. WHATEVER THIS IS, WE'LL GET THROUGH IT. YOU'RE STRONG.

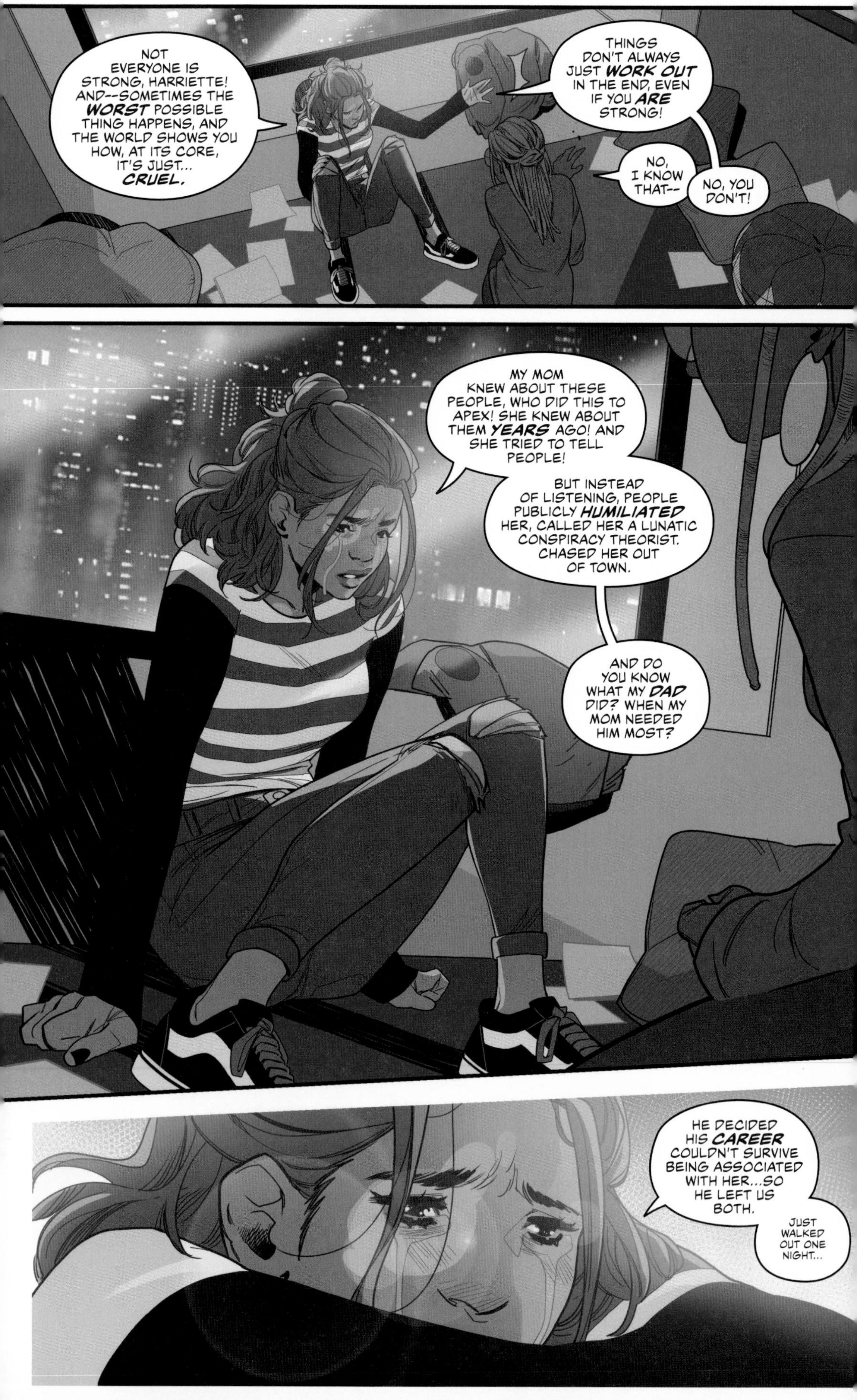
NOT EVERYONE IS STRONG, HARRIETTE! AND--SOMETIMES THE WORST POSSIBLE THING HAPPENS, AND THE WORLD SHOWS YOU HOW, AT ITS CORE, IT'S JUST... CRUEL.
THINGS DON'T ALWAYS JUST WORK OUT IN THE END, EVEN IF YOU ARE STRONG!
NO, I KNOW THAT--
NO, YOU DON'T!
MY MOM KNEW ABOUT THESE PEOPLE, WHO DID THIS TO APEX! SHE KNEW ABOUT THEM YEARS AGO! AND SHE TRIED TO TELL PEOPLE!
BUT INSTEAD OF LISTENING, PEOPLE PUBLICLY HUMILIATED HER, CALLED HER A LUNATIC CONSPIRACY THEORIST. CHASED HER OUT OF TOWN.
AND DO YOU KNOW WHAT MY DAD DID? WHEN MY MOM NEEDED HIM MOST?
HE DECIDED HIS CAREER COULDN'T SURVIVE BEING ASSOCIATED WITH HER...SO HE LEFT US BOTH.
JUST WALKED OUT ONE NIGHT...

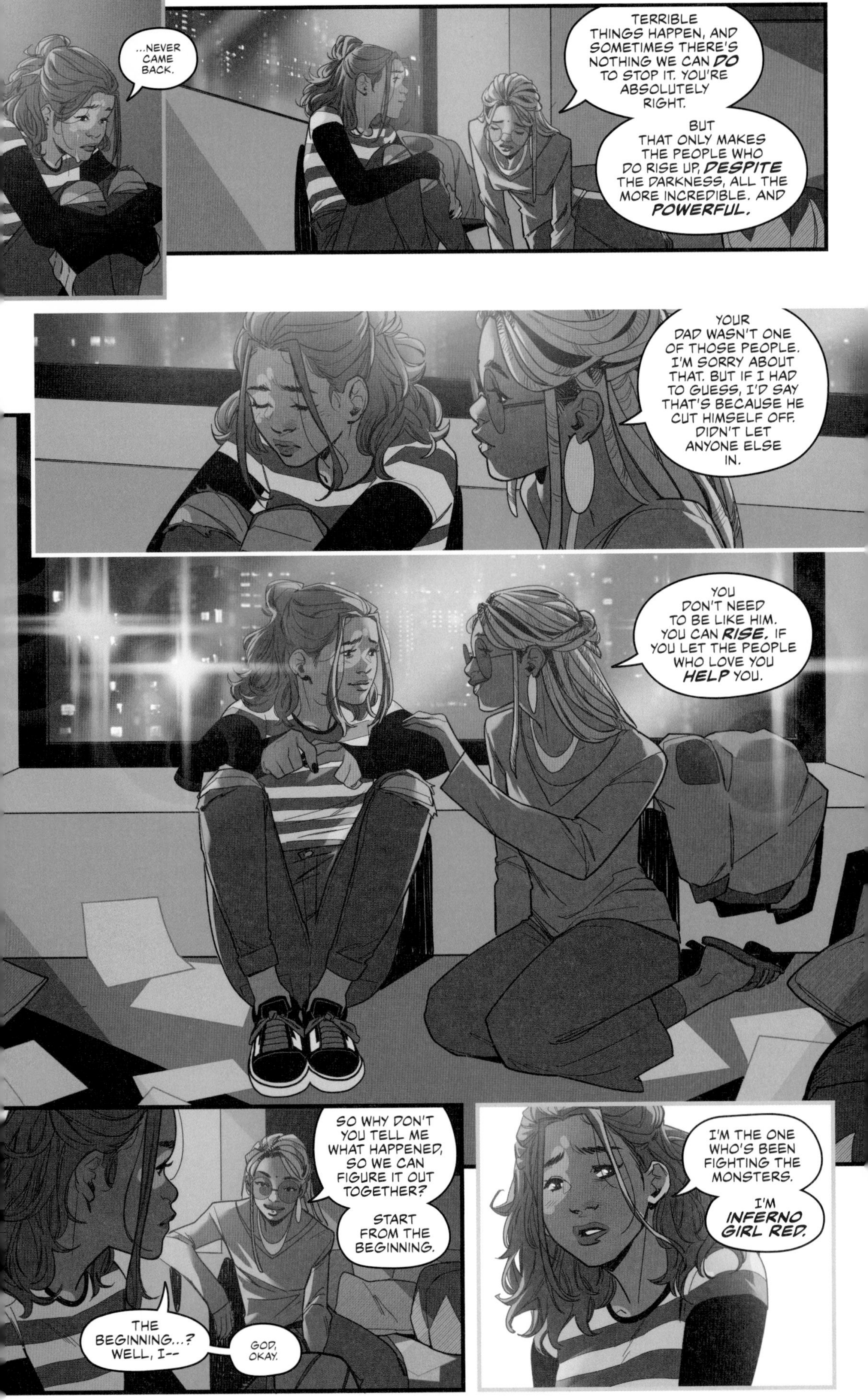

...NEVER CAME BACK.
TERRIBLE THINGS HAPPEN, AND SOMETIMES THERE'S NOTHING WE CAN *DO* TO STOP IT. YOU'RE ABSOLUTELY RIGHT.
BUT THAT ONLY MAKES THE PEOPLE WHO DO RISE UP, ***DESPITE*** THE DARKNESS, ALL THE MORE INCREDIBLE. AND ***POWERFUL.***
YOUR DAD WASN'T ONE OF THOSE PEOPLE. I'M SORRY ABOUT THAT. BUT IF I HAD TO GUESS, I'D SAY THAT'S BECAUSE HE CUT HIMSELF OFF. DIDN'T LET ANYONE ELSE IN.
YOU DON'T NEED TO BE LIKE HIM. YOU CAN ***RISE,*** IF YOU LET THE PEOPLE WHO LOVE YOU ***HELP*** YOU.
SO WHY DON'T YOU TELL ME WHAT HAPPENED, SO WE CAN FIGURE IT OUT TOGETHER?
START FROM THE BEGINNING.
THE BEGINNING...? WELL, I--
GOD, OKAY.
I'M THE ONE WHO'S BEEN FIGHTING THE MONSTERS.
I'M ***INFERNO GIRL RED.***

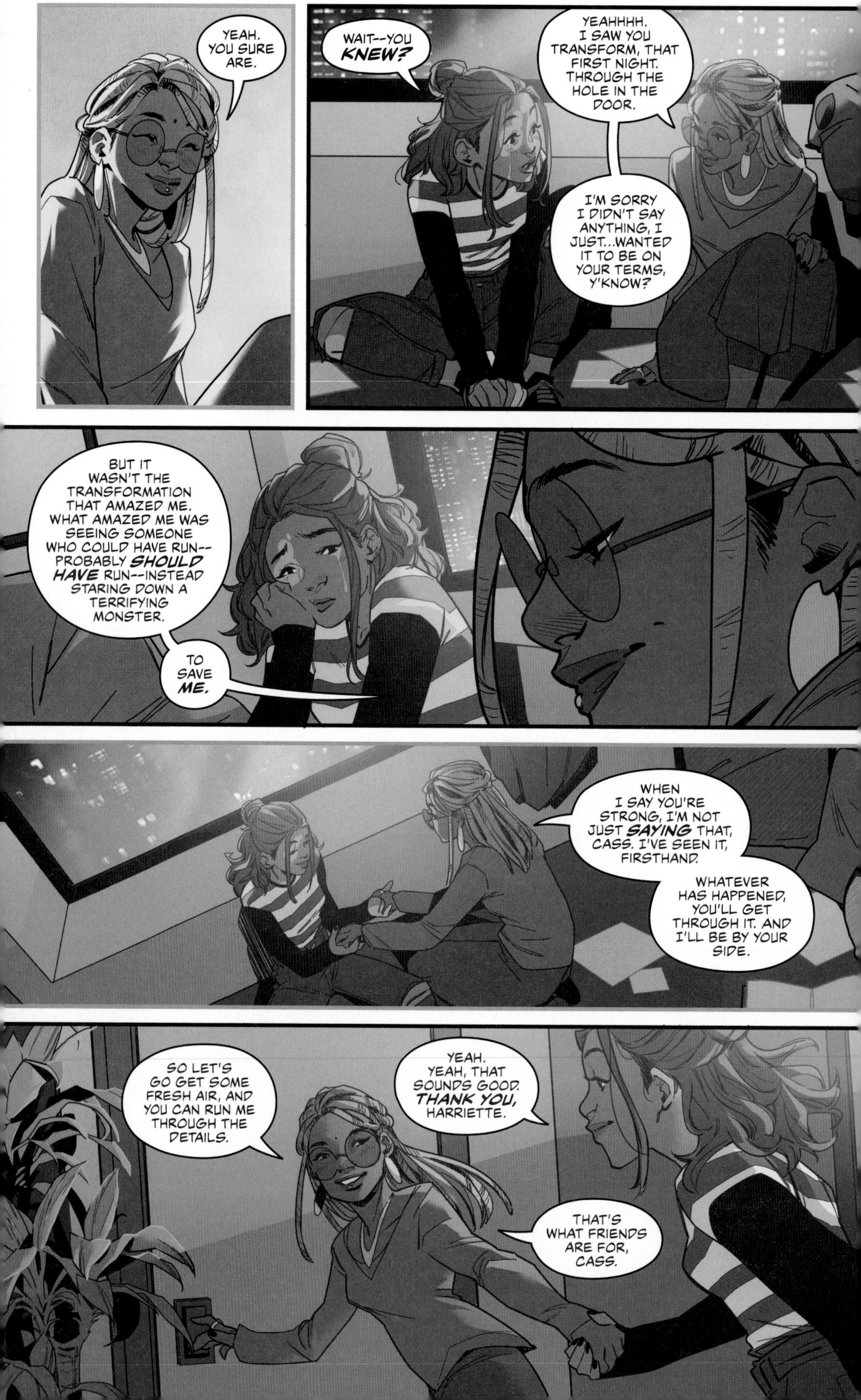
YEAH. YOU SURE ARE.
WAIT--YOU KNEW?
YEAHHHH. I SAW YOU TRANSFORM, THAT FIRST NIGHT. THROUGH THE HOLE IN THE DOOR.
I'M SORRY I DIDN'T SAY ANYTHING, I JUST...WANTED IT TO BE ON YOUR TERMS, Y'KNOW?
BUT IT WASN'T THE TRANSFORMATION THAT AMAZED ME. WHAT AMAZED ME WAS SEEING SOMEONE WHO COULD HAVE RUN--PROBABLY SHOULD HAVE RUN--INSTEAD STARING DOWN A TERRIFYING MONSTER.
TO SAVE ME.
WHEN I SAY YOU'RE STRONG, I'M NOT JUST SAYING THAT, CASS. I'VE SEEN IT, FIRSTHAND.
WHATEVER HAS HAPPENED, YOU'LL GET THROUGH IT. AND I'LL BE BY YOUR SIDE.
SO LET'S GO GET SOME FRESH AIR, AND YOU CAN RUN ME THROUGH THE DETAILS.
YEAH. YEAH, THAT SOUNDS GOOD. THANK YOU, HARRIETTE.
THAT'S WHAT FRIENDS ARE FOR, CASS.

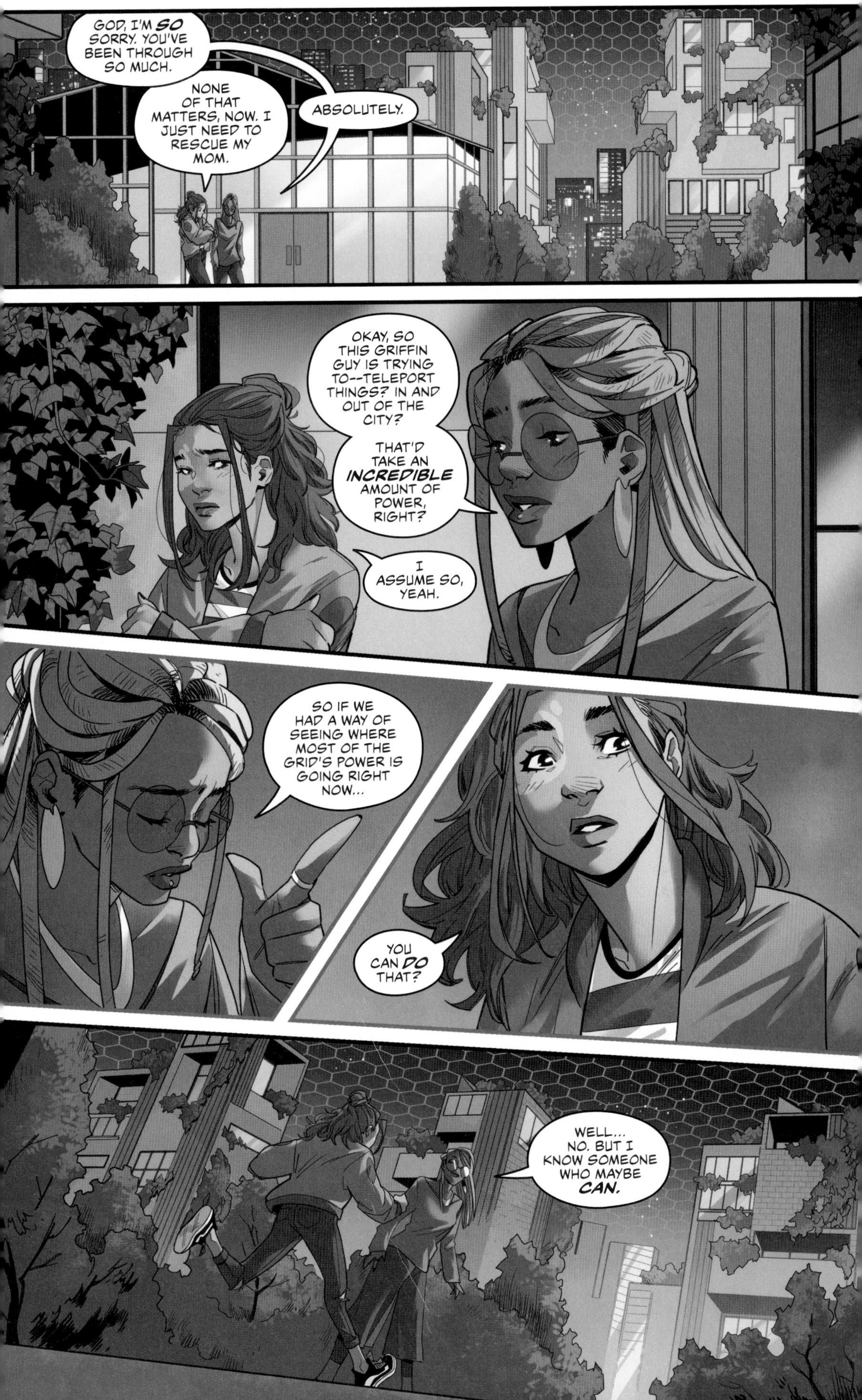
GOD, I'M SO SORRY. YOU'VE BEEN THROUGH SO MUCH.
NONE OF THAT MATTERS, NOW. I JUST NEED TO RESCUE MY MOM.
ABSOLUTELY.
OKAY, SO THIS GRIFFIN GUY IS TRYING TO--TELEPORT THINGS? IN AND OUT OF THE CITY?
THAT'D TAKE AN INCREDIBLE AMOUNT OF POWER, RIGHT?
I ASSUME SO, YEAH.
SO IF WE HAD A WAY OF SEEING WHERE MOST OF THE GRID'S POWER IS GOING RIGHT NOW...
YOU CAN DO THAT?
WELL... NO. BUT I KNOW SOMEONE WHO MAYBE CAN.

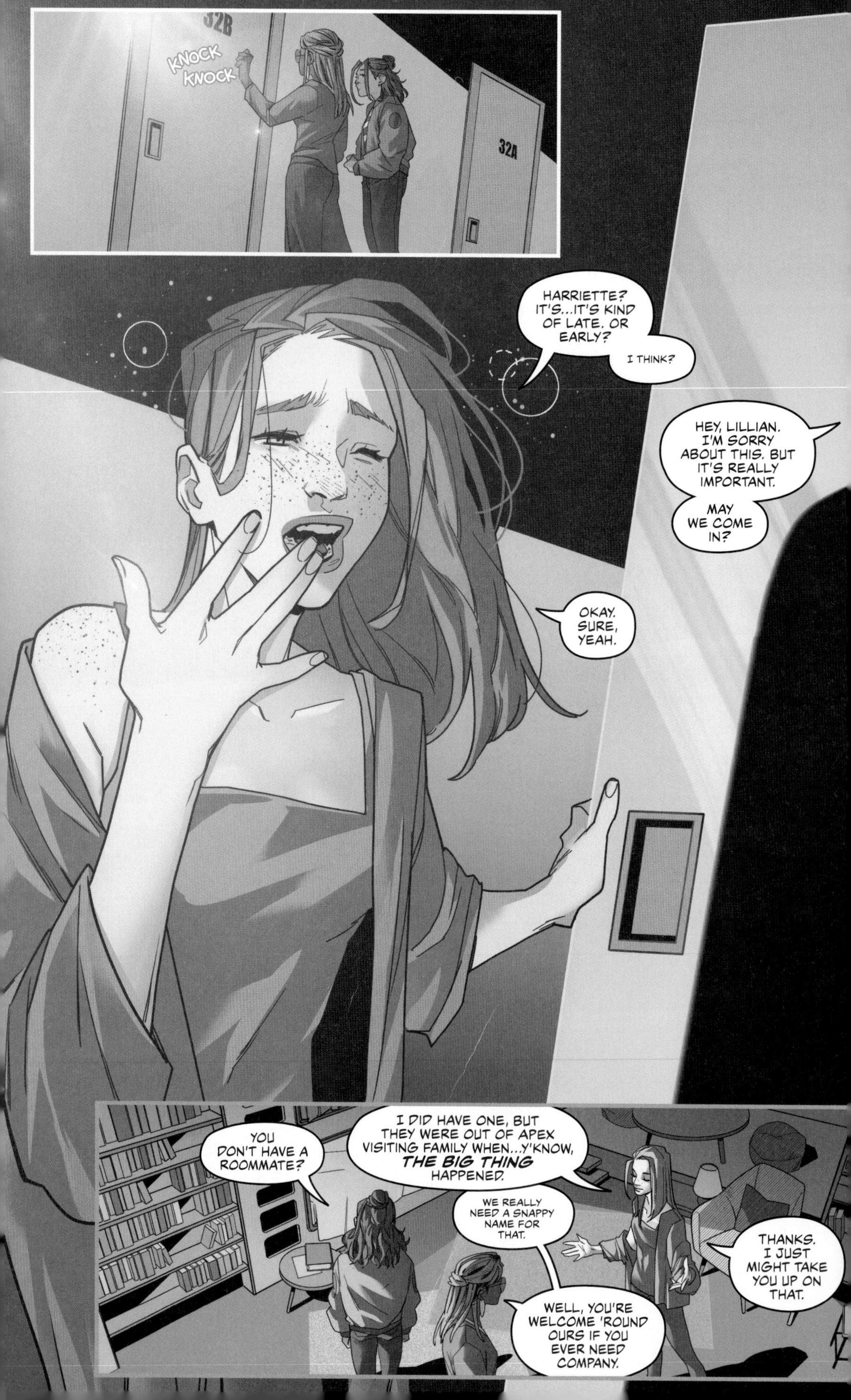
KNOCK KNOCK
32B
32A
HARRIETTE? IT'S...IT'S KIND OF LATE. OR EARLY?
I THINK?
HEY, LILLIAN. I'M SORRY ABOUT THIS. BUT IT'S REALLY IMPORTANT.
MAY WE COME IN?
OKAY. SURE, YEAH.
YOU DON'T HAVE A ROOMMATE?
I DID HAVE ONE, BUT THEY WERE OUT OF APEX VISITING FAMILY WHEN...Y'KNOW, ***THE BIG THING*** HAPPENED.
WE REALLY NEED A SNAPPY NAME FOR THAT.
WELL, YOU'RE WELCOME 'ROUND OURS IF YOU EVER NEED COMPANY.
THANKS. I JUST MIGHT TAKE YOU UP ON THAT.

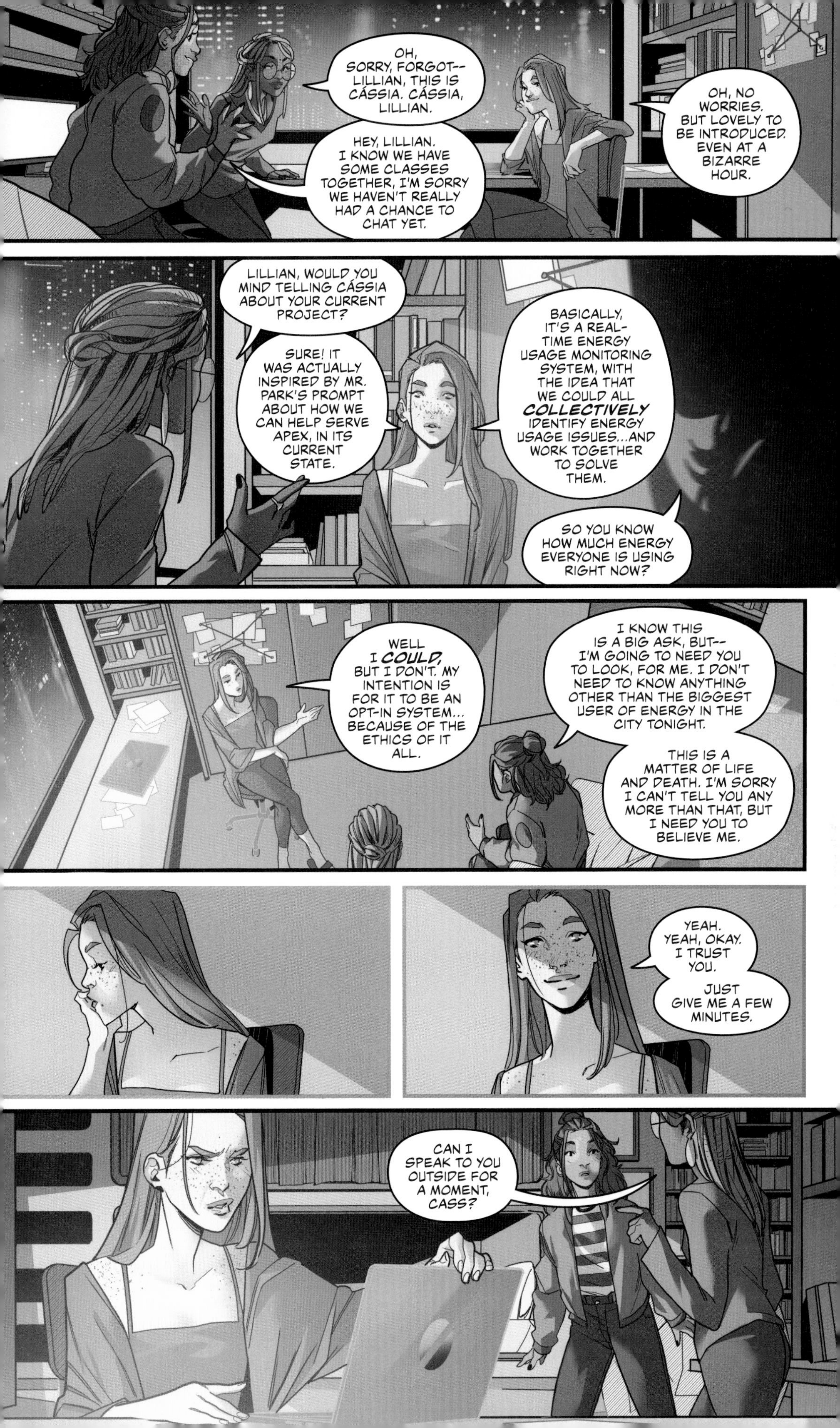
OH, SORRY, FORGOT-- LILLIAN, THIS IS CÁSSIA. CÁSSIA, LILLIAN.
HEY, LILLIAN. I KNOW WE HAVE SOME CLASSES TOGETHER, I'M SORRY WE HAVEN'T REALLY HAD A CHANCE TO CHAT YET.
OH, NO WORRIES. BUT LOVELY TO BE INTRODUCED. EVEN AT A BIZARRE HOUR.
LILLIAN, WOULD YOU MIND TELLING CÁSSIA ABOUT YOUR CURRENT PROJECT?
SURE! IT WAS ACTUALLY INSPIRED BY MR. PARK'S PROMPT ABOUT HOW WE CAN HELP SERVE APEX, IN ITS CURRENT STATE.
BASICALLY, IT'S A REAL-TIME ENERGY USAGE MONITORING SYSTEM, WITH THE IDEA THAT WE COULD ALL ***COLLECTIVELY*** IDENTIFY ENERGY USAGE ISSUES...AND WORK TOGETHER TO SOLVE THEM.
SO YOU KNOW HOW MUCH ENERGY EVERYONE IS USING RIGHT NOW?
WELL I ***COULD,*** BUT I DON'T. MY INTENTION IS FOR IT TO BE AN OPT-IN SYSTEM... BECAUSE OF THE ETHICS OF IT ALL.
I KNOW THIS IS A BIG ASK, BUT-- I'M GOING TO NEED YOU TO LOOK, FOR ME. I DON'T NEED TO KNOW ANYTHING OTHER THAN THE BIGGEST USER OF ENERGY IN THE CITY TONIGHT.
THIS IS A MATTER OF LIFE AND DEATH. I'M SORRY I CAN'T TELL YOU ANY MORE THAN THAT, BUT I NEED YOU TO BELIEVE ME.
YEAH. YEAH, OKAY. I TRUST YOU.
JUST GIVE ME A FEW MINUTES.
CAN I SPEAK TO YOU OUTSIDE FOR A MOMENT, CASS?

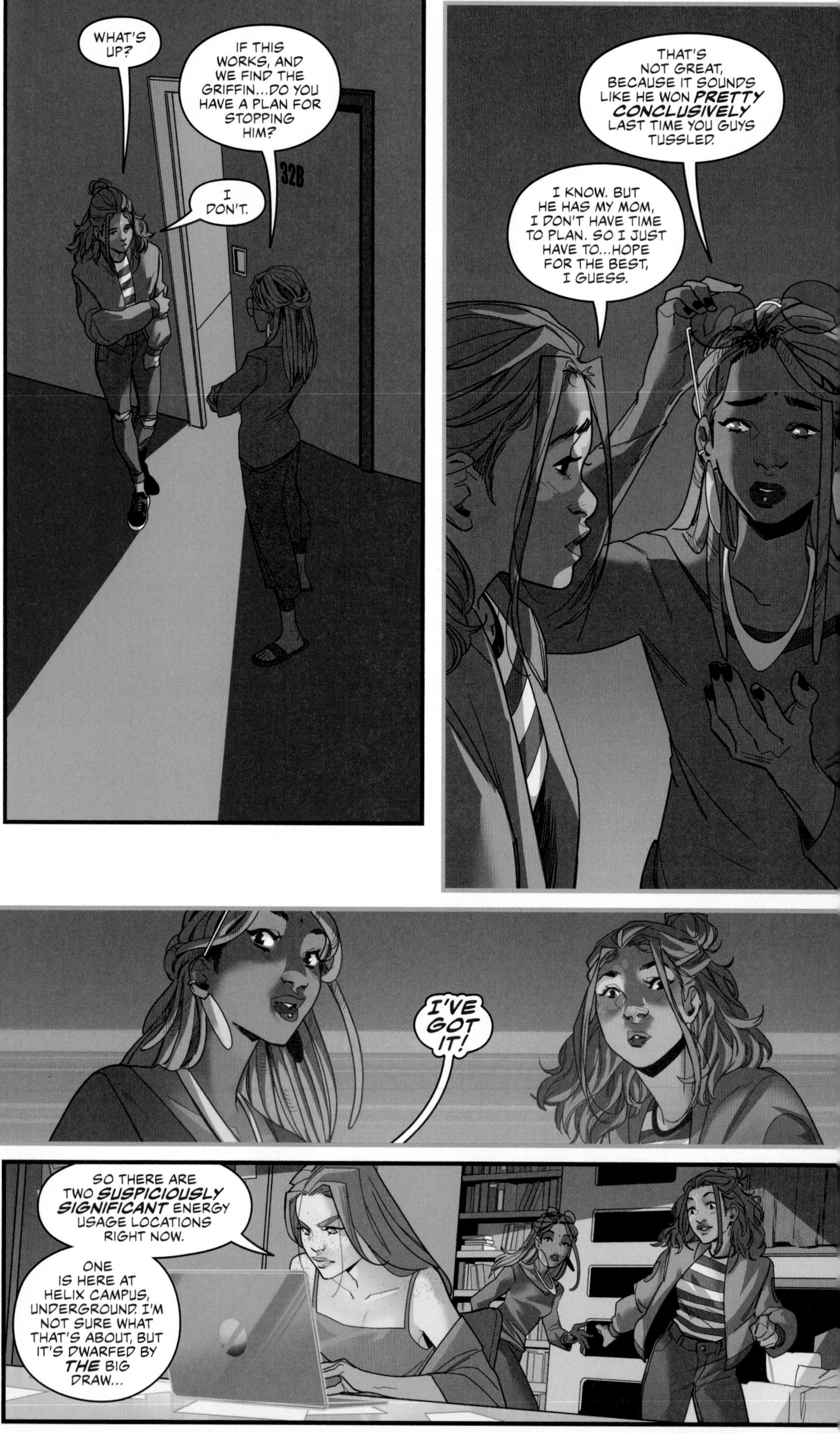
WHAT'S UP?
IF THIS WORKS, AND WE FIND THE GRIFFIN...DO YOU HAVE A PLAN FOR STOPPING HIM?
I DON'T.
32B
THAT'S NOT GREAT, BECAUSE IT SOUNDS LIKE HE WON PRETTY CONCLUSIVELY LAST TIME YOU GUYS TUSSLED.
I KNOW. BUT HE HAS MY MOM, I DON'T HAVE TIME TO PLAN. SO I JUST HAVE TO...HOPE FOR THE BEST, I GUESS.
I'VE GOT IT!
SO THERE ARE TWO SUSPICIOUSLY SIGNIFICANT ENERGY USAGE LOCATIONS RIGHT NOW.
ONE IS HERE AT HELIX CAMPUS, UNDERGROUND. I'M NOT SURE WHAT THAT'S ABOUT, BUT IT'S DWARFED BY THE BIG DRAW...

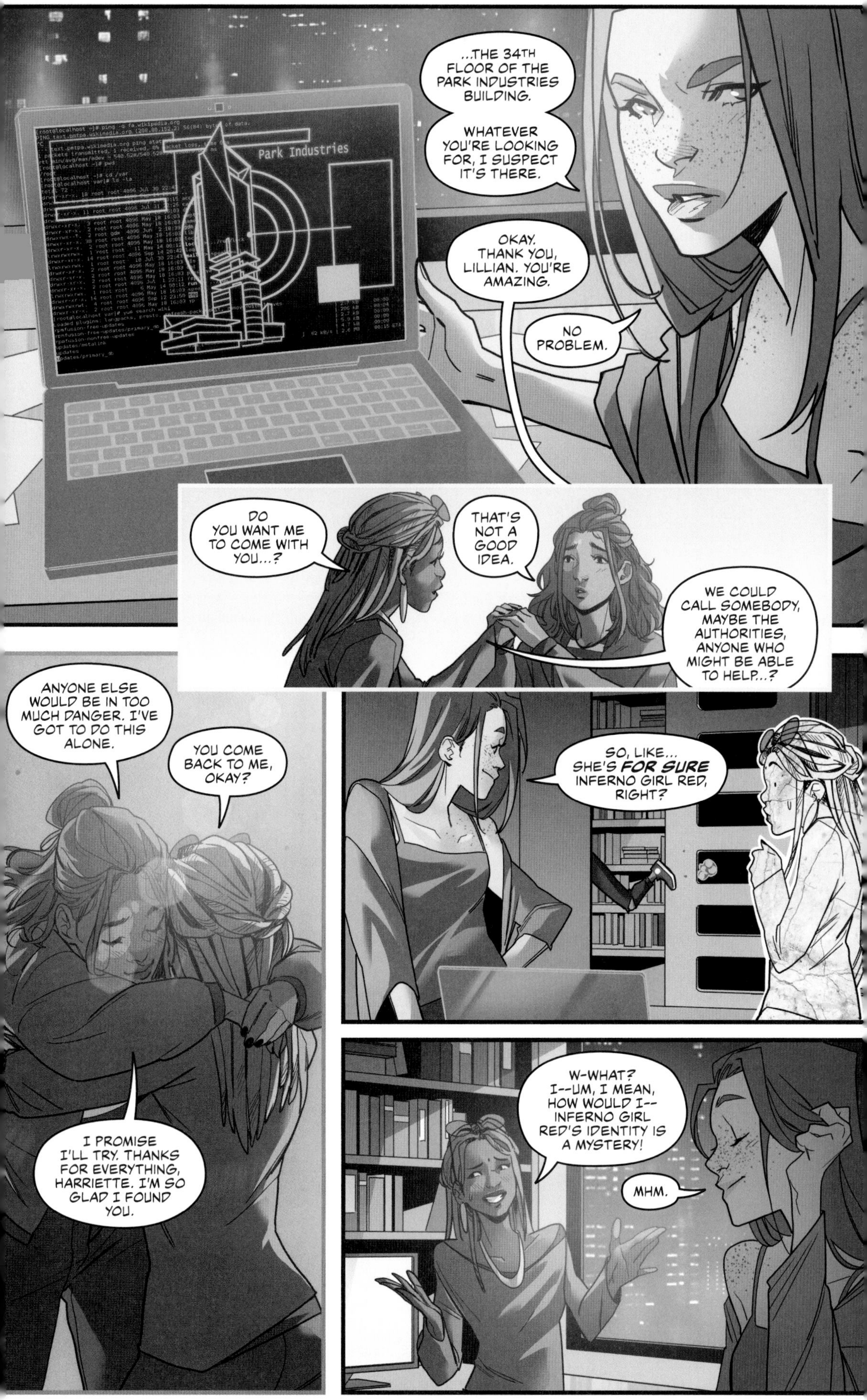

Park Industries
...THE 34TH FLOOR OF THE PARK INDUSTRIES BUILDING.
WHATEVER YOU'RE LOOKING FOR, I SUSPECT IT'S THERE.
OKAY. THANK YOU, LILLIAN. YOU'RE AMAZING.
NO PROBLEM.
DO YOU WANT ME TO COME WITH YOU...?
THAT'S NOT A GOOD IDEA.
WE COULD CALL SOMEBODY, MAYBE THE AUTHORITIES, ANYONE WHO MIGHT BE ABLE TO HELP...?
ANYONE ELSE WOULD BE IN TOO MUCH DANGER. I'VE GOT TO DO THIS ALONE.
YOU COME BACK TO ME, OKAY?
I PROMISE I'LL TRY. THANKS FOR EVERYTHING, HARRIETTE. I'M SO GLAD I FOUND YOU.
SO, LIKE... SHE'S ***FOR SURE*** INFERNO GIRL RED, RIGHT?
W-WHAT? I--UM, I MEAN, HOW WOULD I-- INFERNO GIRL RED'S IDENTITY IS A MYSTERY!
MHM.

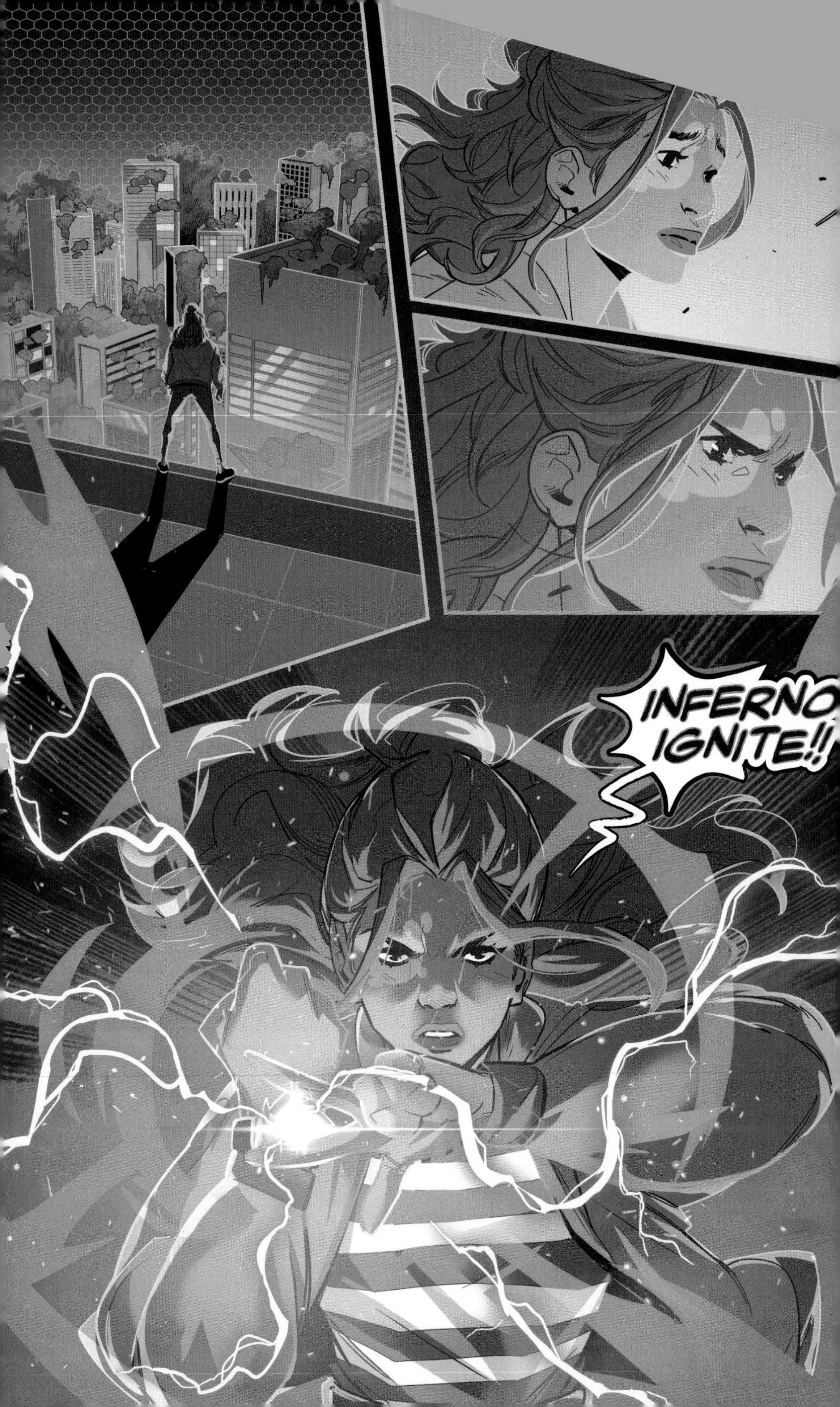
INFERNO IGNITE!!

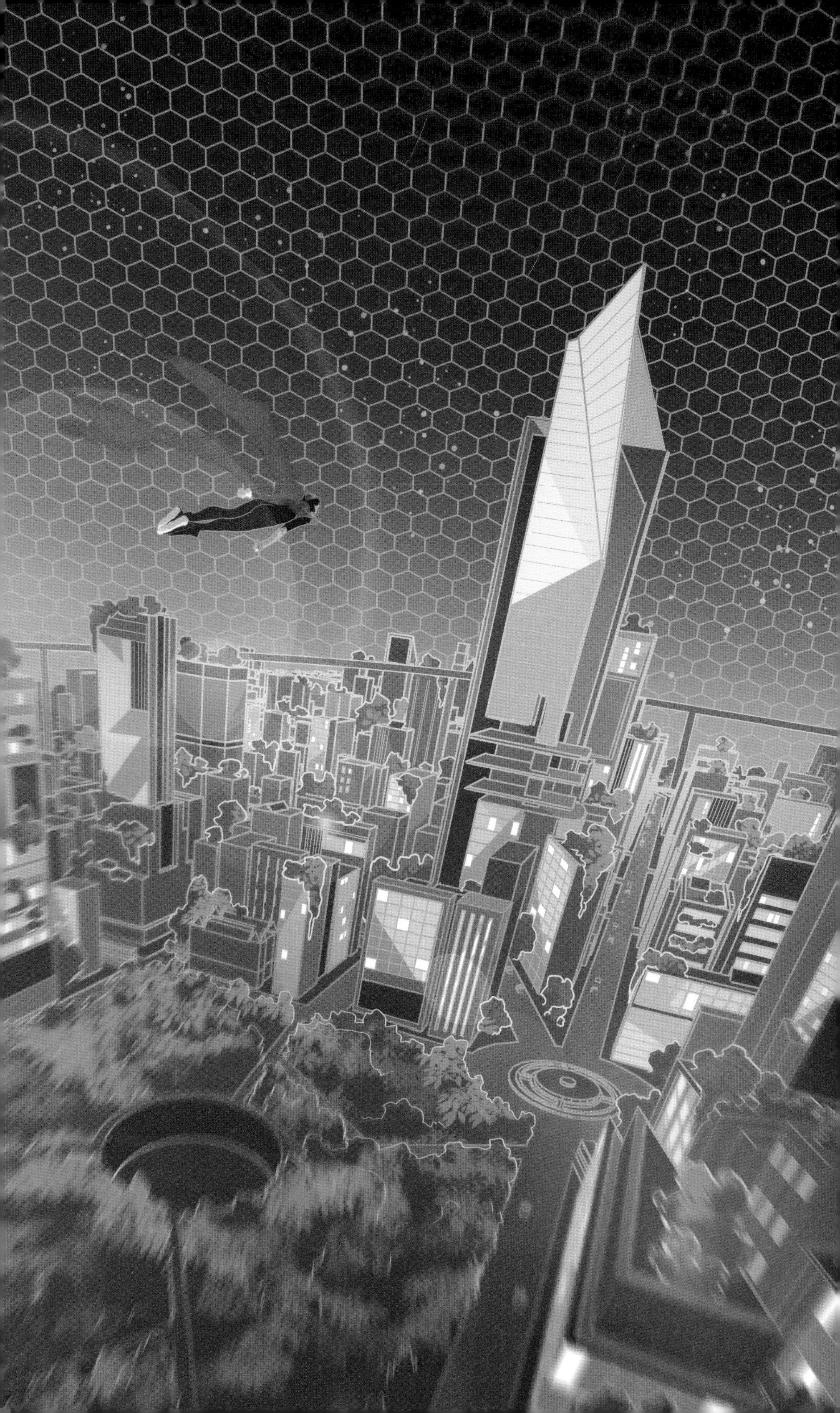

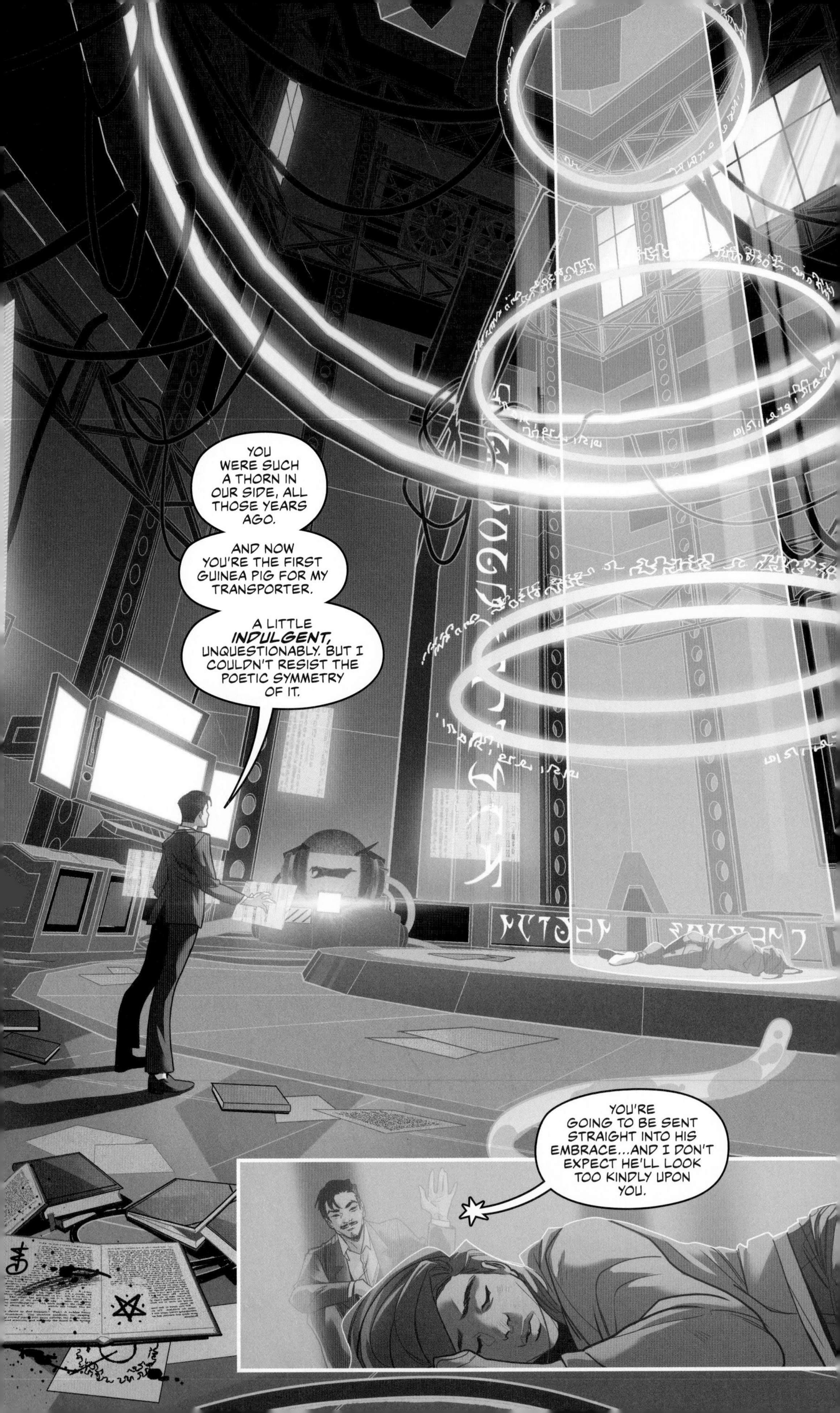
YOU WERE SUCH A THORN IN OUR SIDE, ALL THOSE YEARS AGO.
AND NOW YOU'RE THE FIRST GUINEA PIG FOR MY TRANSPORTER.
A LITTLE ***INDULGENT,*** UNQUESTIONABLY. BUT I COULDN'T RESIST THE POETIC SYMMETRY OF IT.
YOU'RE GOING TO BE SENT STRAIGHT INTO HIS EMBRACE...AND I DON'T EXPECT HE'LL LOOK TOO KINDLY UPON YOU.

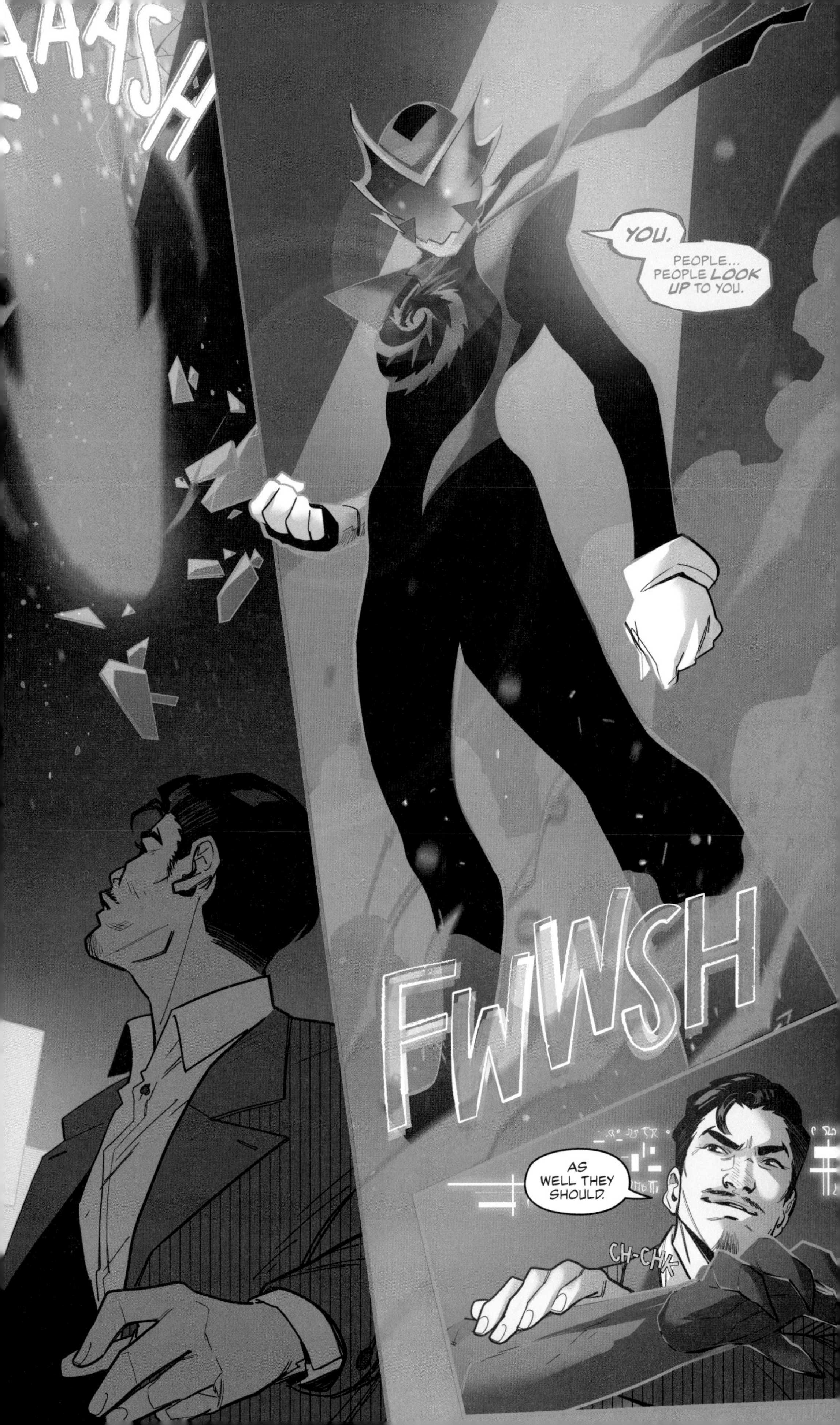
AAASH
YOU.
PEOPLE... PEOPLE LOOK UP TO YOU.
FWWSH
AS WELL THEY SHOULD.
CH-CHK

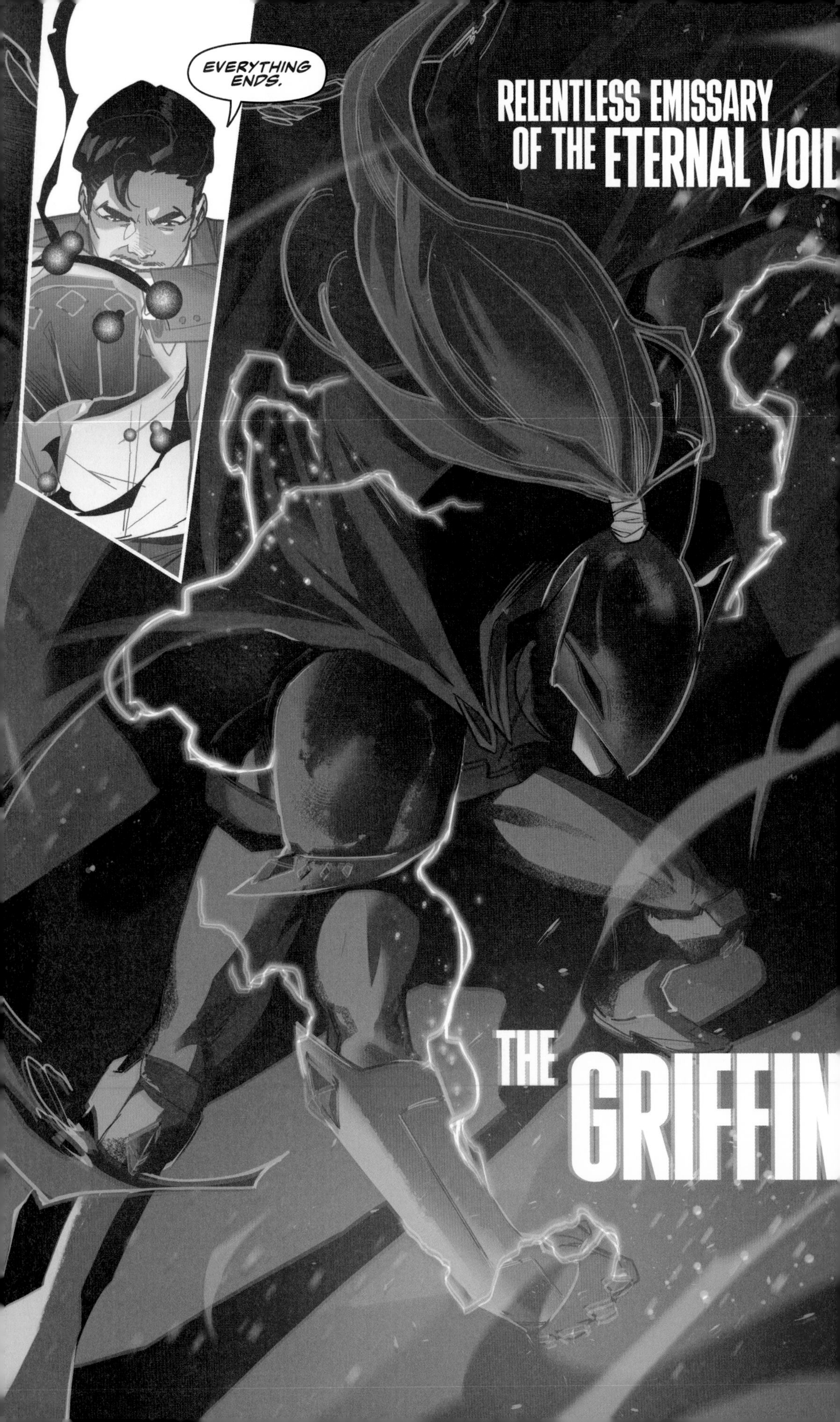
EVERYTHING ENDS.
RELENTLESS EMISSARY OF THE ETERNAL VOID
THE GRIFFIN

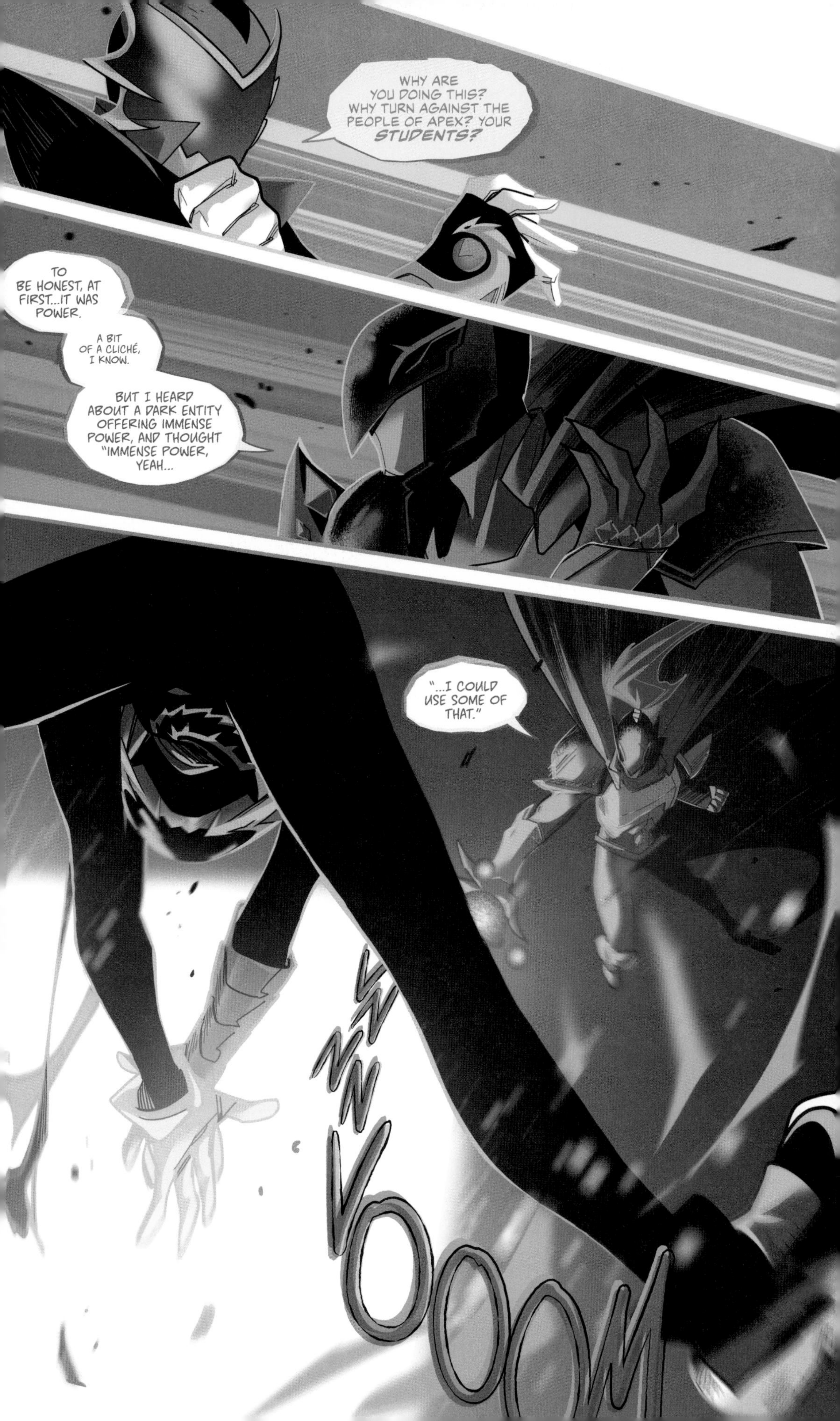
WHY ARE YOU DOING THIS? WHY TURN AGAINST THE PEOPLE OF APEX? YOUR STUDENTS?
TO BE HONEST, AT FIRST...IT WAS POWER.
A BIT OF A CLICHÉ, I KNOW.
BUT I HEARD ABOUT A DARK ENTITY OFFERING IMMENSE POWER, AND THOUGHT "IMMENSE POWER, YEAH...
"...I COULD USE SOME OF THAT."
VVVVVVOOOM

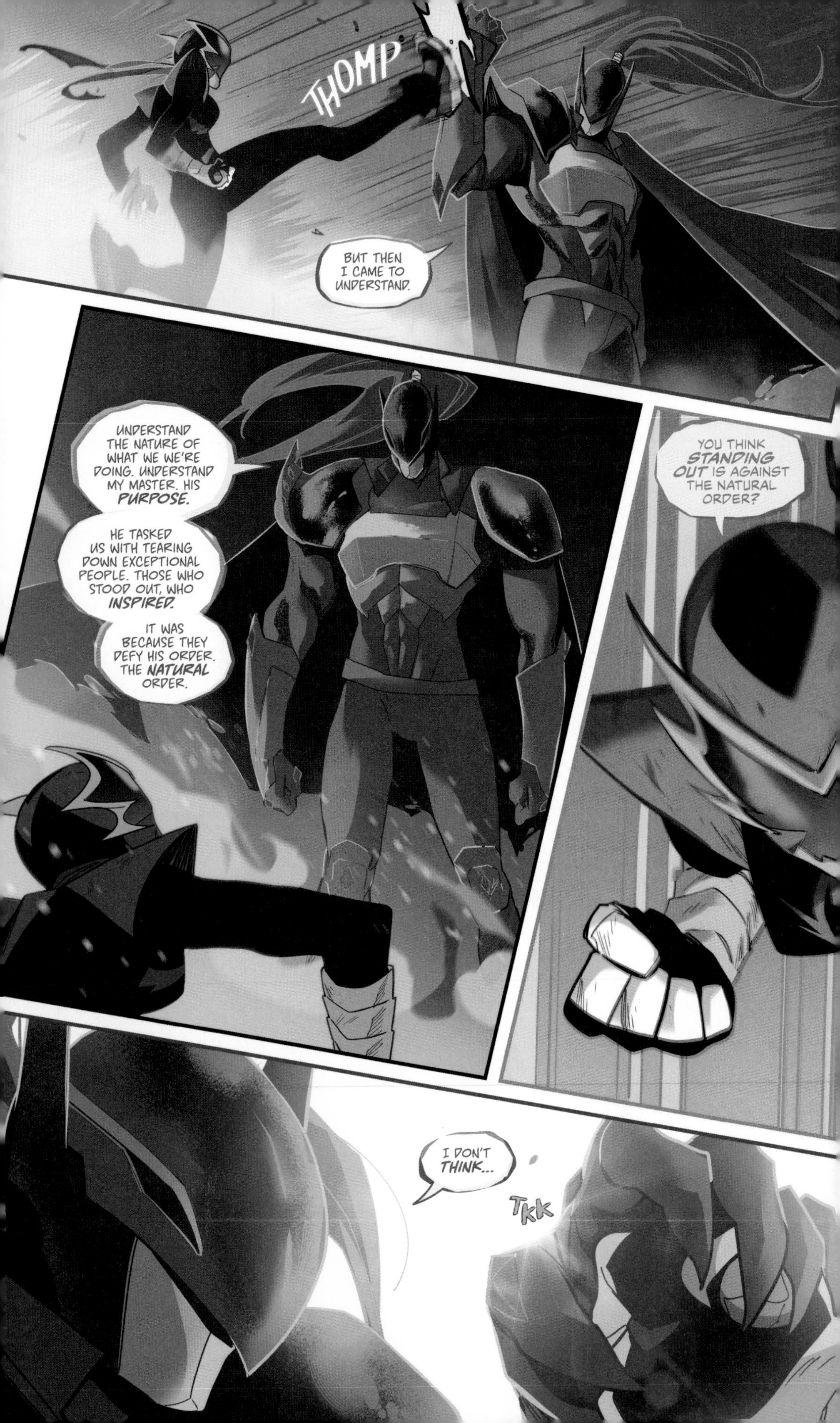
THOMP
BUT THEN I CAME TO UNDERSTAND.
UNDERSTAND THE NATURE OF WHAT WE WE'RE DOING. UNDERSTAND MY MASTER. HIS *PURPOSE.*
HE TASKED US WITH TEARING DOWN EXCEPTIONAL PEOPLE. THOSE WHO STOOD OUT, WHO *INSPIRED.*
IT WAS BECAUSE THEY DEFY HIS ORDER. THE *NATURAL* ORDER.
YOU THINK *STANDING OUT* IS AGAINST THE NATURAL ORDER?
I DON'T *THINK...*
TKK

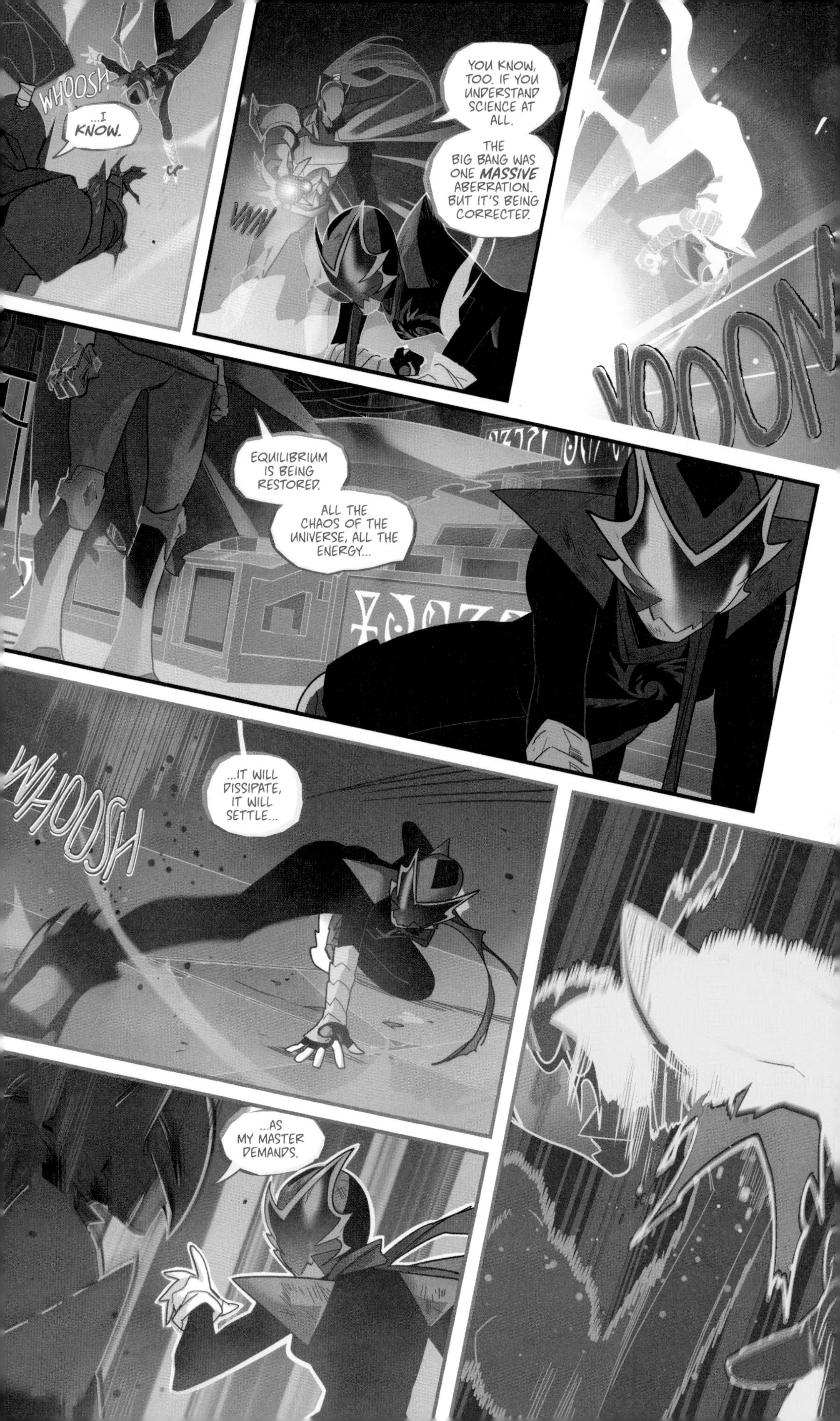
WHOOSH
...I KNOW.
YOU KNOW, TOO. IF YOU UNDERSTAND SCIENCE AT ALL.
THE BIG BANG WAS ONE MASSIVE ABERRATION. BUT IT'S BEING CORRECTED.
VOOOOM
EQUILIBRIUM IS BEING RESTORED.
ALL THE CHAOS OF THE UNIVERSE, ALL THE ENERGY...
WHOOSH
...IT WILL DISSIPATE, IT WILL SETTLE...
...AS MY MASTER DEMANDS.

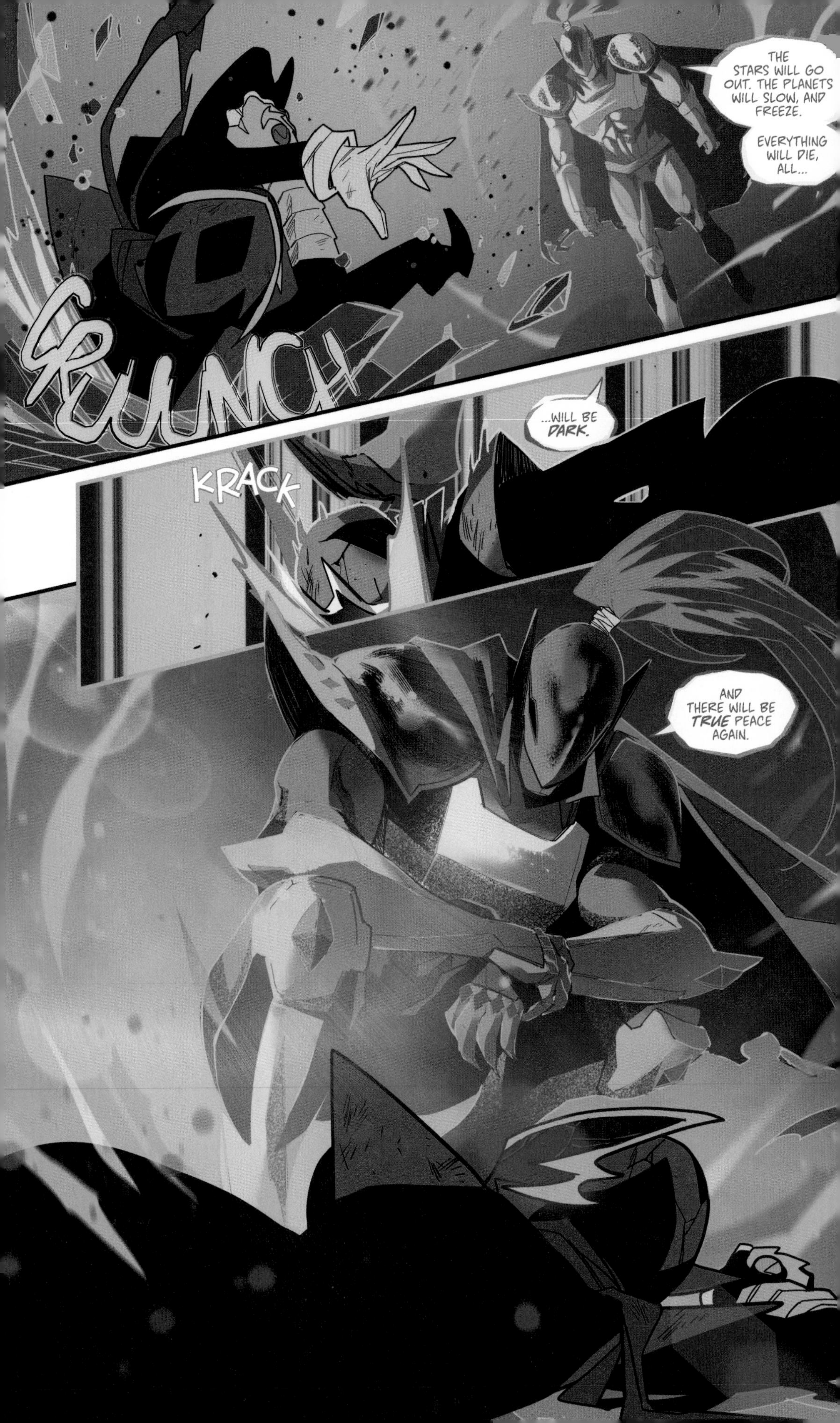
THE STARS WILL GO OUT. THE PLANETS WILL SLOW, AND FREEZE.
EVERYTHING WILL DIE, ALL...
CRUUNCH
...WILL BE DARK.
KRACK
AND THERE WILL BE TRUE PEACE AGAIN.

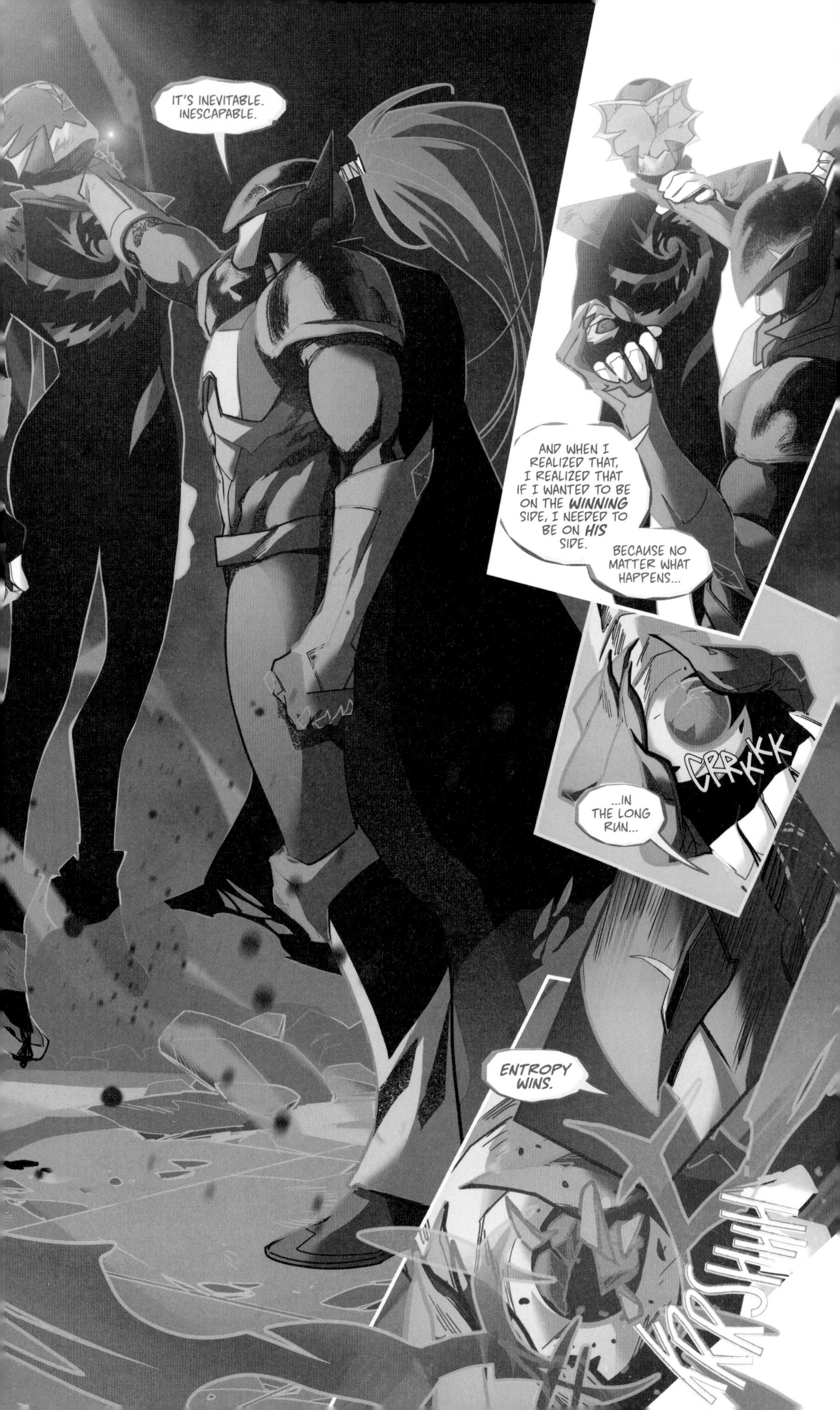
IT'S INEVITABLE. INESCAPABLE.
AND WHEN I REALIZED THAT, I REALIZED THAT IF I WANTED TO BE ON THE WINNING SIDE, I NEEDED TO BE ON HIS SIDE.
BECAUSE NO MATTER WHAT HAPPENS...
CRRKKK
...IN THE LONG RUN...
ENTROPY WINS.
KRASHHH

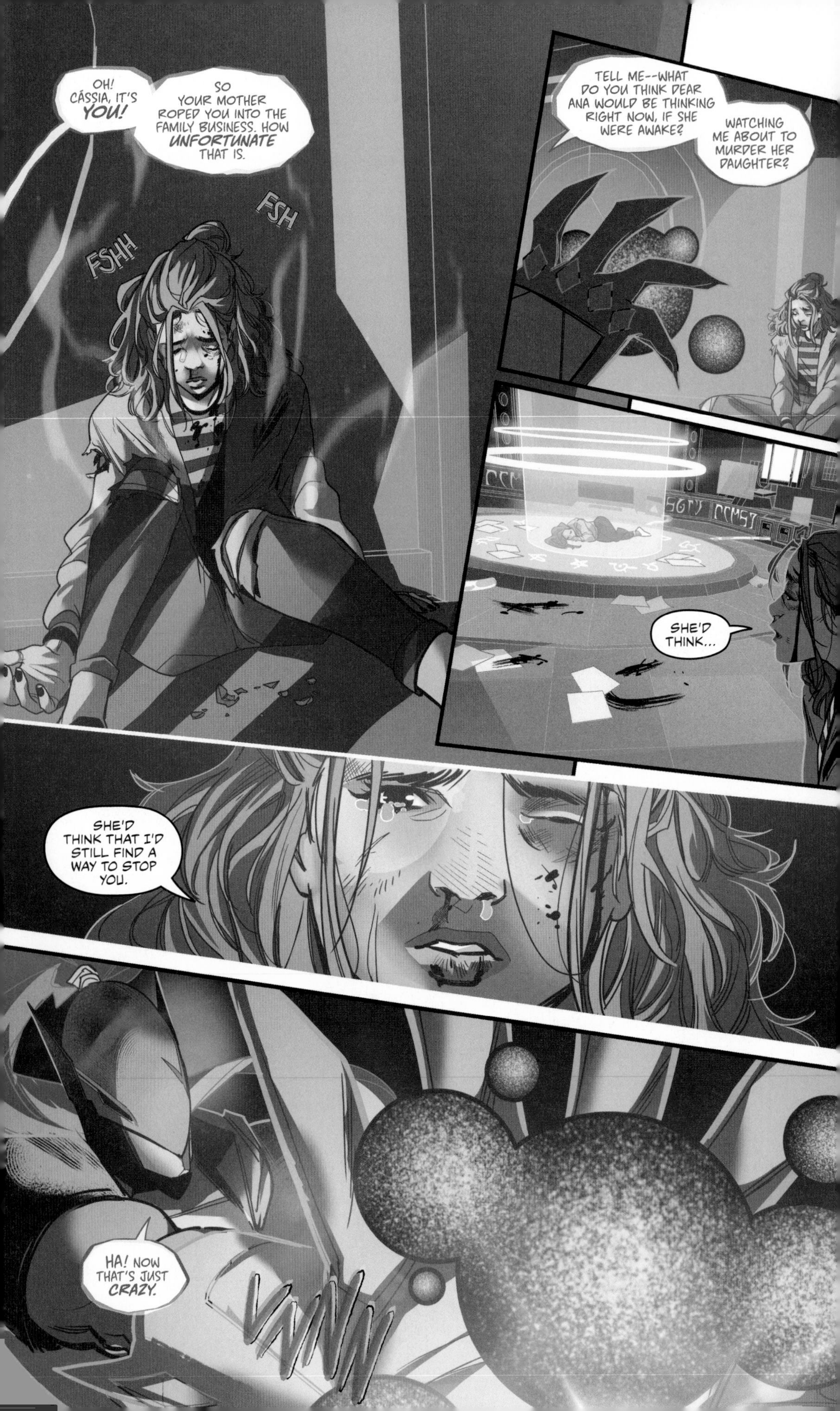
OH! CÁSSIA, IT'S YOU!
SO YOUR MOTHER ROPED YOU INTO THE FAMILY BUSINESS. HOW UNFORTUNATE THAT IS.
FSH
FSHH
TELL ME--WHAT DO YOU THINK DEAR ANA WOULD BE THINKING RIGHT NOW, IF SHE WERE AWAKE?
WATCHING ME ABOUT TO MURDER HER DAUGHTER?
SHE'D THINK...
SHE'D THINK THAT I'D STILL FIND A WAY TO STOP YOU.
HA! NOW THAT'S JUST CRAZY.

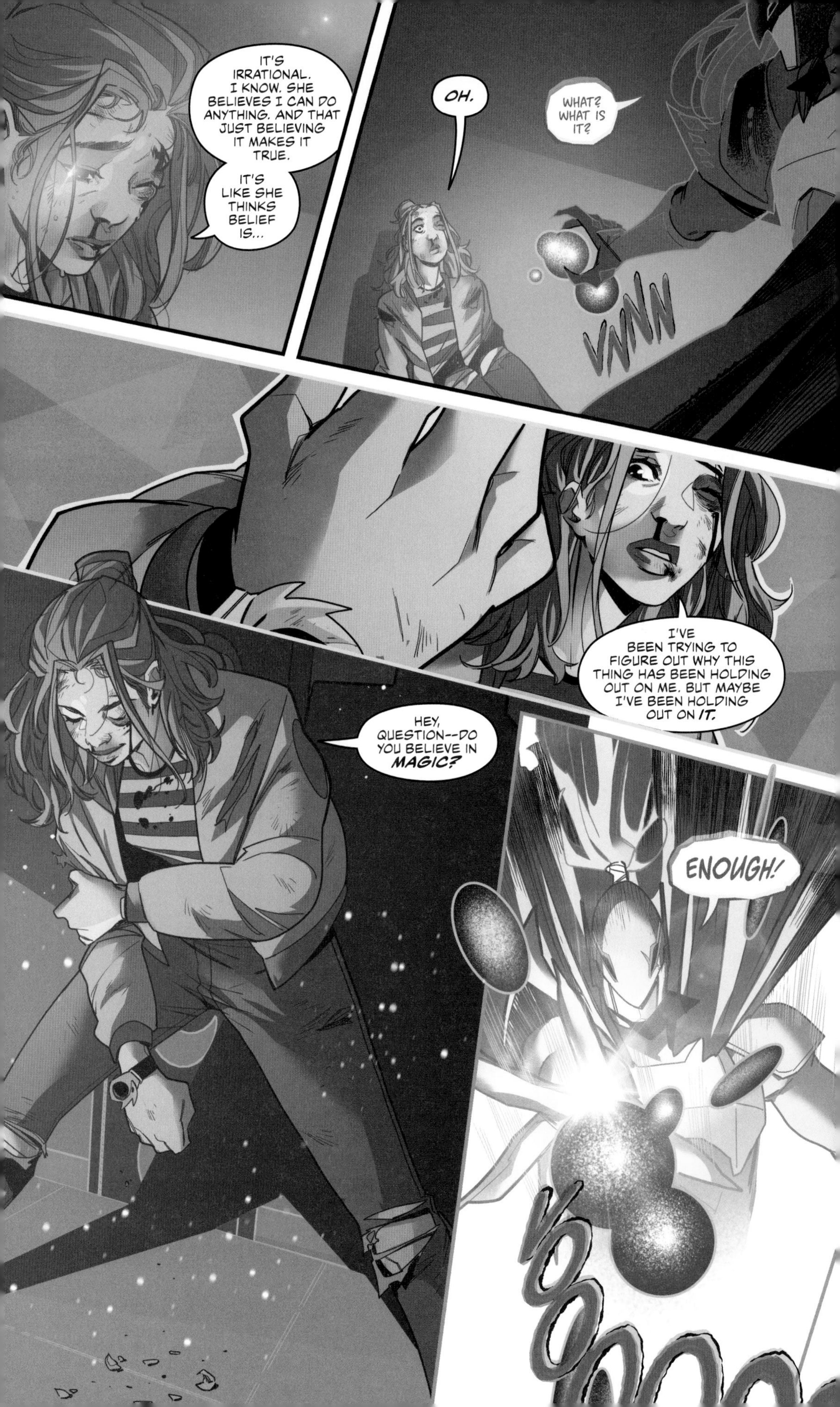
IT'S IRRATIONAL. I KNOW. SHE BELIEVES I CAN DO ANYTHING. AND THAT JUST BELIEVING IT MAKES IT TRUE.
IT'S LIKE SHE THINKS BELIEF IS...
OH.
WHAT? WHAT IS IT?
VNNN
I'VE BEEN TRYING TO FIGURE OUT WHY THIS THING HAS BEEN HOLDING OUT ON ME. BUT MAYBE I'VE BEEN HOLDING OUT ON *IT.*
HEY, QUESTION--DO YOU BELIEVE IN *MAGIC?*
ENOUGH!

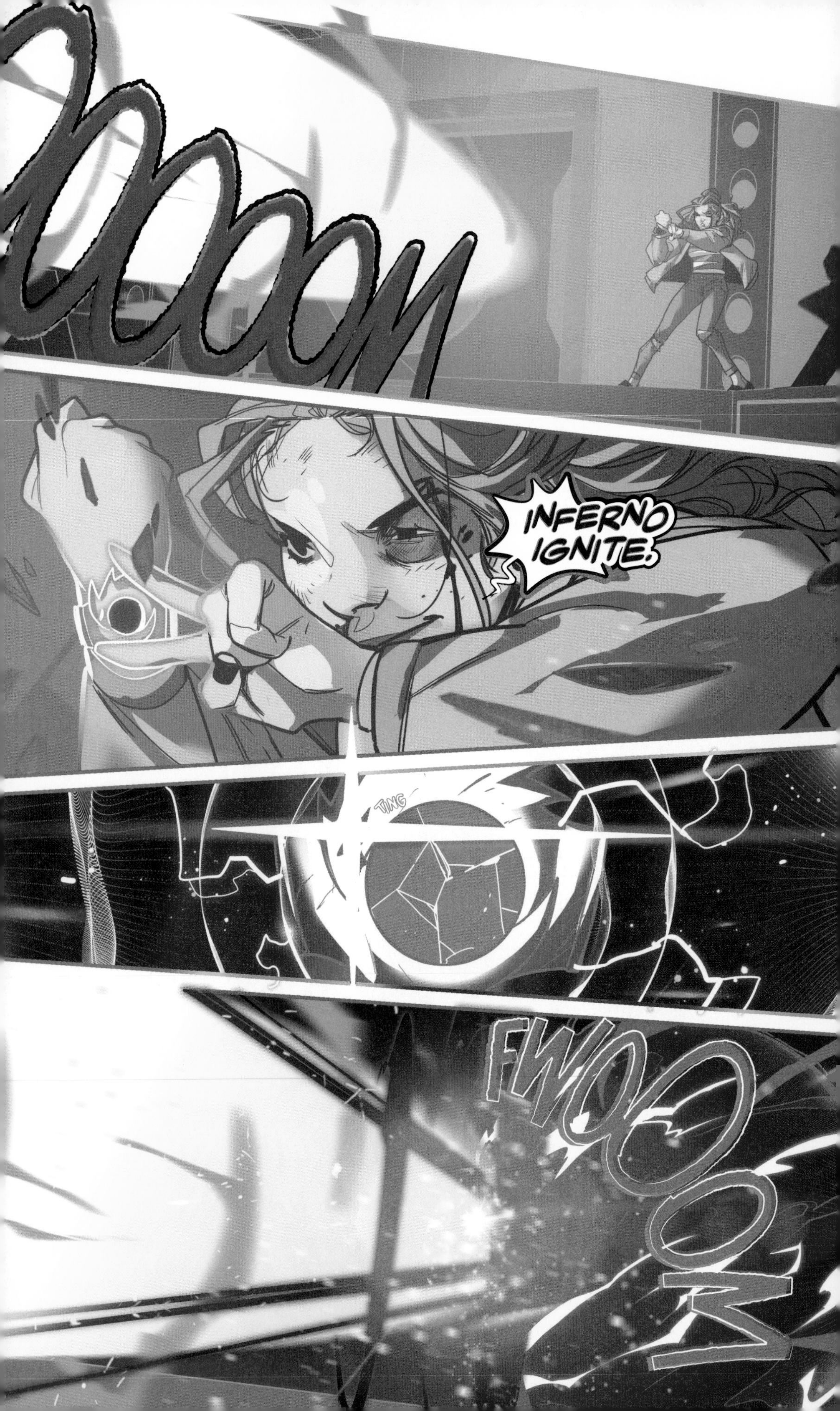

WHOOM
INFERNO IGNITE.
TING
FWOOOM

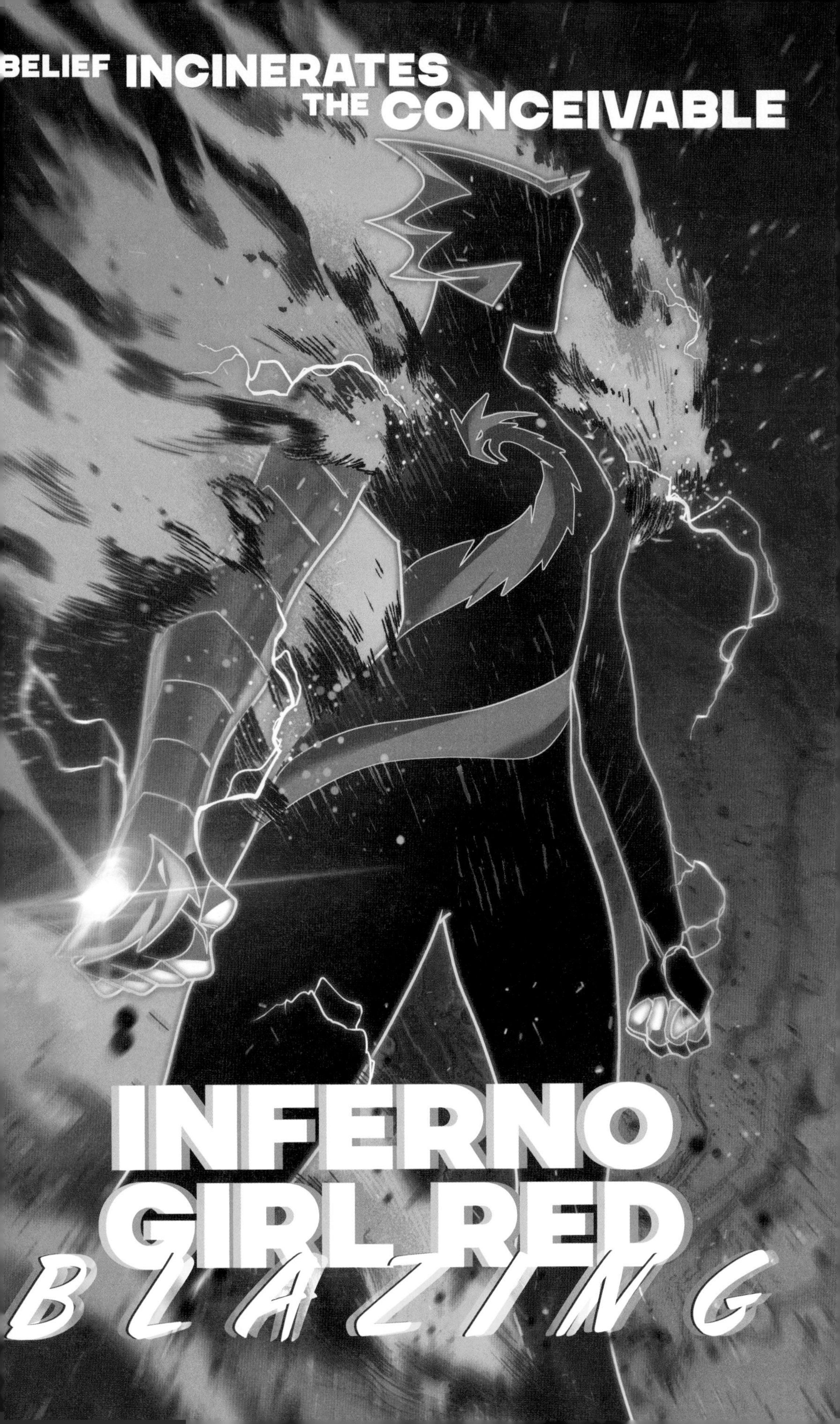
BELIEF INCINERATES THE CONCEIVABLE
INFERNO GIRL RED
BLAZING

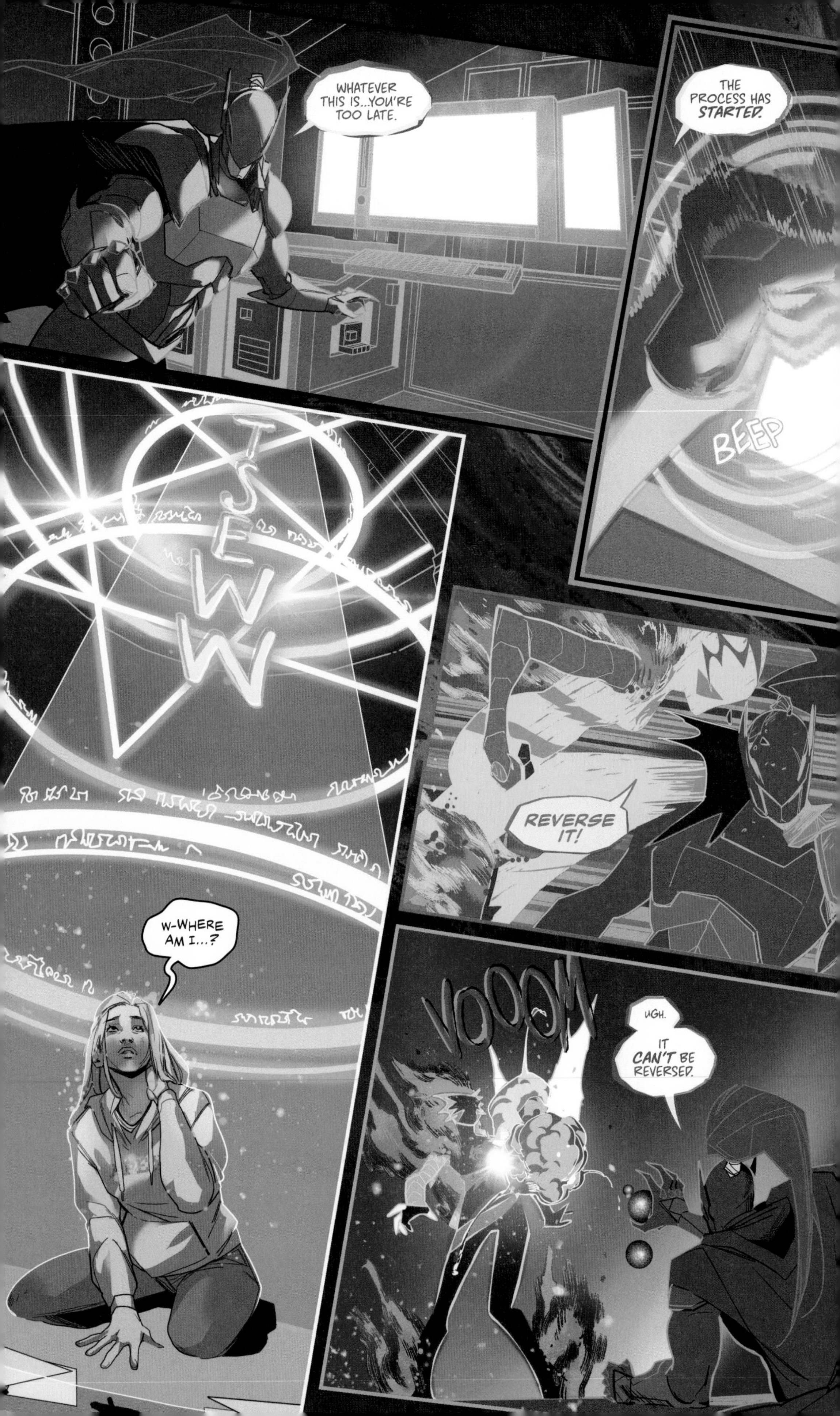

WHATEVER THIS IS...YOU'RE TOO LATE.
THE PROCESS HAS STARTED.
BEEP
TSEWW
REVERSE IT!
W-WHERE AM I...?
VOOOM
UGH.
IT CAN'T BE REVERSED.

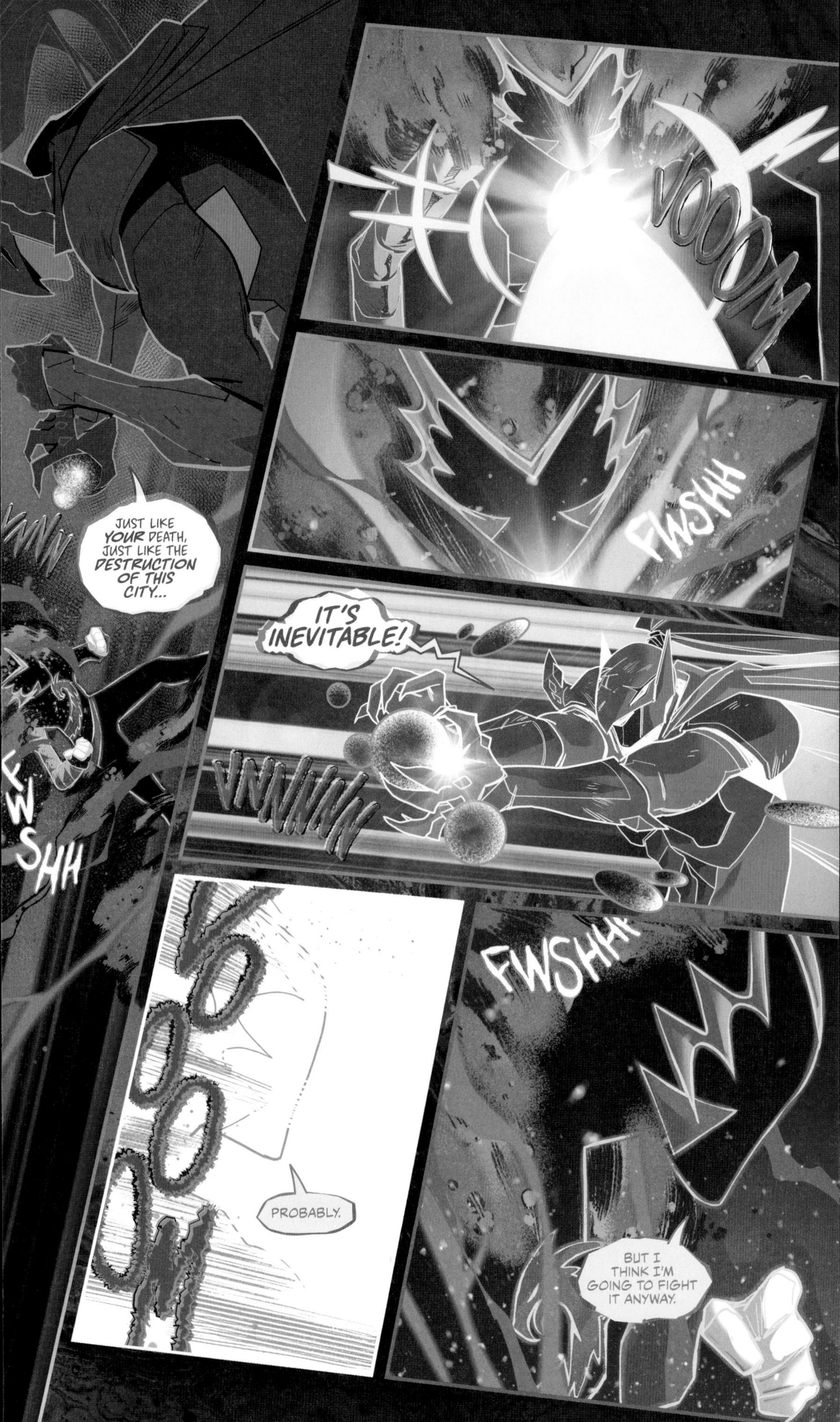
VOOOM
FWSHH
JUST LIKE YOUR DEATH, JUST LIKE THE DESTRUCTION OF THIS CITY...
VNNNN
FWSHH
IT'S INEVITABLE!
VNNNN
PROBABLY.
FWSHH
BUT I THINK I'M GOING TO FIGHT IT ANYWAY.

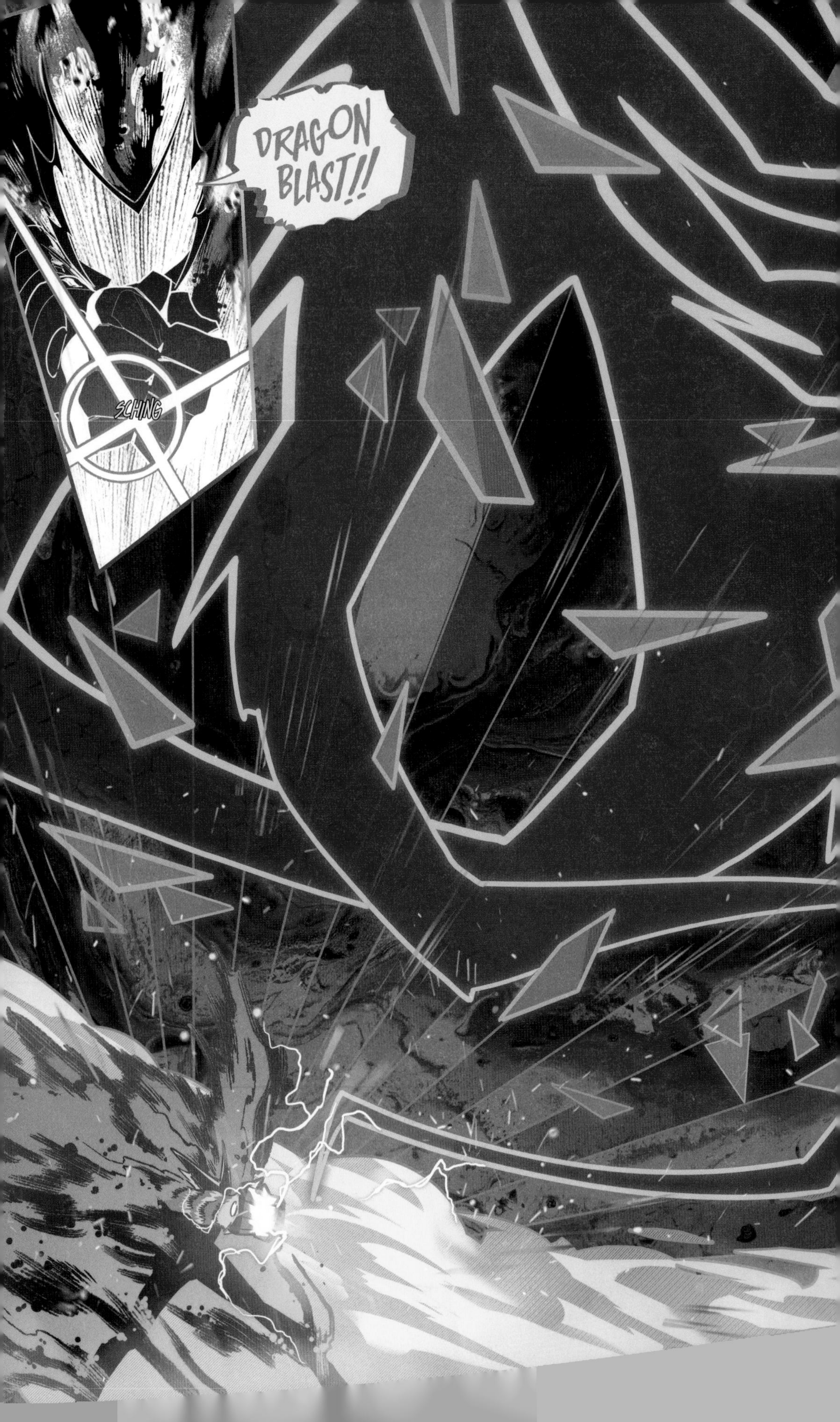
DRAGON BLAST!!
SCHING

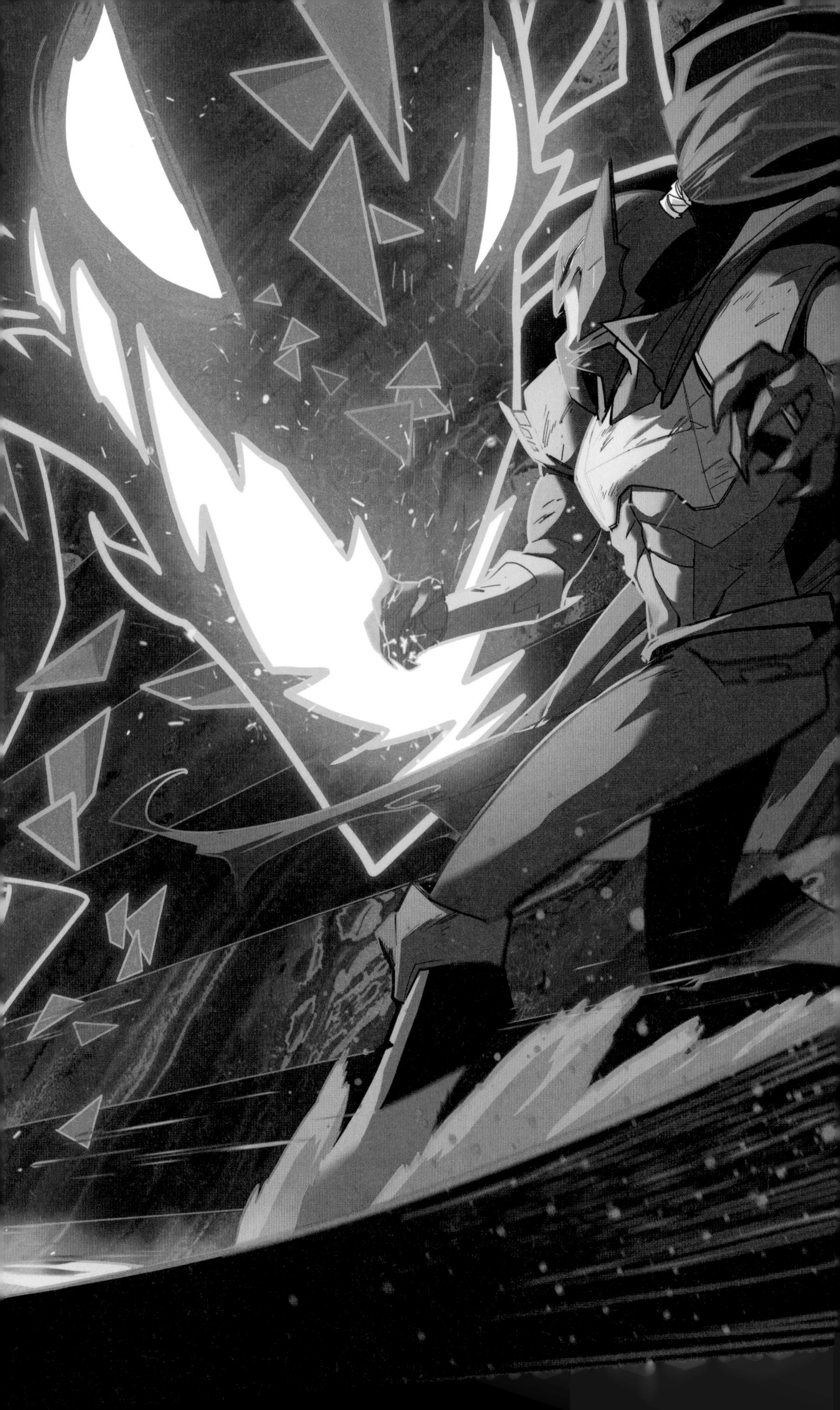

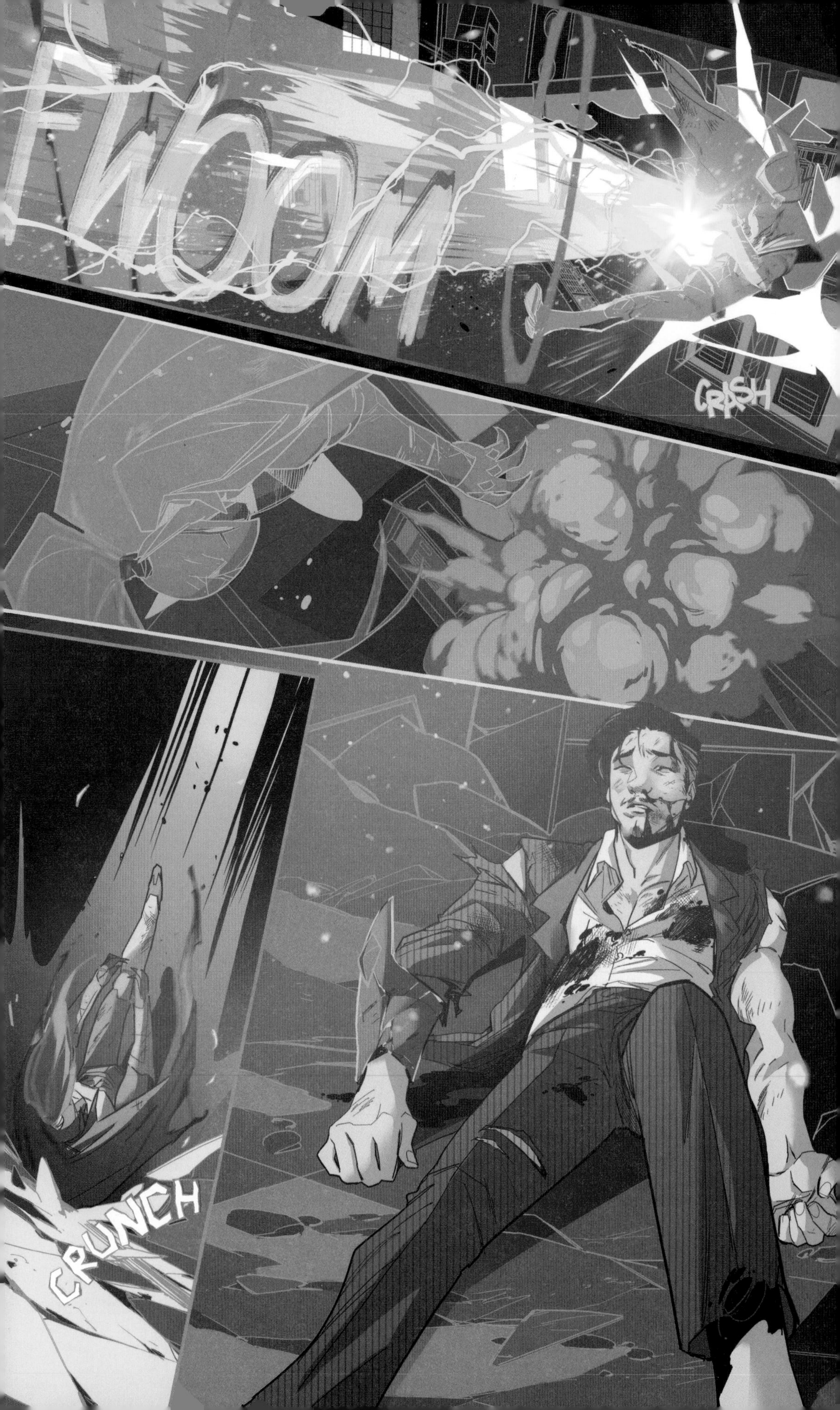
FWOOM
CRASH
CRUNCH

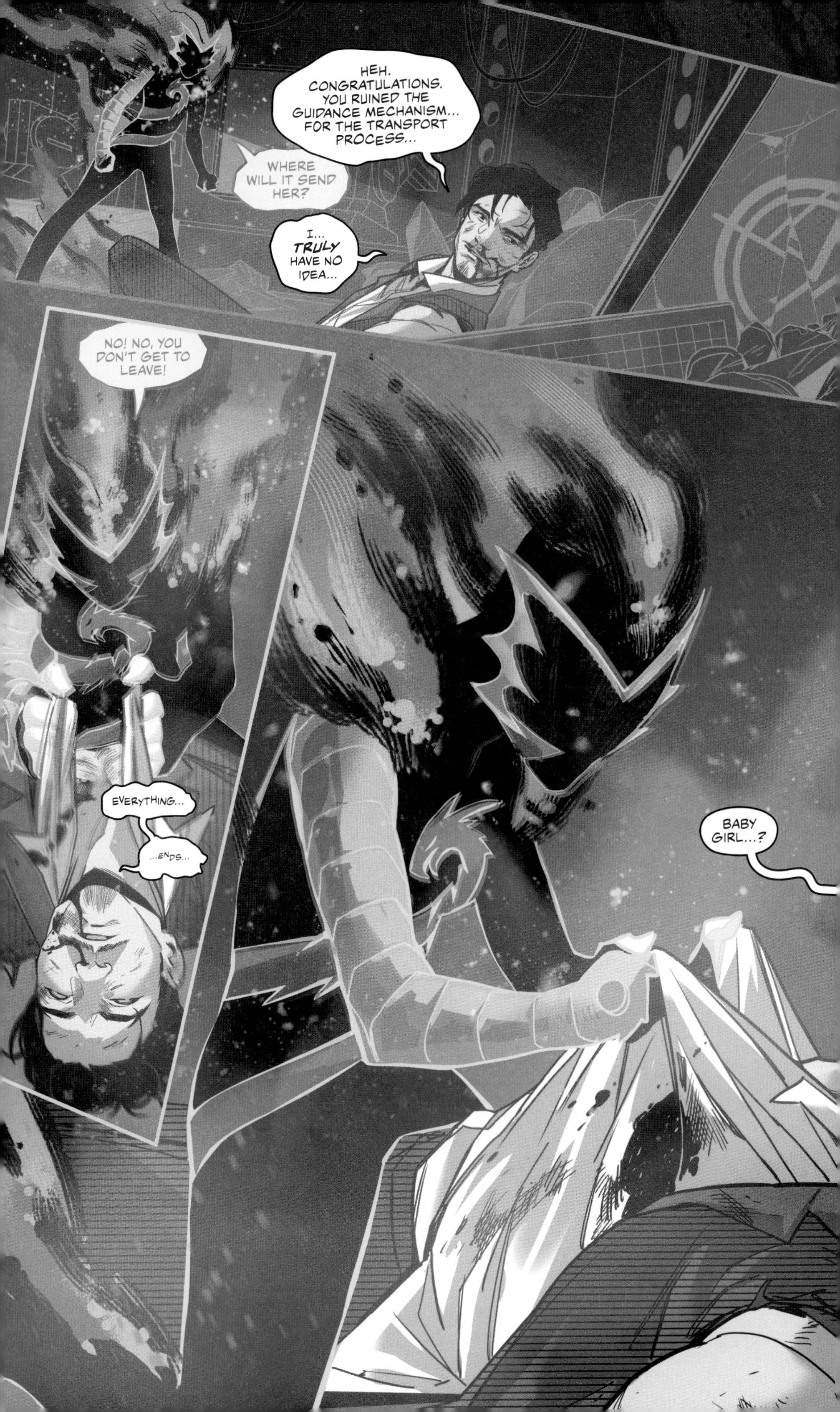
HEH. CONGRATULATIONS. YOU RUINED THE GUIDANCE MECHANISM... FOR THE TRANSPORT PROCESS...
WHERE WILL IT SEND HER?
I... TRULY HAVE NO IDEA...
NO! NO, YOU DON'T GET TO LEAVE!
EVERYTHING...
...ENDS...
BABY GIRL...?

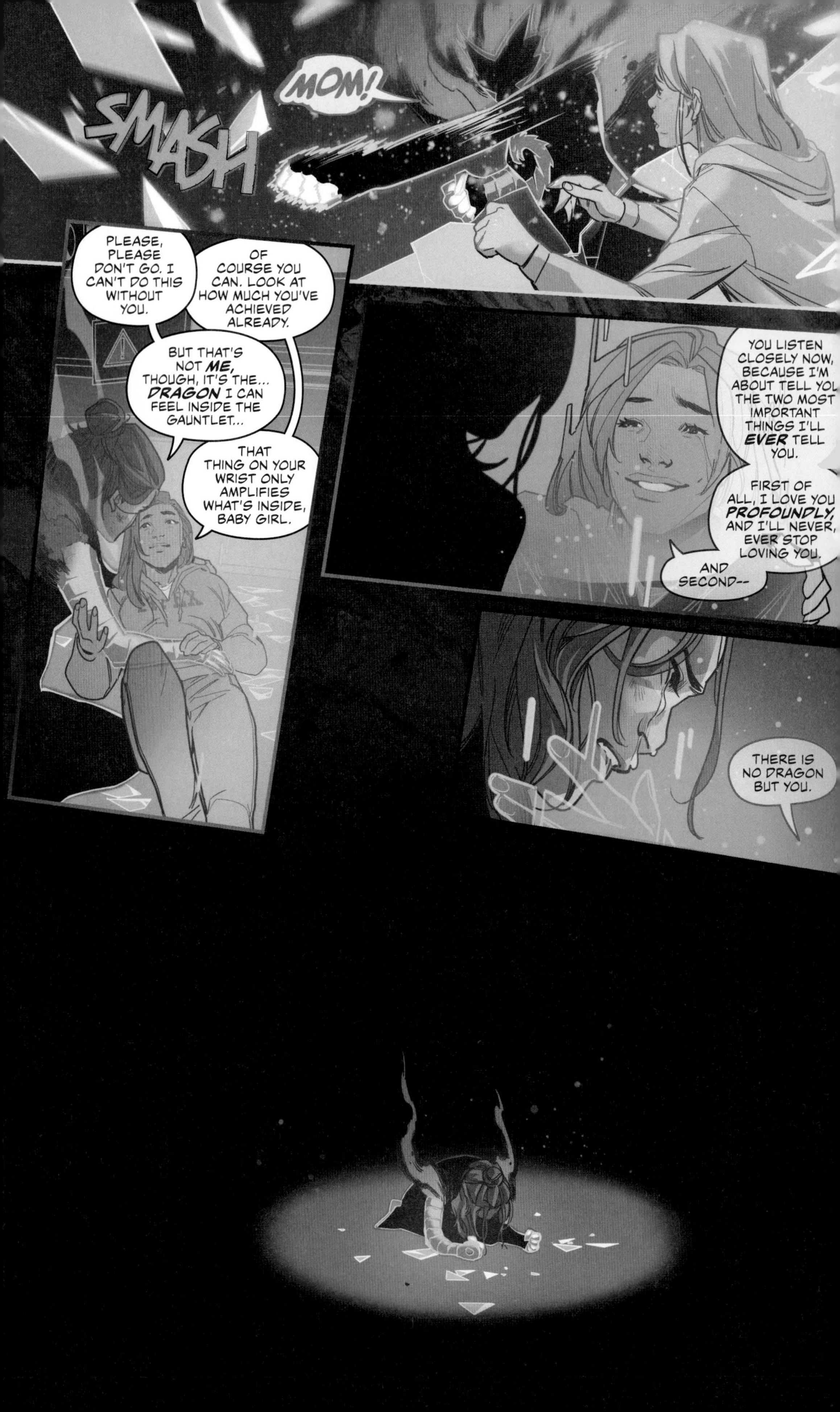
SMASH
MOM!
PLEASE, PLEASE DON'T GO. I CAN'T DO THIS WITHOUT YOU.
OF COURSE YOU CAN. LOOK AT HOW MUCH YOU'VE ACHIEVED ALREADY.
BUT THAT'S NOT ME, THOUGH, IT'S THE... DRAGON I CAN FEEL INSIDE THE GAUNTLET...
THAT THING ON YOUR WRIST ONLY AMPLIFIES WHAT'S INSIDE, BABY GIRL.
YOU LISTEN CLOSELY NOW, BECAUSE I'M ABOUT TELL YOU THE TWO MOST IMPORTANT THINGS I'LL EVER TELL YOU.
FIRST OF ALL, I LOVE YOU PROFOUNDLY, AND I'LL NEVER, EVER STOP LOVING YOU.
AND SECOND--
THERE IS NO DRAGON BUT YOU.

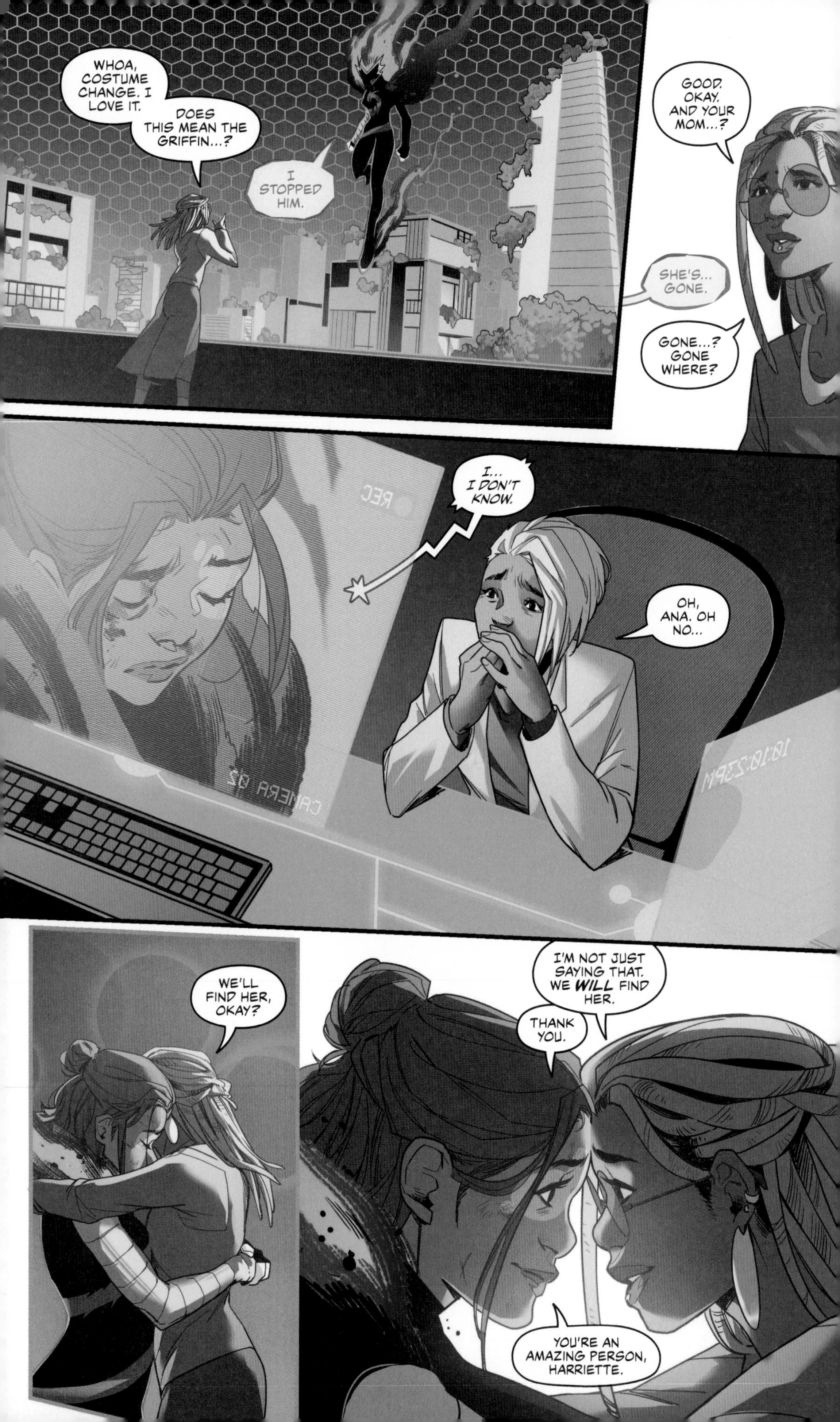
WHOA, COSTUME CHANGE. I LOVE IT.
DOES THIS MEAN THE GRIFFIN...?
I STOPPED HIM.
GOOD. OKAY. AND YOUR MOM...?
SHE'S... GONE.
GONE...? GONE WHERE?
REC
I... I DON'T KNOW.
OH, ANA. OH NO...
CAMERA 02
10:10:23PM
WE'LL FIND HER, OKAY?
I'M NOT JUST SAYING THAT. WE WILL FIND HER.
THANK YOU.
YOU'RE AN AMAZING PERSON, HARRIETTE.

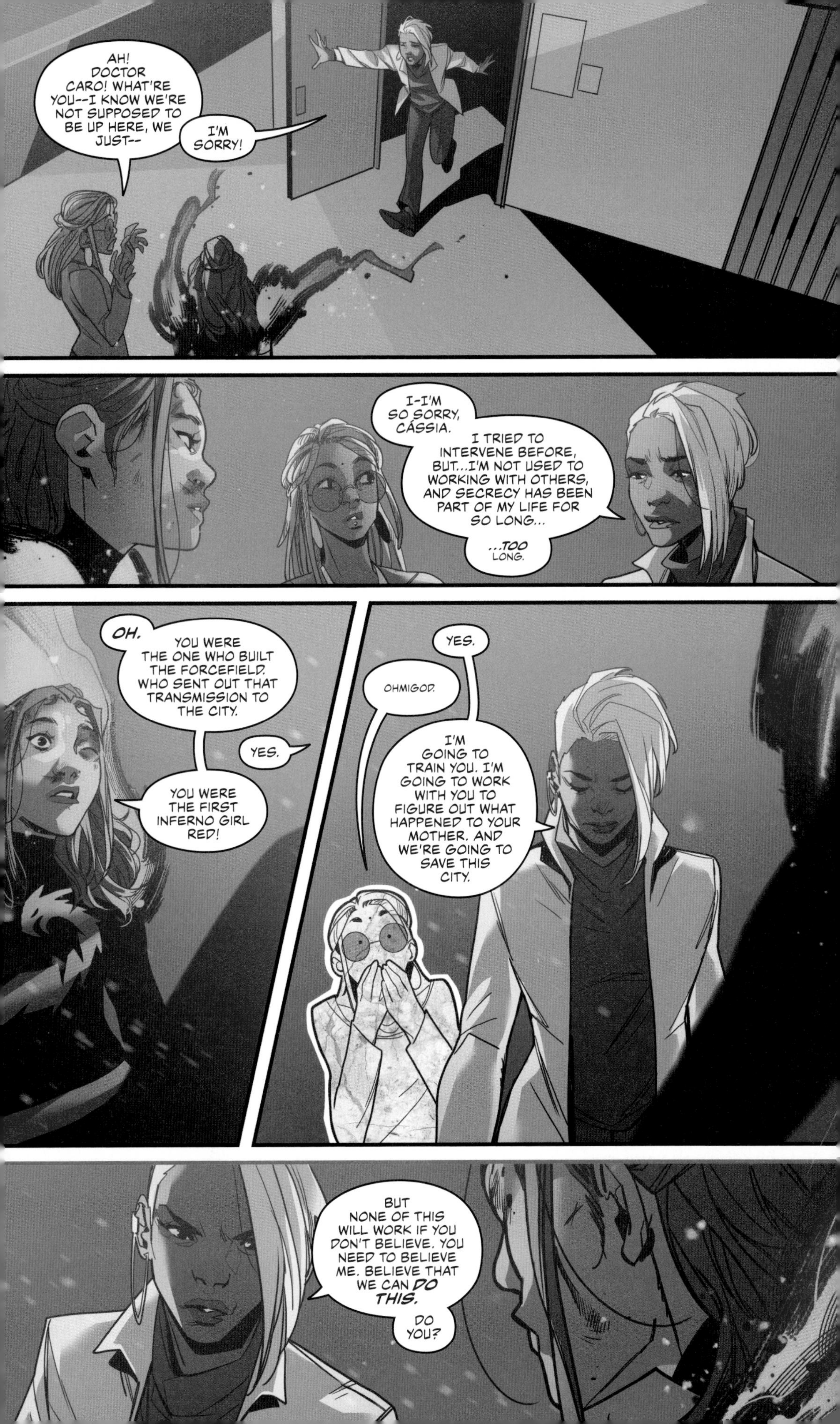
AH! DOCTOR CARO! WHAT'RE YOU--I KNOW WE'RE NOT SUPPOSED TO BE UP HERE, WE JUST--
I'M SORRY!
I-I'M SO SORRY, CÁSSIA.
I TRIED TO INTERVENE BEFORE, BUT...I'M NOT USED TO WORKING WITH OTHERS, AND SECRECY HAS BEEN PART OF MY LIFE FOR SO LONG...
...TOO LONG.
OH.
YOU WERE THE ONE WHO BUILT THE FORCEFIELD. WHO SENT OUT THAT TRANSMISSION TO THE CITY.
YES.
YOU WERE THE FIRST INFERNO GIRL RED!
YES.
OHMIGOD.
I'M GOING TO TRAIN YOU. I'M GOING TO WORK WITH YOU TO FIGURE OUT WHAT HAPPENED TO YOUR MOTHER. AND WE'RE GOING TO SAVE THIS CITY.
BUT NONE OF THIS WILL WORK IF YOU DON'T BELIEVE. YOU NEED TO BELIEVE ME. BELIEVE THAT WE CAN DO THIS.
DO YOU?

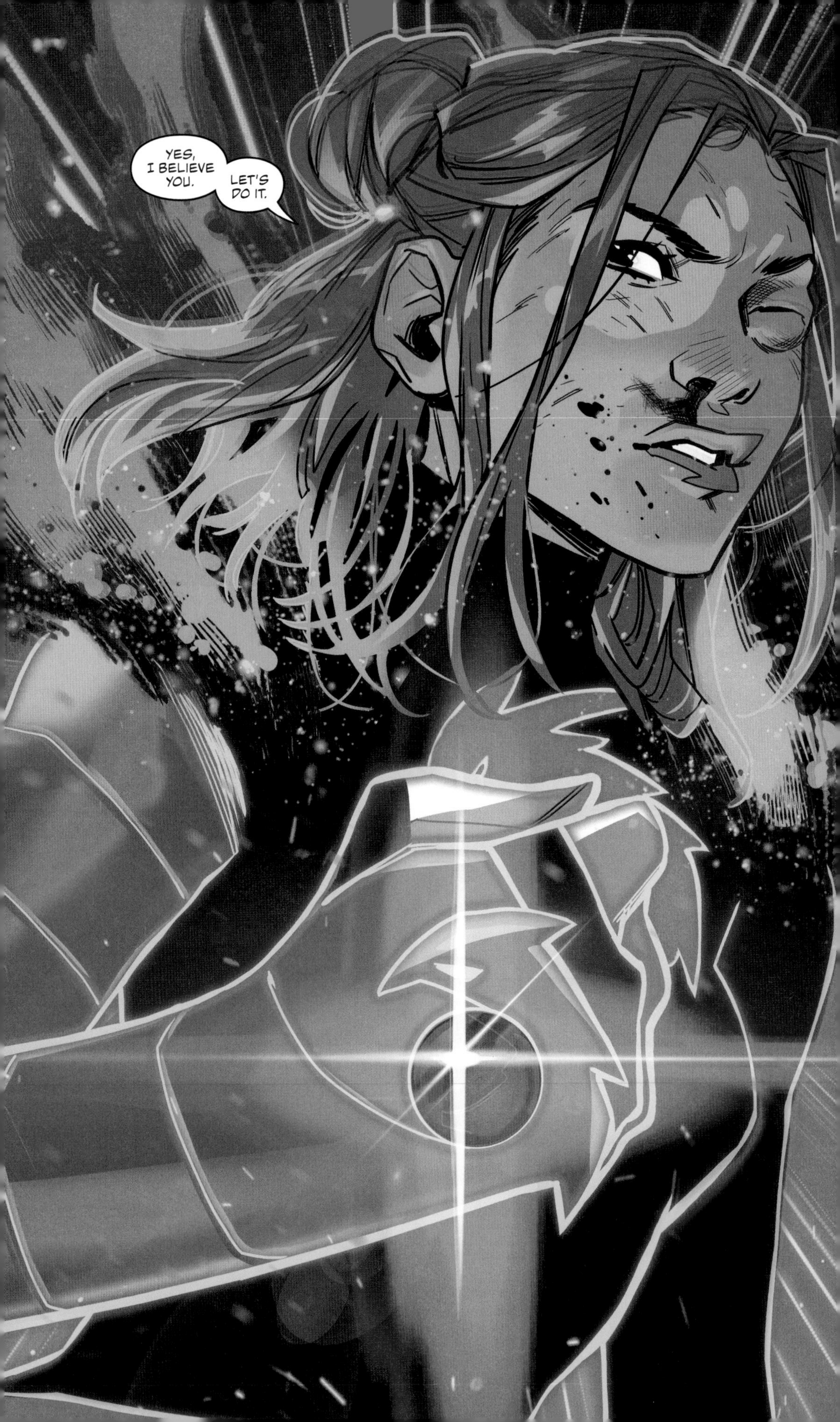
YES, I BELIEVE YOU.
LET'S DO IT.

INFERNO GIRL RED

WILL
RETURN.

 BLACK MARKET NARRATIVE For The People

IMAGE COMICS, INC. • **Robert Kirkman**: Chief Operating Officer • **Erik Larsen**: Chief Financial Officer • **Todd McFarlane**: President • **Marc Silvestri**: Chief Executive Officer • **Jim Valentino**: Vice President • **Eric Stephenson**: Publisher / Chief Creative Officer • **Nicole Lapalme**: Vice President of Finance • **Leanna Caunter**: Accounting Analyst • **Sue Korpela**: Accounting & HR Manager • **Matt Parkinson**: Vice President of Sales & Publishing Planning • **Lorelei Bunjes**: Vice President of Digital Strategy • **Dirk Wood**: Vice President of International Sales & Licensing • **Ryan Brewer**: International Sales & Licensing Manager • **Alex Cox**: Director of Direct Market Sales • **Chloe Ramos**: Book Market & Library Sales Manager • **Emilio Bautista**: Digital Sales Coordinator • **Jon Schlaffman**: Specialty Sales Coordinator • **Kat Salazar**: Vice President of PR & Marketing • **Deanna Phelps**: Marketing Design Manager • **Drew Fitzgerald**: Marketing Content Associate • **Heather Doornink**: Vice President of Production • **Drew Gill**: Art Director • **Hilary DiLoreto**: Print Manager • **Tricia Ramos**: Traffic Manager • **Melissa Gifford**: Content Manager • **Erika Schnatz**: Senior Production Artist • **Wesley Griffith**: Production Artist • **Rich Fowlks**: Production Artist • **IMAGECOMICS.COM**

INFERNO GIRL RED BOOK ONE

Artist / Co-Creator	**ERICA D'URSO** IG: @erucchan
Writer / Co-Creator	**MAT GROOM** TW: @mathewgroom
Colorist	**IGOR MONTI** IG: @igor.monti
Background Assistant	**LORENZO TAMMETTA** IG: @lorenzo_tammetta
Color Assistant	**SABRINA DEL GROSSO** IG: @colors.factory
Letterer	**BECCA CAREY** TW: @becca_see
Editor	**KYLE HIGGINS** TW: @kyledhiggins
Assistant Editor	**MICHAEL BUSUTTIL** TW: @m_busuttil
Design	**FOR THE PEOPLE** IG: @forthepeople.agency

INFERNO GIRL RED, BOOK ONE. First Printing. June 2023. Published by Image Comics, Inc. Office of publication: PO BOX 14457, Portland, OR 97293. Copyright © 2023 Erica D'Urso & Mat Groom. All rights reserved. Contains material originally published in single magazine form as INFERNO GIRL RED BOOK ONE #1-3. "Inferno Girl Red," its logos, and the likenesses of all characters herein are trademarks of Erica D'Urso, unless otherwise noted. "Image" and the Image Comics logos are registered trademarks of Image Comics, Inc. No part of this publication may be reproduced or transmitted, in any form or by any means (except for short excerpts for journalistic or review purposes), without the express written permission of Erica D'Urso & Mat Groom, or Image Comics, Inc. All names, characters, events, and locales in this publication are entirely fictional. Any resemblance to actual persons (living or dead), events, or places, without satirical intent, is coincidental. Printed in the USA. For international rights, contact: foreignlicensing@imagecomics.com. ISBN: 978-1-5343-2481-7.

MESSAGES FROM THE TEAM

MAT

As you probably figured out, INFERNO GIRL RED is a story about belief. And to be honest, it's required a lot of belief to get IGR to you. At times, it was a rocky journey.

But the passion of my two principle collaborators on this project – Erica and Igor – kept my spirits buoyed throughout. Their enthusiasm for (and belief in) this project was seemingly unshakeable – no matter what went wrong, it would only ever take a quick conversation with them to reassure me that what we were doing was both worthwhile and possible.

Also, I happen to think they're both masters of their craft and should be looked at as the trailblazers of their generation. But perhaps I have a compromised perspective, there.

With all that in mind, for my part, I dedicate IGR: BOOK ONE to Erica and Igor.

ERICA

To our 1,593 Kickstarter backers – 1,593 thank yous (if not more) for helping make this book real. Since we launched the Kickstarter, a lot happened and the world changed. Meanwhile, so did I. I got through a lot of stuff, but the only constant that kept me going was the care and affection from every person around me. From loved ones and strangers alike, I never stopped reading or hearing supportive words and this most beautiful thing fired my soul. Thank you, from the bottom of my heart, to everyone who's holding this book and believed in us.

IGOR

IGR, the acronym for this novel, is literally my name without the "O". Thanks a lot to Mat for the enormous goodness, Kyle for the amazing opportunity, Michael for being our captain, Erica for all these amazing pages and Becca for giving voice and sounds to the great emotions inside this story. I hope you will have a great experience reading it, at least half as much as we enjoyed working on it. To be honest, it wasn't easy to be by my side even on the heavy days – so last, but not least, I want to thank my girlfriend Chiara, for always being supportive every single day (and night) I worked on the pages.

Now it's your turn – have a nice trip to the city of Apex.

COVER
GALLERY

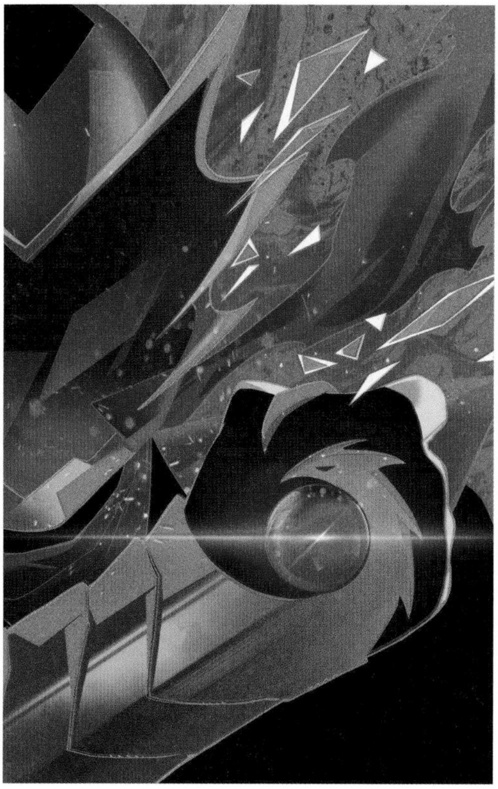

1A ERICA D'URSO W/ IGOR MONTI

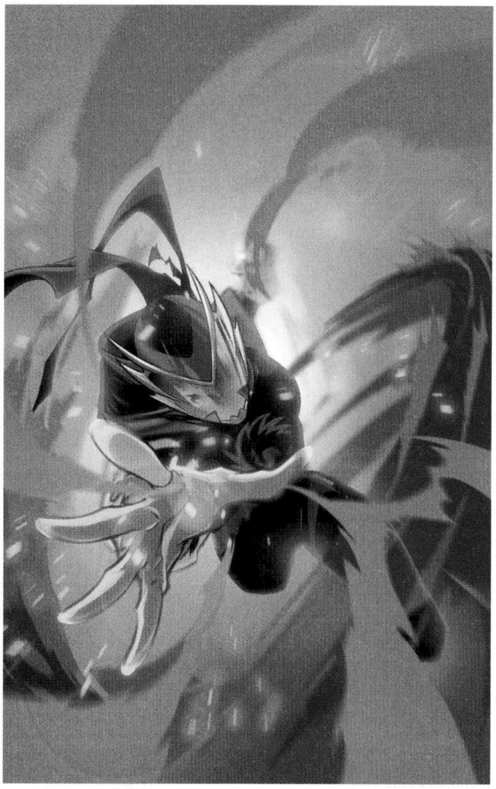

1B FRANCESCO MANNA W/ IGOR MONTI

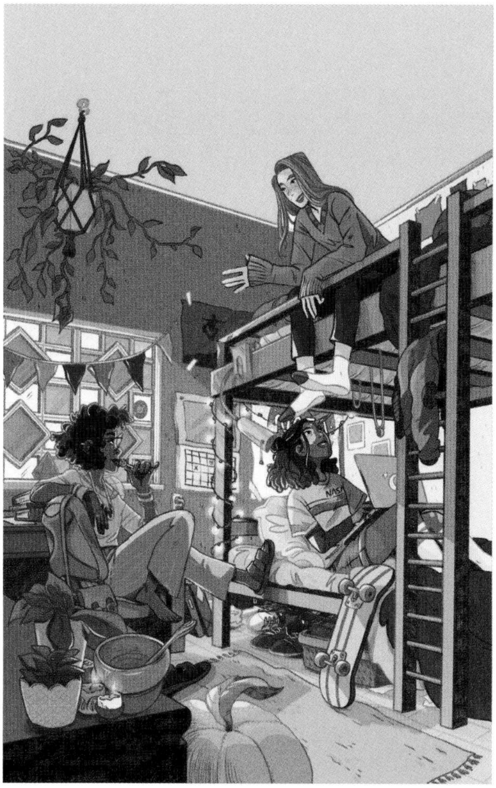

1C NICOLE GOUX

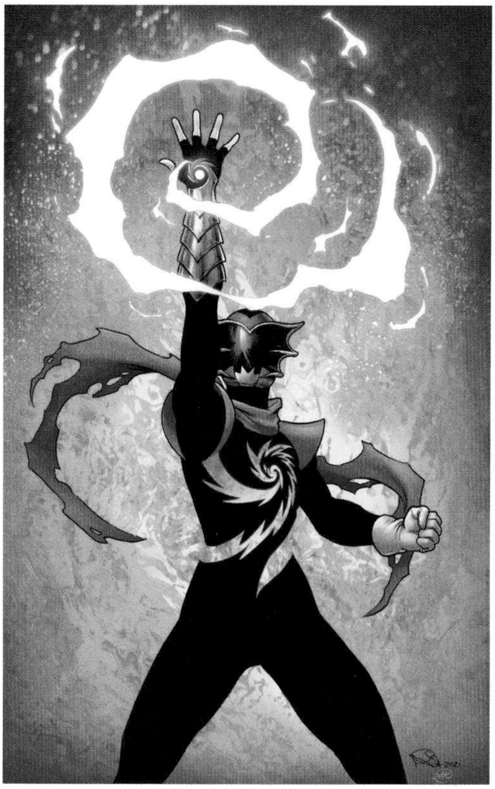

1D NICOLA SCOTT W/ ANNETTE KWOK

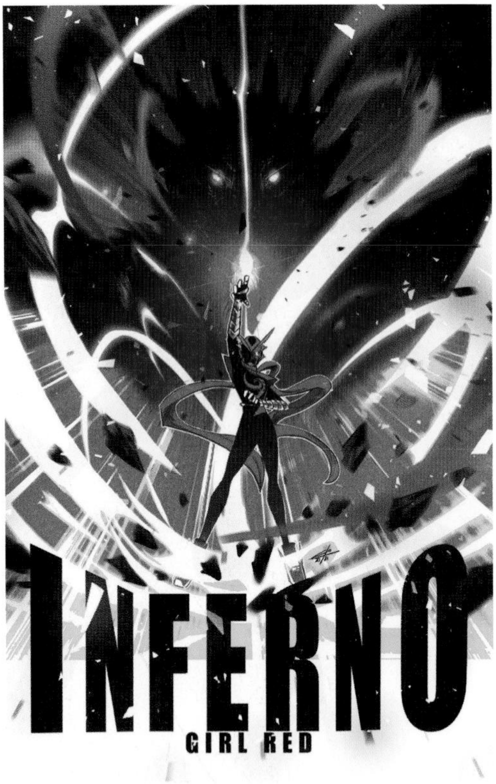
INFERNO
GIRL RED

1E ELEONORA CARLINI

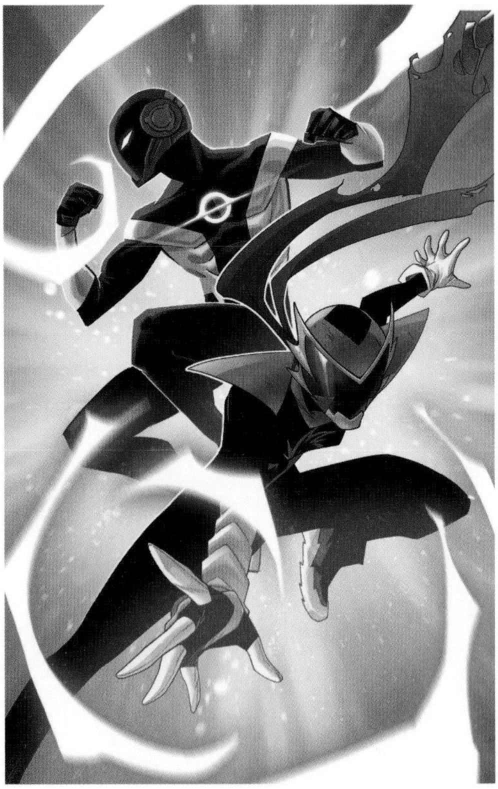

1F FRANCESCO MANNA W/ IGOR MONTI

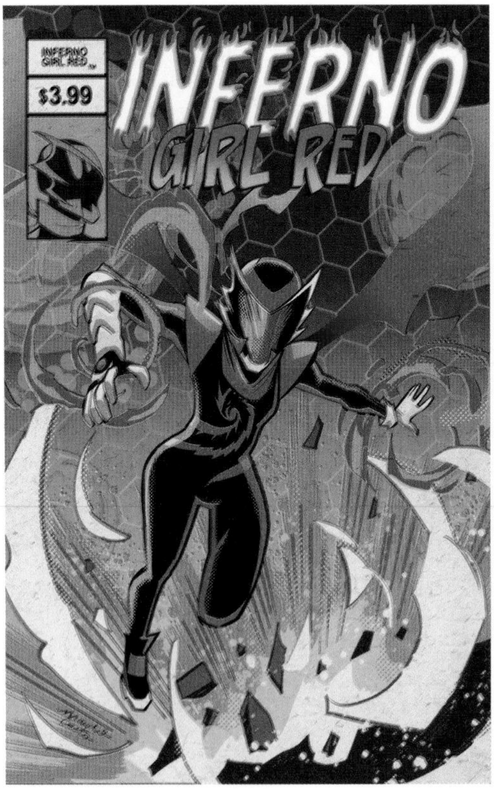
INFERNO GIRL RED
$3.99
INFERNO
GIRL RED

1 MARCELO COSTA

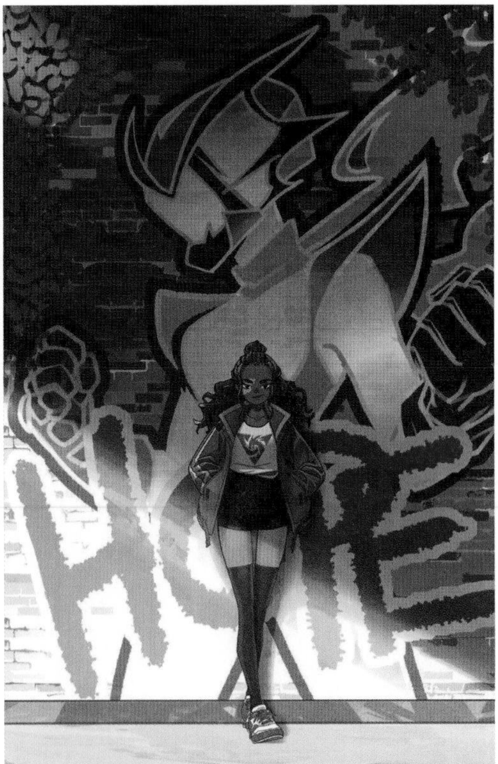

1 DEAD SLUG

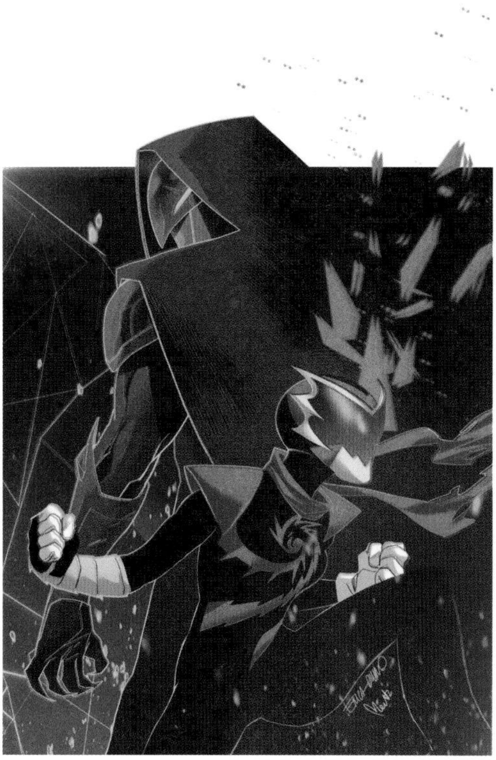

2A ERICA D'URSO W/ IGOR MONTI

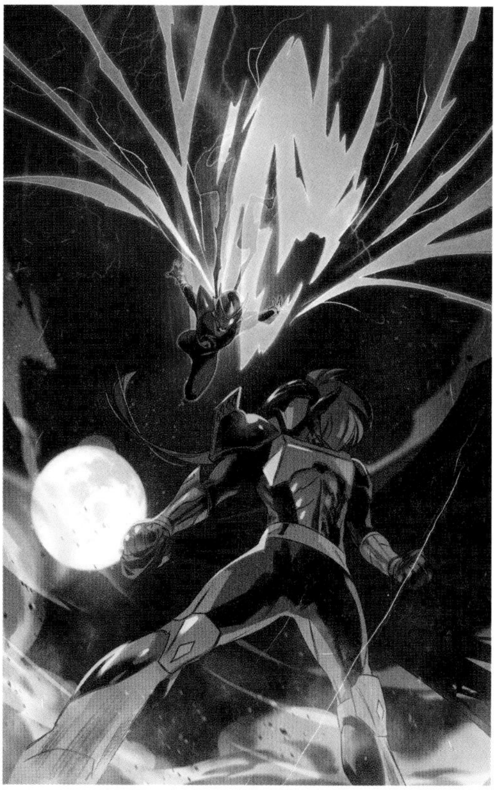

2B FRANCESCO MANNA W/ IGOR MONTI

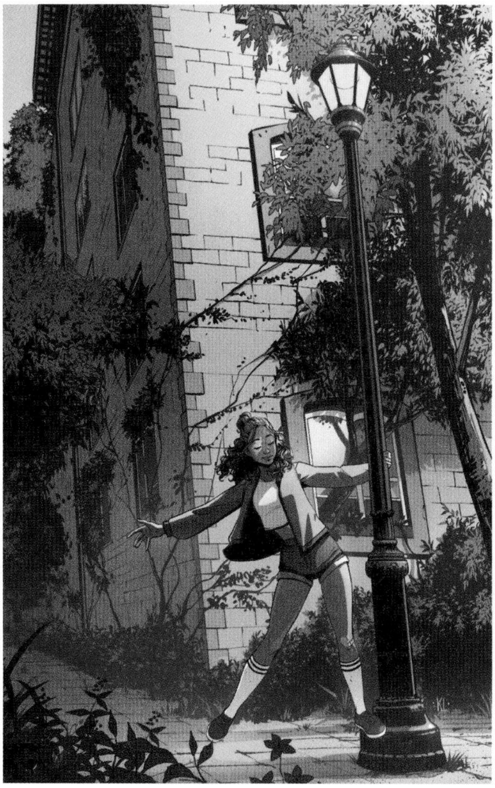

2C NICOLE GOUX

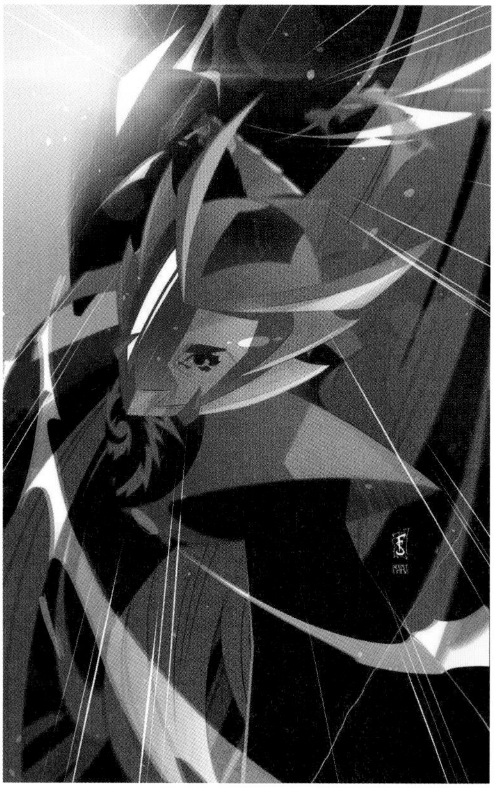

2D NICOLA SCOTT W/ ANNETTE KWOK

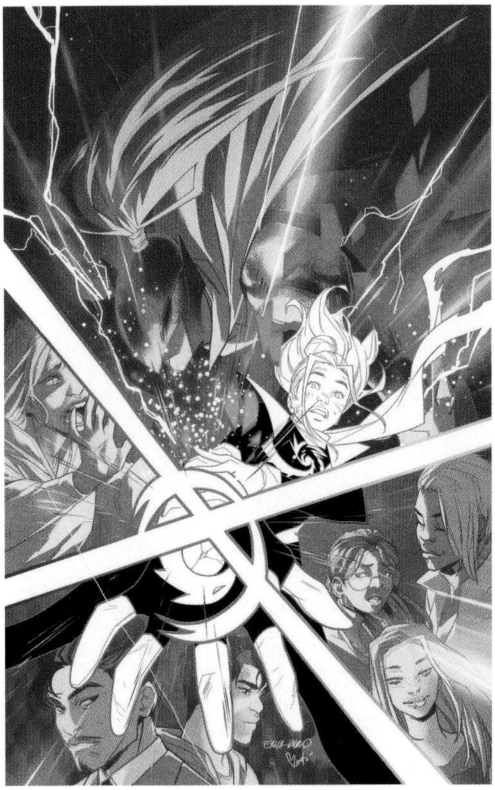

3A ERICA D'URSO W/ IGOR MONTI

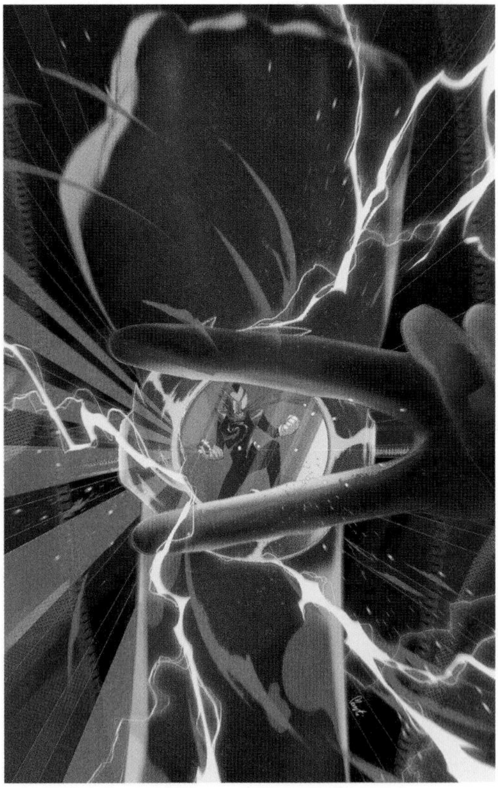

3B IGOR MONTI

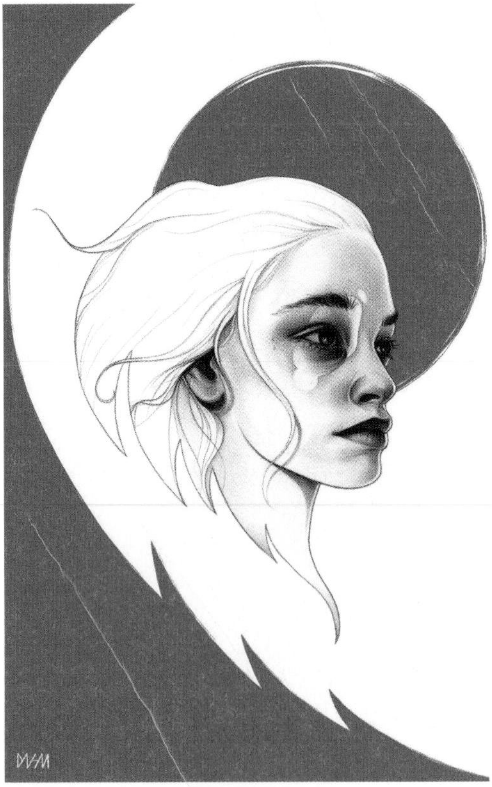

3C DASH O'BRIEN-GEORGESON

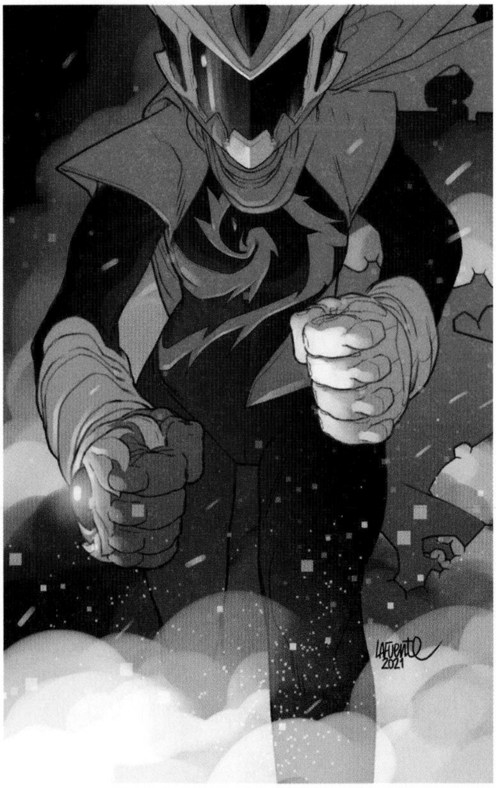

3D DAVID LAFUENTE

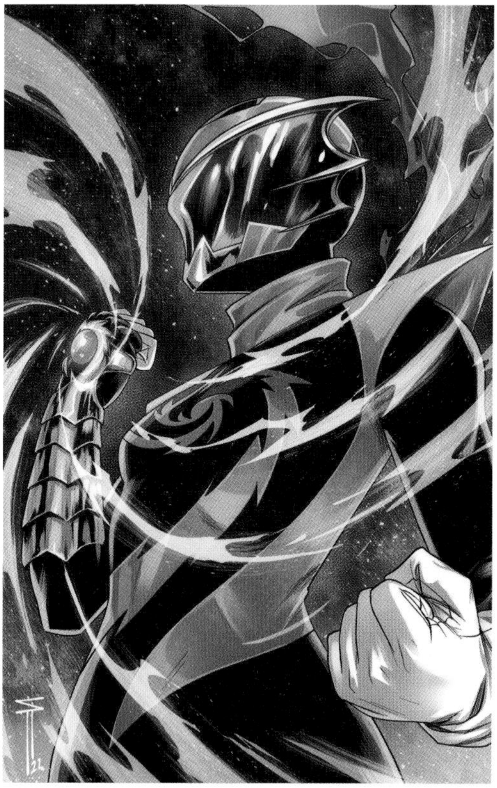

\-   SERGE ACUÑA

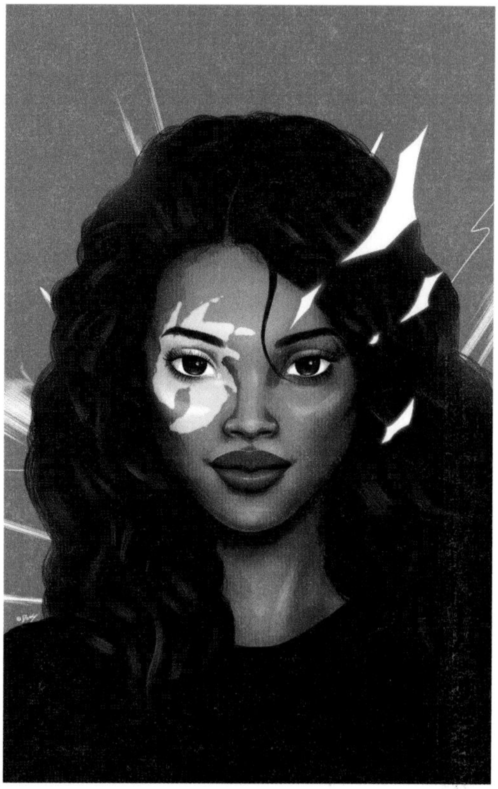

\-   DOALY

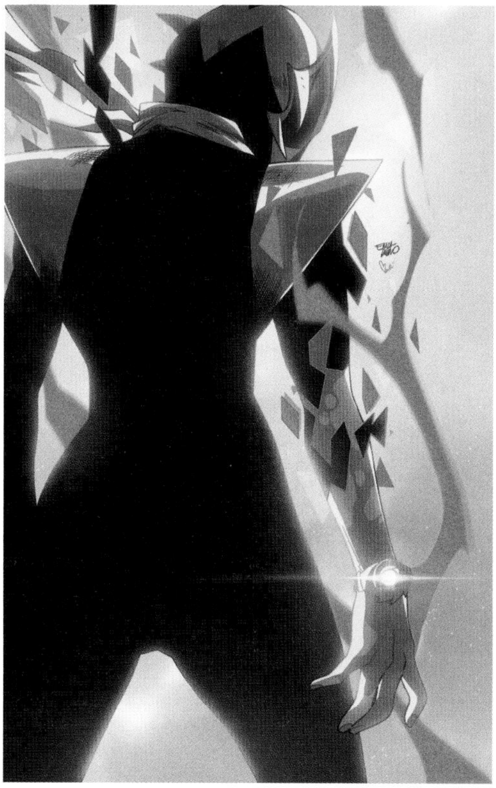

\-   ERICA D'URSO W/ IGOR MONTI

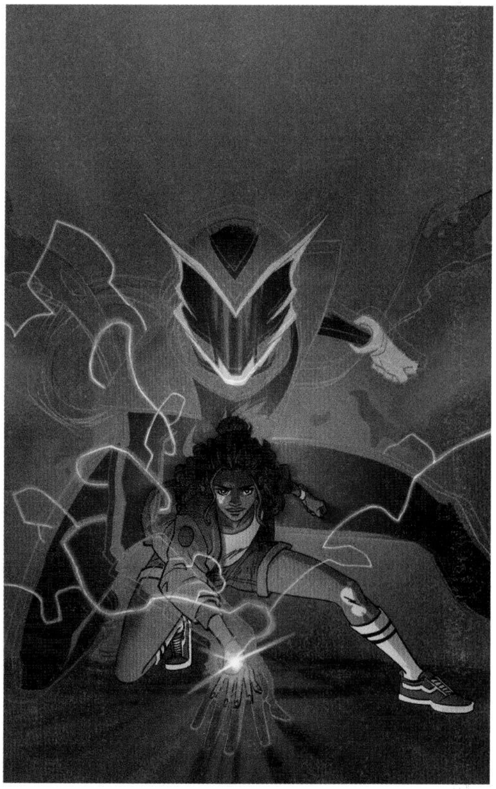

\-   EDUARDO FERIGATO

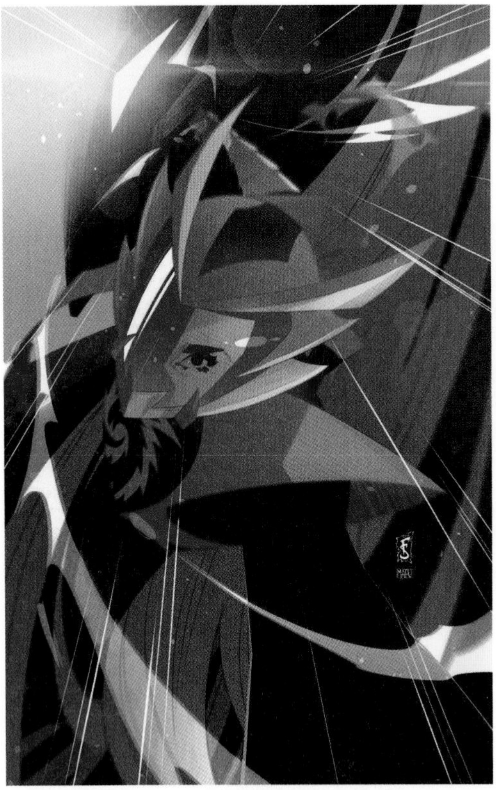

\- FEDERICO SABBATINI W/ MAFURIAH

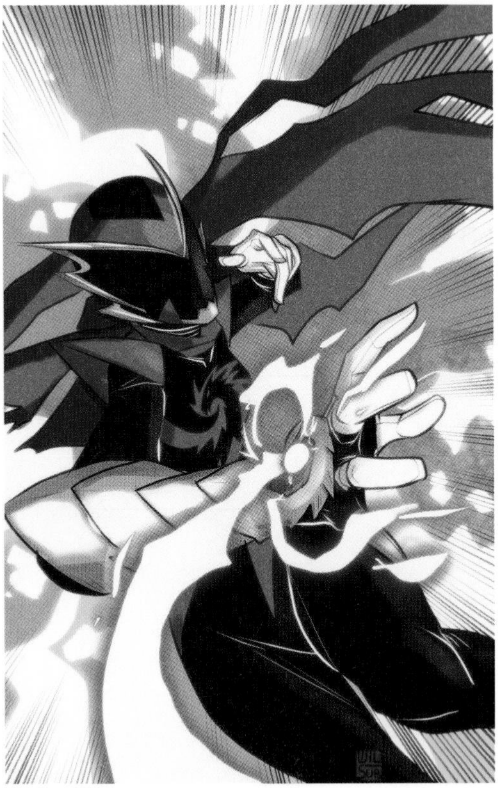

\- WIL SUR

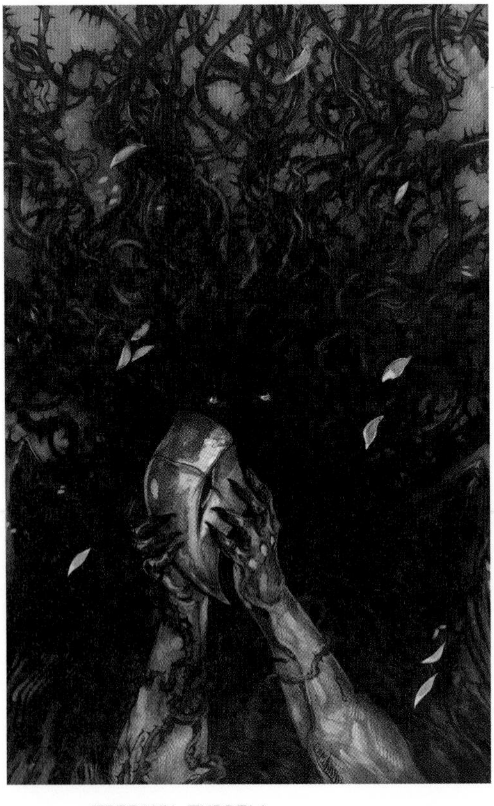

\- TIFFANY TURRILL

Thank you so much for reading. We put a whole lot of love, and a whole lot of ourselves, into this book... so it means the world to us that people like you are taking a chance on a new story and spending some of your time in our world.

If you'd like to keep up-to-date on where and when Cássia will appear next, make sure to subscribe to our newsletter at infernogirlred.com. Otherwise, thanks again – and burn bright!

–Mat Groom
(on behalf of Team IGR)